Austin Echema

Anointing of the Sick and the Healing Ministry

Austin Echema

Anointing of the Sick and the Healing Ministry

The Nigerian Pastoral Experience

IKO – Verlag für Interkulturelle Kommunikation

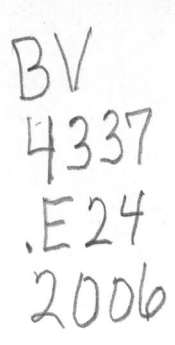

Bibliographische Information der Deutschen Bibliothek
Die Deutsche Bibliothek verzeichnet diese Publikation in der Deutschen
Nationalbibliographie; detaillierte bibliographische Daten sind im Internet über
http://dnb.ddb.de abrufbar.

© IKO - Verlag für Interkulturelle Kommunikation
   Frankfurt am Main • London, 2006

      Frankfurt am Main   London
      Postfach 90 04 21   70 c, Wrentham Avenue
      D - 60444 Frankfurt   London NW10 3HG, UK

      e-mail: info@iko-verlag.de • Internet: www.iko-verlag.de

      ISBN: 3-88939-831-6 (978-3-88939-831-4)

Umschlaggestaltung: Volker Loschek, 61184 Karben
Herstellung: Schaltungsdienst Lange, 12277 Berlin

Contents

General Introduction 1

Chapter One: Contextual Considerations 7
1.1   Anointing of the Sick 7
1.2   The Healing Ministry 10
1.3   The Nigerian Context 12
1.4   The Quest for Healing 15
1.4.1 Influence of Indigenous Cosmology 15
1.4.2 Reality of Socio-economic and Political Difficulties 18
1.5   Methods Employed by Healers 19
Summary 29

Chapter Two: Survey of Various Attitudes towards Sickness and Healing 31
2.1   Pre-biblical Times and Sickness 31
2.2   Sickness and Healing in African World View 32
2.3   Secularized Notion of Sickness 35
2.4   Some Modern Insights into Sickness and Healing 38
2.4.1 Relationship between the Physical and Spiritual 38
2.4.2 The Role of Social Structures 39
2.4.3 The Practice of Faith-Healing 40
Summary 41

Chapter Three: Biblical Insight into Sickness and Healing 43
3.1   Sickness and Healing in the Hebrew Tradition 43
3.2   Sickness and Healing in the New Testament 49
3.3   Healing in the Apostolic Age 55
3.4   Early Christian Community and its Care for the Sick 58
Summary 61

Chapter Four: Historical Review of the Church's Attitude to Sickness and Healing 63
4.1   The Patristic Church 63
4.2   Carolingian Renaissance 70
4.3   The Scholastic Period 73
4.4   Council of Trent to Vatican 11 75
4.5   Ecumenical Convergence 77
Summary 80

Chapter Five: The Revised Rites for the Sick 83
5.1   Pastoral Care of the Sick.. 84
5.2   Visits to the Sick (Chapter 1)... 87
5.3   Visits to a Sick Child (Chapter 2) 89
5.4   Communion of the Sick (Chapter 3)... 91
5.4.1   Communion in Ordinary Circumstances 92
5.4.2   Communion in a Hospital or Institution 94
5.5   Anointing of the Sick (Chapter 4).. 96
5.6   Important Questions Concerning Anointing 106
5.6.1   The Condition for Reception 106
5.6.2   For Sickness other than Physical?.. 108
5.6.3   Repetition of the Sacrament... 110
5.6.4   The Proper Minister of the Sacrament... 110
5.7   New Problems Raised by the Revised Rite 113
5.7.1   Anointing as Sacrament for the Dying?...................................... 113
5.7.2   Sacramental and Charismatic Healing... 117
Summary 120

Chapter Six: Theological Meaning of Sickness and Healing........... 123
6.1   Dualism of Body-Spirit... 124
6.2   Repentance and Healing 129
6.3   Suffering and Dying under the Sign of the Cross....................... 136
6.4   Jesus' Ministry to the Sick 143
6.5   Jesus' Ministry Continues in the Church 148
Summary 157

Chapter Seven: Pastoral Implications (Practical Inculturation)...... 163
7.1   Misunderstandings of the Sacraments 164
7.2   Abuses in the Celebration of the "Last Rites" 168
7.3   Inculturating Anointing of the Sick 169
7.3.1   Use of Locally Produced Oil... 171
7.3.2   Sacramental Use of Oil Blessed by the Bishop 171
7.3.3   Lay Anointing 172
7.3.4   Anointing of the Sick and Liturgical Celebration....................... 173
7.4   Ongoing Catechesis on the Revised Rites 174
7.5   Healthy Self-Critique of the Church's Healing Ministry............ 176
7.6   Present Day Healers and the Example of Jesus 179
Summary 186

General Conclusion 189
Bibliography 193

Acknowledgments

The production of this book has once more proved to me the ancient, ever true saying that "nobody is an island" or that "a tree does not make a forest." From the beginning to its completion this book benefited from the goodness, inspiration and expertise of so many people, whom I doubt whether the entire space for acknowledging those who worked behind the scene could contain all their names.

I begin with those who remotely contributed to the writing and completion of the book. First and foremost are the members of the CIWA Governing Council, the Rector Very Rev. Dr. James S. Moti, the Dean of Theology Rev. Dr. Dr. A. N. Odoemene, my HOD Very Rev. Msgr. Dr. J. T. Ogunduyilemi, my colleagues and all the students. All agreed unanimously that I was due for sabbatical leave after ten solid years of service to the Institute. I am extremely grateful for their permission and support, without which I do not think the book would have been written. I thank my local ordinary His Grace, Most Rev. Dr. A. J. V. Obinna, who is also a member of CIWA Governing Council for his support both at home and abroad (i.e. CIWA and Limburg diocese).

In the same vain, I remain in debt to the diocese of Limburg, Germany for enthusiastically welcoming me again for one year and giving me a place to stay and carry out this study. I thank especially Pfarrer Helmut Wanka (Dezernat Personal) for his understanding and humane approach to issues. I will ever remain grateful to the bishop Dr. Franz Kamphaus who in conjunction with the Institute of Missiology, MISSIO Aachen financed my doctoral studies between 1988 and 1994 in the Philosophisch-Theologische Hochschule, St. Georgen Frankfurt.

I spent my sabbatical year as a chaplain of the Herz-Jesu-Krankenhaus (Heart of Jesus Hospital) Dernbach, a hospital belonging to the Arme Dienstmägde Jesu Christi (Poor Handmaids of Jesus Christ). The Catholic atmosphere, the efficiency and expertise of the workers were simply wonderful to behold. The prayerful spirit and generosity of the Sisters made me once to think of joining the congregation but for my being a male. I cannot but mention some of them by name. Sr. Dominica Arbeiter worked with me in the Pastoral Department. But she made her computer available to me from my first day and spent hours with me type-setting and correcting this work and my other articles. I thank her immensely for her generosity with time and readiness to help. But more importantly her dedication to the patients was a source of inspiration to me. I am grateful to Srs. Christina Krasson, Ulrike Paoe and Irmgild Jassner for constantly inviting me to festive meals and coffee and providing for me in times of scarcity, especially when I forgot to go shopping. Their good neighbourliness will remain ever green in my memory. I wish to thank Sr. Alsmunda who always surprised me with fresh bread from the Sisters' kitchen and indeed all the Sisters with whom I celebrated daily and Sunday Masses. I learnt a lot of positive things from these holy women.

To the immediate contributors to the completion of this book counts in the first place Prof. Dr. Manfred Probst, SAC. I cannot thank him enough for the interest he showed in my theme from the first day I approached him to guide me in my writing, being himself a master in the field of the anointing of the sick and a renowned professor of liturgy. I am grateful to him for his humane guidance, generosity with his time and resources throughout the process of the birth of this book. My special thanks go to Sr. Philothea Dittmer for making all her books dealing on caring for the sick and dying available to me. I thank Srs. Ugochi Ozurumba and Lilian Onuoha for typing some parts or chapters of this book. My sincere and very special gratitude is due Sr. Simone Weber who organized the typing team and made sure that the work was at no time interrupted. I am very grateful to Mr. J. T. Velady for being so generous with his time and expertise on computer and for being a wonderful neighbour. In the same way, I sincerely thank Herr Joachim Hemme and his dear wife Anne who generously formated the entire manuscript and made it ready for the publication.

I want to say a word of thanks to my numerous friends in Germany, America and Belgium for giving me a home in their families and hearts. They all occupy special places in my heart. I cannot resist mentioning some of them: Families Maria Böing-Messing, Waltraud and Gerhard Kempermann, Eva-Maria and Bernhard Olbrich, Anni and Walter Dinges, Maria and Helmut Hintner, Anni and Helmut Storck, and Thea and Ernst Eisinger (Germany), Vivian Ontiveros (America) and Petra and Alex Emenogu (Belgium). I am especially grateful to Pfarrer Ludwig Janzen for his genuine friendship and generosity since we first met in 1994. I thank Pfarrer Rudi Müller for offering me summer jobs in his parish and for his generosity.

I must also give special thanks to my friends at home who have always stood by me with their sincere encouragement and advice. Rev. Prof. P. D. Akpunonu whom I have known and respected since my theology student days as my rector and teacher; a man who recognizes talents in persons rather than where they come from has continued to inspire me with his advice and encouragement. My brother priests and friends Rev. Dr. R. Madu, Rev. Dr. J. C. Ike, Rev. Dr. G. C. Okeke, Frs. Pius Kii, A. Alamezie, A. Okoroafor, G. Agbagwa, Rev. V. Arisiukwu and a host of others have remained true friends all these years. Special thanks go to Fr. Christian

Okwuru (a doctoral student in Leuven, Belgium) for promptly assisting me with relevant materials from his famous Katholik University Leuven (KUL) library, and for housing me during my research trip to Leuven. My sincere thanks are also due my former student Fr. Hubert Opara (a doctoral student in Goethe University Frankfurt) for generously accepting to read through the whole work. I benefited from his courageous and objective criticisms.

I wish to thank members of my family, especially my late parents whom I fondly remember every day for sowing the seed of faith in me; my eldest sister Theresa who with her late husband Emmanuel Onyekwere provided me with everything I needed from my first day in Elementary School till I became a priest in 1986. I am especially grateful to my niece Uloma Ejike for her selfless services to me and the entire members of my family for their warmth, care and love.

Finally, I prayerfully remember all the patients of Herz-Jesu-Krankenhaus between 25.10.05 and 30.09.06, who requested and worthily received the sacrament of anointing of the sick. They did not realize how much they were teaching me along the way. Most of them went back to their "temporary" homes happily, while others passed on to our eternal home. To all of them, I dedicate this book.

Dernbach, 25th May 2006   Dr. Austin Echema
Solemnity of Ascension of the Lord

Abbreviations

AFER	African Ecclesial Review (Eldoret/Kenya)
BTS	Bigard Theological Studies (Enugu/Nigeria)
CBCN	Catholic Bishops' Conference Nigeria
CCC	Catechism of the Catholic Church
Cf	Confer
CIC	Codex Iuris Canonici (Code of Canon Law, 1983)
CIWA	Catholic Institute of West Africa (Port Harcourt/Nigeria)
Co	Company
DS	H. Denzinger and A. Schönmetzer, eds. Enchridion Symbolorum, Definitionum et Declarationum. 33rd edition. (Rome: Herder, 1965)
Ed/s	Editor/s
Etc	Et Cetera
Hrsg	Herausgegeben
Ibid	Ibidem (The same reference)
JIT	Journal of Inculturation Theology (CIWA Port Harcourt/Nigeria)
LG	Lumen Gentium (Vatican II Dogmatic Constitution on the Church)
Mansi	J. D. Mansi, ed. Sacrorum Conciliorum nova et amplissima Collectio. 31 Vols. Florence and Venice: 1757-1798. Reprinted and continued by L. Petit and J. B. Martin to 53 Vols. (Paris: 1889-1927)
No/s	Number/s
NT	New Testament
OT	Old Testament
PL	Patrologia Latina. Edited by J. P. Migne. 217 Vols; with 4 vols. of indices. Paris: 1878-1890
SC	Sacrosanctum Concilium (Vatican Council II Constitution on the Sacred Liturgy)
Sr/s	Sister/s
Trans	Translated by
TV	Television
Vol/s	Volume/s

Foreword

Research students from Black-African continent are familiar faces in most of the Faculties of Theology in the Federal Republic of Germany. But it is rare to find someone who is already in the field like Dr. Austin Echema from the Catholic Institute of West Africa, Port Harcourt, on Sabbatical year coming to Germany to research on a liturgical issue and eventually to write a great work on the subject. His primary focus is on the phenomenon of healing and healers both inside and outside the Catholic Church in Nigeria and its relation with the celebration of the sacrament of the anointing of the sick.

I considered myself greatly honored and privileged when Dr. Echema approached me and requested if I could dialogue with him over his project. We quickly came into intensive discussion over the phenomenon of healers in Africa, their methods of practice and their successes. What readily came to my mind was the practice of spiritual healers, charismatic healing Masses and blessings for the sick in Germany.

At the background of this lively discussion was the question of what the Catholic Church could learn from the practice of the healers by way of inculturating its liturgy and how this could eventually be absorbed into the celebration of the anointing of the sick. We agreed on most of the issues, for example, on the role of the laying on of hands with its reach biblical foundation and how it could be emphasized in the celebration of the anointing of the sick.

There were also subjects on which we differed in setting our individual accent. Thus, for example, my colleague stressed the use of locally produced oil in the anointing of the sick; while the application of the oil on the particular sick part of the body appeared to me to be of great importance.

Considered generally, it was a good and fruitful interaction on inter and intra-cultural practices from which both of us immensely profited. I am very grateful to Dr. Austin Echema for this wonderful exchange of ideas and information. I wish him the strength and courage in his efforts to concretize the acquired knowledge in his local Church; of course, after due consultation with the bishops and authorities of the Church in his native country, whose responsibility it is to put these into practice.

Vallendar, 12th May 2006   Dr. Manfred Probst SAC,
                                 Professor of Liturgy

General Introduction

The saving-healing dimension of the sacrament of anointing of the sick is particularly evident in both scripture and considerable portions of the liturgical tradition. The Lord Jesus came into the world that women and men might have life and have it to the full (Jn 10:10). To this end he "went about doing good and curing all who had fallen into the power of the devil" (Acts 10:38) and were victims of all manner of diseases and disabilities in body, mind, and spirit. Jesus shows a special concern to the sick (cf. Mk 1:32-34). His compassion towards the sick and his numerous healings of every kind of infirmity are a sign that "God has visited his people" (Lk 7:16; cf. also Matt 4:24) and that the kingdom of God is close at hand.[1] He came to heal the whole person, soul and body. He is indeed the physician, the healer par excellence whom the sick have need of (cf. Mk 2:17). In his healing activities, Jesus made use of signs: spittle and the laying on of hands (cf. Mk 7:32-36; 8:22-25), mud and washing (cf. Jn 9:6-7).The sick tried to touch him, "for power came forth from him and healed them all" (Lk 6:19; cf. Mk 1:41; 3:10; 6:56).

Jesus' preferential compassion for the sick did not cease with his earthly life. He transferred it not only to his apostles but also to his disciples. Luke the physician and evangelist speaks not only of the mandate to heal given to the twelve apostles but also to that given to the seventy-two others (disciples). After bringing back to life the daughter of Jairus, Jesus "called the twelve together and gave them power and authority to overcome the devil and to cure diseases, and sent them to proclaim the kingdom of God and to heal ... and everywhere they told the Good News and healed the sick" (Lk 9: 1-6). Later Jesus appointed a further seventy-two other disciples and sent them ahead in pairs with the same instructions to "heal the sick, and say, 'The kingdom of God has come'" (Lk 10:1-9). Other relevant passages of scripture where Jesus mandated his apostles to heal include Matt 10:6-7; Mk 16:17-18, 16:20, etc.

The example of Jesus influenced the mission of the early Church (cf. Acts 3:5,15f). The concern for the sick, caring for and accompanying them with

---

[1] CCC, 1503.

prayers, as well as the building of hospitals and hospices remain a characteristic feature of the Church up till today. Thus, in the following of Jesus, the visitation of the sick is from the beginning of Christianity, one of the seven corporal works of mercy (cf. Matt 25:36). As time went on, the apostolic Church developed its own rite for the sick, attested to by St. James (5:14-15). Since then, tradition has always recognized in this rite one of the seven sacraments of the Church.[2] Both the East and the West testify to the practice of anointing the sick with blessed oil that they may recover from their illness. However, in the course of time the anointing was administered more and more exclusively on those at the point of death. As a result it received the name "Extreme Unction." This unfortunate development obscured the therapeutic dimension of the rite for centuries, especially in the West. People were frightened and thus postponed its reception until towards the very last breath.

The Second Vatican Council, however, restored the emphasis of healing. According to the Council,

> 'Extreme Unction,' which may also and more fittingly be called 'Anointing of the Sick,' is not a sacrament for those only who are at the point of death. Hence, as soon as anyone of the faithful begins to be in danger of death from sickness or old age, the fitting time for him to receive this sacrament has certainly already arrived.[3]

The biblical text frequently quoted in support of the sacrament is even clearer regarding its healing power (cf. James 5:14-15). The fifth sacrament is indeed very closely linked with healing.

In spite of the efforts of Vatican II, the misunderstanding of the anointing of the sick has persisted. The general experience all over the Catholic world is to postpone the reception of the sacrament until there is no more hope of survival. For many people – both priests and laity – calling the priest (sick call) means "I will soon die." In addition to the sacrament of the anointing of the sick, the Church has also hospital apostolate which seems to be its own version of the healing ministry. But the two ministries do not seem to

---

[2] Cf. Council of Constantinople II (553): DS 216; Council of Florence (1439): 1324-1325; Council of Trent (1551): 1695-1696; 1716-1717.
[3] Vatican II, Sacrosanctum Concilium, 73.

emphasize enough the healing aspect of Christ's mission.

The situation in Nigeria and Africa is not different. Perhaps the only difference lies in the way people are searching for healing from their possession of evil spirits and from all known types of sickness. The reason for this fascination for healing is the supreme value attached to life and the belief in the role of spirits to affect this life for better or for worse. Consequently, many Nigerians including Christians go to any length to have life prolonged when afflicted by disease or evil spirits. This explains among other reasons why so many Spiritual Churches, Prayer Houses and Miracle Centres spring up almost on daily basis in the Nigerian scene.

In recent times the mainline Churches including the Roman Catholic have joined the healing ministry. One of the reasons adduced by Catholic priest-healers as the motive behind this development is to prevent Catholics drifting to the sects and the many Pentecostal healing centres booming all over the place. But this reason fails to explain the many abuses that have crept into the ministry. Some of the priests who originally joined the healing ministry in order to save Catholics are not different from the Pentecostal preachers and the so- called healers. The craze was becoming out of control and so the Nigerian Bishops' Conference in 1997 issued Guidelines for the Healing Ministry in the Catholic Church in Nigeria. It is left to anybody's guess whether the situation has improved since then. However, the present situation is not the first of its kind. Throughout history the Church's practices of healing and exorcism have always been a source of ambivalence. One can say that:

> *the Church ... has always had some difficulty in discovering how it should respond to its Lord's command to heal. In contrast to the other imperatives – to preach, teach, and baptize, whose implementation has presented no problems – the imperative to heal has always created some confusion.*[4]

Perhaps, one of the reasons for this difficulty is the failure of theology to incorporate the ministry for the sick as an integral part of the Church's total mission. It has not succeeded in grasping how intimately and inseparably

---

[4] J. McGilvray, The Quest for Health and Wholeness, German Institute for Medical Missions, Tübingen, 1981, 1.

interwoven are the kerygma of salvation and the healing ministry to the sick.

This study, therefore, intends to examine the Church's sacrament of anointing of the sick and its relation with the present day healing ministry in the Nigerian context. It will attempt to find out the reason why many Christians in Nigeria and Africa generally prefer prayer houses and African traditional healers to the mainline Churches and their sacraments. To achieve this aim, our pastoral experience, interaction with some healers, and actual participation at healing sessions of some of the healing centres will be brought to bear on this work so that it will not just be book work or what some people call armchair theology. Most of the reports and in formations in this book have been obtained and observed at first hand.

Chapter one situates the context of the study by examining the key phrases of our theme. But more importantly it presents the Nigerian situation which mirrors the African condition also with its quest for healing and the reasons for this quest. The methods and techniques of the healers are also examined. Chapter two is a survey of the various attitudes towards sickness and healing from both a religious and a human point of view. It begins with those of both the ancient Greek and Islamic cultures; delves into the African world view, then that of the secularized world which was prevalent from the 16th century onwards deriving basically from the birth of modern sciences, particularly medicine; and ends with the modern insights on sickness and healing.

Chapter three offers a detailed discussion on the biblical understanding of sickness and healing. It reveals that biblical revelation is concerned with the religious meaning of sickness and healing in the plan of salvation. An historical synopsis of the Church's long tradition of anointing the sick will be reviewed. Our aim is to show that this sacrament just like every other sacrament is a living phenomenon which is continually adapted to the concrete situation of any given historical epoch. The development of the sacraments cannot be considered apart from the ideas, values, and thought systems that characterize the continual development of humanity. Sometimes these ideas, values, and thought systems contribute to a healthy development of a sacrament; at other times they can work against that development. This was the fate of the fifth sacrament of the Church and constitutes the subject matter of chapter four.

Chapter five elaborately examines the revised rites for the sick as it evolved from the reforms of the Second Vatican Council, promulgated by the Roman Congregation for Divine Worship in 1972, and accompanied by the Apostolic Constitution Sacram unctionem infirmorum of Paul VI. At the end of this consideration it is hoped that enough evidence will be gathered to delineate the ritual meanings of the anointing of the sick and charismatic healing. In addition, other related themes like repentance and healing, suffering and dying under the sign of the cross, Jesus' own ministry to the sick which is continued in his Church are all discussed in chapter six.

Chapter seven draws pastoral implications from the entire investigation. Following the spirit of aggiornamento of Vatican II, it tries to translate the Church's faith into terms understandable to the culture of the African and Nigerian (Igbo) people by making concrete suggestions in the actual and practical exercise of inculturation. The general conclusion reiterates the major points raised in the entire book and brings it to a final end.

Chapter One
Contextual Considerations

"No one speaks from nowhere" is a famous dictum credited to the philosopher Paul Ricoeur. This basic truth compels us to begin our discussion by situating the context of study. The major phrases and terms of our topic need to be explained; not so much from their dictionary or encyclopedic meaning but more from their contextual and sociological relevance. These include Anointing of the Sick, the Healing Ministry, and the Nigerian Pastoral Experience. It is important to note, for example, that the anointing of the sick as one of the sacraments of the Church did not evolve from nowhere. The use of oil was already in vogue at the time of Jesus. In other words, he was simply making use of materials in his culture and transforming them into something salvific.

In the same way, the healing ministry is nothing new in the Church. It has been part and parcel of the Church's proclamation of the Good News of the Kingdom of God. But how and why this ministry has assumed a dramatic and spectacular dimension in Nigeria today needs to be investigated. The Nigerian situation, therefore, will be analyzed with its galaxy of problems which many believe are responsible for the quest for healing observable in the land. All these will form the basis of discussion in this first chapter.

1.1 Anointing of the Sick

The phrase "Anointing of the Sick" will be used throughout this book to refer to the fifth sacrament of the Church. Of all the sacraments, the anointing of the sick is perhaps the least understood. An indication to this effect is the fact that its name has been changed so often: Extreme Unction, Anointing of the Sick. At a time it was called "Last Rites."

With each subsequent change of name, the Church seeks to clarify the purpose of this sacrament. Over the centuries the sacrament was "conferred more and more exclusively on those at the point of death"[1] and that led to

---
[1] CCC, 1512.

its name "Extreme Unction," though, erroneously so called. This surely led to a misunderstanding of the sacrament.

Even with Vatican II and its reforms, the misunderstanding has persisted. Most people still regard this sacrament as intended only for those on their deathbed. But nothing could be further from the mind of the Church. Anyone who is seriously ill is eligible.[2] Anointing of the sick is according to the confession and teaching of the Catholic Church one of the seven sacraments of the New Testament. It was instituted by Christ our Lord as Paul VI wrote in his Apostolic Constitution Sacram unctionem infirmorum, with which he presented to the whole Church, the reform of the rite of the "Last Anointing" on the 30th of November 1974. As we shall see later, the rite is very biblical in its theology and origins. Already a reference is made to the anointing of the sick in Mark's Gospel: The disciples "anointed with oil many that were sick and healed them" (6:13). A similar scene is read in the passage according to James (5:14ff).

The oil used in the anointing of the sick is ordinarily blessed by the Bishop on Holy Thursday Chrism Mass, during the Eucharistic prayer, supported by all the presbyterium.[3] Like most blessings, it is both anamnetic and epicletic, that is, it both recalls by way of memorial the use of oil in salvation history and invokes the power of God upon the oil. Thus sanctified, the oil becomes capable of producing its healing effects for those who use it. During his time, Jesus approved the use of oil and other bodily contacts that were regarded as an important part of the healing process. He also practiced anointing as well as the use of saliva (cf. Jn 9:6). His disciples inherited the custom which eventually developed into a rite of its own and thus became one of the seven sacraments of the Church.

This use of oil was generally recognized in ancient time as a healing aid. In addition to oil, grain (bread) and wine were the most important agricultural products of the Jewish culture so much that Deuteronomy specifically mentions them in its enumeration of the blessings of God (7:13). In Jewish mythology, after the deluge, the olive leaf which the dove brought back to Noah was the first sign of the appearance of the new world (cf. Gen 8:11).

---

[2] CCC, 1514-1515.
[3] Rites of Anointing, 221.

According to the Apocryphal writing of Enoch, the tree of life in Eden was an olive tree and the rivers of paradise flowed with oil and wine (2 Enoch 8:5). The Apocalypse of Moses contains a moving account of Adam longing for the "oil of mercy" which flows from this tree of life (9:3). It reports that Eve and Seth returned to paradise to beg God to grant them this oil of mercy; a plea to which the archangel Michael responds: "Do not tire yourself begging and praying for the tree from which flows this oil to anoint your father. It will not be given to you now, but only at the last days. Then all flesh from Adam to that great day will rise up, all who are a righteous people. Then all the delights of paradise will be given to them" (13:1-3).

It is not surprising then, that oil which was so widespread and vital in the economic life of the people of Israel, took on their symbolic life the meaning of life from and with God. Endowed with such symbolic meaning, oil is obviously preferable for use in ritual action at the event of life, whether physical or spiritual when threatened.[4] In addition, oil was employed in various religious ways. It was used in the coronation of Kings (Jgs 9:8; 1 Sam 9:16, 10:1; 2 Kgs 9:3, 6, Pss 23:5, 45:8, 89:21, etc.); in the ordination of priests (Ex 28:41, 29:7, 29, 30:30-33, 40:13; Lv 4:3, 6:13, 7.36, 8:12; Num 3:3; Dn 9:25; Sir 45:15); in the installation of a prophet (1 Kgs 19:16; Is 61:1; Lk 4:18); consecration of objects of cult (Gen 28:18, 31:13; Ex 29:36, 30:23-29; Num 7:1, 10, 88; Dn 9:24, etc.); care of wounds (Is 1:6; Lk 10:34; Lev 14:15-18, 26-29); embalming the body (Mk 16:1; Lk 24:1).

These varied uses are not completely lost even today. Among the Igbo of Nigeria, the use of oil especially the one extracted from palm kernel in preservation, care of wounds and embalming the body is very common. It is equally widely acknowledged as an antidote for convulsion. Palm oil is used throughout Africa for cooking and eating. The Italians still boast of their olive oil today. Oil provided illumination for lamps; till today the Eastern Orthodox Rite of Unction is still referred to as the Rite of the Lamp, as the oil of anointing may be taken from oil lamps hanging before icons. Today oil serves as a cleansing substance in bathing similar to soap. As Cyprian Anyanwu observes, "People put on oil or cream after a refresh-

---

[4] Cf. G. Lawler, Symbol and Sacrament: A Contemporary Sacramental Theology, New York/Mahwah: Paulist Press, 1987, 156-7.

ing bath, they use perfumed sprays or creams before going for a party."[5]
Such uses of oil led to the origin of the prebaptismal oil of the catechumens with its exorcist and purgative meaning. Oil was also a cosmetic. Chrism is a kind of sacred perfume with a rich symbolism retained in the Greek language: through chrismation we are conformed to Christ (Anointed One) and become Christians (anointed ones). Oil was indeed an indispensable element in the economic life of the ancient Orient. Its pride of place is maintained even today. Perhaps, what could be compared to its ancient all-purpose medium might be "petroleum with its multiple uses for industry, heating, fuel for vehicles, and synthetic products.[6]

1.2 The Healing Ministry

The healing ministry has been part of the mandate of Christ to the Church. It is an old tradition which the Church inherited from its founder. What is probably new is the proportion and dimension it has assumed all over the world today and particularly in Nigeria. It is rooted in the healing diakonia of Jesus himself whose "compassion toward all who suffer goes so far that he identifies himself with them: "I was sick and you visited me" (Matt 25:36).[7] The Church received this charge of healing the sick from the Lord. And ever since then, it strives to carry out this ministry by taking care of the sick. Even today the ministry of healing is still very much alive in the Church, for Christ's commission to his Church to preach the Kingdom of God and to heal the sick was a single commission. The one (preaching) did not continue, while the other (healing) was suspended. Apart from the Church possessing the gift as a community, individual Christians, priests or laity can also receive this charism. One proof of this fact is that the Church uses healing as one of the tests for canonization of its saints. The problem is how and to what extent an individual can practice and establish the heal-

---

[5] C. Anyanwu, The Rites of Initiation in Christian Liturgy and in Igbo Traditional Society, Frankfurt: Peter Lang, 2004, 204-5.
[6] C. W. Gusmer, And You Visited Me: Sacramental Ministry to the Sick and the Dying, Collegeville, Minnesota: The Liturgical Press, 1990, 6.
[7] CCC, 1503.

ing ministry in his/her home, parish, uncompleted building or even in public places like stadium and market squares.

The healing ministry did not originate from the Pentecostals as many people tend to believe. Indeed, there was a time in their history when the phenomenon of healing was denied and rejected by some of their founders. It was not until the nineteenth century AD that healing began to be accepted by non-Catholics. However, it must be said that the Pentecostals popularized the practice. With the popularity came also the many abuses. Naturally, the Church which has experienced so many schisms and heresies in its history retreated to the background and became skeptical of the new trend or should one say boom of the healing ministry. Ever since then, the Church has continued to reflect on the nature and place of healing in its mission. This culminated in the promulgation on November 18, 1965 of the decree *Apostolicam Actuositatem* (Decree on the Apostolate of the Laity) of Vatican II. The Church recognizes that the Holy Spirit allots special and varied gifts to the faithful as he wills (1 Cor 12:7) but it insists that,

It is for the pastors to pass judgment on the authenticity and good use of these gifts, not certainly with a view to quenching the Spirit but to testing everything and keeping what is good (cf. 1 Thess 5:12, 19, 21).[8]

One fact that must always be kept in mind is that Jesus did not make healing the most important or even the only significant feature or sign of Christianity. The apostles and the apostolic Fathers never considered healing to be the foundation on which to build the Church of Christ. Moreover, the Church's mission in the world is a holistic one which comprises its loving, healing, reconciling presence with special concern and affection for the helpless, the sick, the infirm, and the aged. The Church's option is and should always be first and foremost for the poor and the lowly.

This overall ministry of reconciliation and healing entails a prophetic and humanizing influence on social and environmental issues which often is so easily neglected, such as adequate housing for the poor, a more equitable sharing of food with the hungry, the prevention of drug and alcohol abuse, coping with AIDS pandemic, a better equitable distribution of natural re-

---

[8] Vatican II, Apostolicam Actuositatem, 3.

sources, and nuclear disarmament. All this can be realized when deeply rooted in the entire reality and message of the kingdom of God. As is evident here, healing is just one of the ministries of the Church. Therefore, the Church cannot enthrone healing over and above the other ministries. It remains one of the ministries and sacraments in the Church. As Charles Gusmer points out "the Church's ministry of healing should not be isolated or viewed apart from the rest of its mission to be visible sign of Christ's continued presence in the world."[9] And the views of T. Onoyima are also very relevant:

> *Healing has always been a part of the Church but it must be controlled by those authorities concerned especially when healing ministries become a centre of many abnormalities and aberrations.*[10]

1.3 The Nigerian Pastoral Experience

It is important to situate the context of our discussion on the Anointing of the Sick and the Healing Ministry. That context is Nigeria and the situation of the Church in grappling with its divine imperative to heal. Although, healing has been in vogue since the emergence of the African Independent Churches[11] at the beginning of the twentieth century, it was the Pentecostals who popularized the phenomenon in Nigeria. Pentecostalism which began in the USA in 1901 made its debut in Nigeria in the 1970s.

Initially, people laughed at such groups which were springing up in every corner like mushrooms. No wonder they were called names like "Mushroom Churches," "Church of Clapping Worshippers," "Alleluia Churches," etc. Today, however, the phenomenon has become so widespread that it is a

---

[9] C. W. Gusmer, And You Visited Me: Sacramental Ministry to the Sick and the Dying, 1990, 155.

[10] T. Onoyima, "Priestly Formation, Charismatism, Pentecostalism and the Healing Ministry: New Trends in African Christianity" in V. M. Okeke (ed.), Bigard Diamond Jubilee Essays, Nsukka: Fulladu Publishing Company, 2001, 276.

[11] To the African Independent Churches (some call them African Indigenous Churches, or African Initiated Churches) belong the Aladura, Cherubim and Seraphim, Faith Tabernacle, etc.

mere waste of energy trying to count the number of those who operate Churches, healing centers or prayer houses.[12] These are littered virtually in almost every street in Nigerian towns and cities. Most of the uncompleted buildings, abandoned ware houses, cinema houses that are in disuse, garages, town halls, etc. are all used as Churches or healing places. Some even operate in their private homes. The phenomenon has eventually found its way into the Catholic Church thanks to the founding of the Catholic Charismatic Renewal in 1974.[13] With this last straw, the Carmel's back was broken. It seemed that the opportune time of liberation from the "tyranny" and control of the hierarchy had arrived. Members of the group claimed that they have had a religious experience distinct from their reception of the sacraments of initiation. They felt that "their lives as members of the historic Church lack some forgotten factor which they are no longer content to do without."[14] Part of the "forgotten factor" was probably the realization that they possessed various charismatic gifts especially that of healing which no authority had any right to control.

In order "to provide an alternative for Catholics who defected to the Aladura Churches"[15] and other Charismatic groups, Father Godwin Ikeobi and Monsignor Matthew Obiukwu started some form of prayer ministry in Onitsha area. Soon thereafter many priests especially the younger ones joined the bandwagon of healing ministry so much so that today "there is hardly any Catholic diocese in Nigeria that has not one or more healing centers organized by Catholic priests or by some lay Cathoics."[16] The situation has become so chaotic that it has led to the break down of discipline and the abuse of the sacraments and liturgical celebrations in some dio-

---

[12] A. Nwabekee tried to do so and could only "mention but a few." See his "Liturgical Formation in the Seminary" in V. M. Okeke (ed.), Bigard Diamond Jubilee Essays, 2001, 258.

[13] Courtesy of the Dominican Fathers in Nigeria who started the movement shortly after a visit of one of their own, Francis MacNutt, OP, the then renowned American priest who was actively involved in the healing ministry. See A. I. Umoren, Jesus and Miracle Healing Today, Ibadan: Intec Printers, 2000, 33.

[14] J. V. Taylor, The Go-Between God: The Holy Spirit and The Christian Mission, London: SCM Press, 1972, 198.

[15] H. C. Achunike, The Influence of Pentecostalism on Catholic Priests and Seminarians in Nigeria, Lagos: Rex Charles and Patrick, 2004, 78.

[16] A. Nwabekee, "Liturgical Formation in the Seminary," 2001, 258.

ceses. It is only understandable that the Church's hierarchy and indeed any sane observer will be worried. Bishop Alexius Makozi expresses the concern of his brother bishops in the following way:

> *The Church hierarchy has over the past few years been worried about the increasing number of healing ministries. It is known that some self-seeking priests and pastors are responsible for the break down of discipline in some Churches.*[17]

It was this worry that necessitated the National Theological and Pastoral Seminar on Healing Ministry held at Enugu, from 12th-14th February 1992. After further study and deliberation, the Bishops' Conference later issued in 1997 some pastoral Guidelines for the Healing Ministry in the Catholic Church in Nigeria. Since then, many seminars and conferences have been organized on the theme.[18] Many books and articles have in recent times been published by both sympathizers[19] and critics[20] of the phenomenon. The present effort, however, is geared towards locating the healing ministry where it properly belongs, namely, in the Church's holistic ministry of salvation.

Despite these worries, the ministry has continued to multiply geometrically and to sustain its irresistible attraction both for the healers themselves and their clients. The latter are in constant search for solutions to their problems which seem to increase on daily basis, but unfortunately do not seem to get the desired solution.

---

[17] A. O. Makozi, Foreword to the book: The Healing Ministry by Pius Kii, Enugu: Snaap Press, 2004, VI.

[18] For instance, the 8th National Theological Conference held at the National Missionary Seminary of St Paul, Gwagwalada, Abuja, April 13-16, 1993; The Missiology Symposium on Healing and Exorcism: The Nigerian Experience organized by the Spiritan International School of Theology (SIST), Attakwu, Enugu, May 18-20, 1989, with the proceedings published later in 1992 and many other conferences held in individual dioceses.

[19] H. C. Achunike sees his book as sympathetically looking "at healing as it is practised by priests." See his already cited work: The Influence of Pentecostalism, 2004, 76.

[20] N. I. Ndiokwere, Search for Security, Benin City: Ambik Press, 1990; B. A. C. Obiefuna, Endure to the End: Charismatics and the Hard Times, Enugu: Pearl Functions, 1997; Fidelis Obiora, The Divine Deceit: Business in Religion, Enugu: Optimal Publishers, 1999, etc.

1.4 The Quest for Healing

The Nigerian situation prompts one to ask why this upsurge of healing ministry? Why has this phenomenon invaded the Catholic Church? Why are many young priests lured to the ministry or put the other way round why is the ministry of healing holding such an attraction to Catholic priests? Why are many Nigerian Christians - Catholics and non-Catholics alike flocking to the healing ministries no matter where they are found? These are some of the questions which this section will attempt to find answers. A lot has been written on this issue. However, we shall treat just two factors that we consider the most important.

1.4.1 Influence of Indigenous Cosmology

Generally speaking, people flock to the healing ministry and prayer houses in search of solutions to their various problems which could be spiritual, psychological, emotional or even economical. These range from diseases, psychosomatic illnesses, barrenness, to protection from enemies and the fulfillment of their ambitions and hopes. This is why today, one finds people of varying social and economic positions including engineers, lawyers, magistrates, politicians, senior police and army officers patronizing these healers.

At the background of the search for security and well-being is the influence of the African Traditional Religion. As we shall see in chapter two, African peoples believe that all forms of misfortune including sickness, barrenness, mental disorder, premature death, unhappy family life, accident, absence of material well-being, etc. are caused by the activities of ubiquitous evil spirits, angry gods, vengeful ancestors and evil forces operating through the agency of witchcraft or magic. Being a people whose indigenous cosmology is "'heavily anthropocentric' (that is primarily and largely centered on human beings and their general well-being)," [21] the people resist all calamities that impede their well-being with all available resources including pla-

---

[21] C. I. Ejizu, "Cosmological Perspective on Exorcism and Prayer-Healing in Contemporary Nigeria," in C. U. Manus (ed.) et al, Healing and Exorcism: The Nigerian Experience, Enugu: Snaap Press, 1992, 17.

cating the gods and spirits.

This explains to a large extent the presence of uncountable deities in African Traditional Religion. Indeed, among the Igbo of Nigeria, no traditional priest knows the names of all the gods. This fact is illustrated by the conclusion of prayer in Igbo religion, which sometimes assumes the form of threat of abandonment in search of another deity, should the one being petitioned fail to fulfill the desire of the petitioner.[22] M. J. C. Echeruo confirms that the Igbo "are a thoroughly iconoclastic people" who acknowledge the power of the gods, and cultivate that power, but should the gods consistently fail to prove themselves powerful, the people reserve the right to discard them and seek out new gods. In fact, circumstances greater than the gods themselves will eventually take care of the matter.[23]

This pragmatic religious outlook is not peculiar to the Igbo alone. Many African traditional societies share the same world view in which religion is above all, a practical problem solver. The practice of medicine and healing is thus, perceived as essentially religious. These indigenous Africans embraced Christianity with the burden of their cosmology. One would have expected that after so many centuries of the advent of Western culture, other faiths, science and technology, etc. new outlooks, belief-system and value orientations could have prevailed over the traditional ones. No! The old religious ideas and influences have refused to die, confirming Durkheim's assertion that "there is something eternal in religion which is destined to survive all the particular symbols in which religious thought successfully enveloped itself."[24] The pragmatic religious attitude of the African reveals itself thus in the proliferation of healing ministries and Churches. But the riddle is that most of these Churches are reverting to the renounced "pagan" practices.

There is today a resurgence and revival of African Traditional Religion in modified and complicated forms. Many of these healers, including Catholic priests could easily pass for "dibia priests" of the old African Traditional

---

[22] A. Echema, Corporate Personality in Traditional Igbo Society and the Sacrament of Reconciliation, Frankfurt: Peter Lang, 1995, 10.

[23] M. J. C. Echeruo, "A Matter of Identity" in Ahiajoku Lecture, Owerri: Government Press, 1979, 19.

[24] E. Durkheim, Elementary Forms of the Religious Life, London: George Allen and

Religion. They employ practices like burying of crucifix, salt, sacramentals, animals, mutilating some parts of the body to effect cure, blaming people's ill-luck or misfortune on particular trees or objects in their neighborhood and opting for the destruction of such, digging up of objects from the ground of compounds of the sick people, etc. All these are reminiscent of the old African Traditional Religion.[25] It has been observed that the reality of this religion reveals itself in moments of crisis such as cases of childlessness, sickness, death, witchcraft, failure in business, accident or natural disaster. At such periods, Christians of both Catholics and non-Catholics betray their faith. They make clandestine visits not only to healing Churches or homes believed to bring the desired results but even also to sorcerers and magicians.

All these underline the Igbo principle that "the essence of the godhead is power."[26] The concept of being as action predisposes the Igbo or any other African for that matter to the acceptance of a wide range of deities. The attitude of "shopping" or "prostituting" from one healing centre to the other and consulting one diviner or marabouts again goes to prove the pragmatic nature of African Traditional Religion which is still influencing most African Christians. I do not quite agree with Anthony Umoren that consulting "traditional oracles, witch doctors and healers" by Christians is a last resort when efforts to get "solutions to their problems from the miracle centers" fail.[27] To my mind no avenue is left out in the pursuit of solution to problems. The same is also true of the healers; they employ all sorts of practices - orthodox and unorthodox alike. This agrees with the Igbo saying "Ma Chi ma Ekwensu zowa, onye zotaranu ya ewere" (Let both God and Satan be involved in the struggle whoever wins, let him take). Our view is confirmed by Healey and Sybertz who reported about East African people that "when a serious need arises, local people will try everything – any medicine, any cure, any religion, the advice of any healer."[28] But Umoren is

---

Unwin, 1915, 427.
[25] See M. Jiwike (ed.), The Challenges of the Pastoral Ministry in a Pluralistic Society, Owerri: Assumpta Press, 2004, 65.
[26] D. I. Nwoga, "Nka na Nzere: The focus of Igbo World View," in Ahiajoku Lecture, Owerri: Government Press, 1984, 19.
[27] A. I. Umoren, Jesus and Miracle Healing Today, 200, 46.
[28] J. Healey and D. Sybertz, Towards an African Narrative Theology, Nairobi: Pauli-

right and I agree with him that "just as in the traditional setting, if the Christian is not satisfied with the particular Church or healing centre, he or she moves to the next one in search of a more powerful and more experienced miracle healer."[29]

Very closely related to the foregoing reason why many Christians in Africa flock to the healing Churches and centers is the reality of poverty, hunger, illiteracy, sickness, and other human-made problems in the land. It is to these problems that we will turn in the next section.

1.4.2 Reality of Socio-economic and Political Difficulties

Africa is "a continent full of bad news."[30] It is a continent of misery. This reality is not an exaggeration or one of those plots by foreign media to look down on Africa. The African Synod Fathers caught the picture vividly:

One common situation, without any doubt, is that Africa is full of problems. In almost all our nations, there is abject poverty, tragic mismanagement of available scarce resources, political and social disorientation. The results stare us in the face: misery, wars, despairs.[31]

In Nigeria, for example, the situation is the same. There is a total collapse of social and economic infrastructure, decadence of educational system, erosion of moral values, enduring state of political instability, general insecurity of lives and property, unemployment, low wages and income, delayed payment of salaries, poor health care delivery, high mortality rate, etc. The list of misery is inexhaustible.

Fulton Sheen once remarked that poverty has other inconveniences outside food and drink. One of such inconveniences is the inability to consider a medical option in the event of sickness. Our people are "caught in a web of poverty and misery, disease and ignorance,[32] that many are unable to solve their health and economic problems. In such a situation of wretchedness

---

nes Publications Africa, 1995, 294.
[29] A. I. Umoren, Jesus and Miracle Healing Today, 2000, 45.
[30] John Paul II, Encyclical Letter Ecclesia in Africa (14 September 1995), 40.
[31] Ibid.
[32] C. J. Uzor, Living Between Two Worlds: Intrapersonal Conflict Among Igbo Semi-

and despair, they turn to the God of miracle whom they are taught is able "to make the impossible possible."[33] In any case, most villages have no access to medical facilities. Even where there are hospitals which are mostly in the major cities, these are characterized by non-existent or ineffective equipment, fake and expired drugs, under-staffing and quackery. Most of them are merely consulting homes and serve better as mortuaries. The few good ones are naturally unaffordable to the masses. Poverty is one of the major factors that drive most people to healing Churches.

However, very closely related to poverty is illiteracy and ignorance. Up till today many people among the Igbo of Nigeria still believe that certain illnesses are not cured in the hospital. For example, things like stroke, paralysis (mba muo), hospital treatment is out of the question. They attribute such illnesses to evil spirits or to a witch and so bring such cases to healing houses or centers. Many healers capitalize on the ignorance of our people and brainwash and manipulate them with false teaching, giving them false hope that never gets fulfilled.

Indeed, the two factors mentioned above, namely, the indigenous cosmological underpinnings and the reality of abject poverty are the major reasons why people surge to Pentecostal Churches and healing centers. On these two factors depend all other reasons like the search for security,[34] misinterpretation of the Bible on miraculous healing,[35] etc.

1.5 Methods Employed by Healers

As we have mentioned earlier, many healers, both Catholics (priests inclusive) and Pentecostals employ practices which seem dubious, unorthodox and often reminiscent of African traditional dibia priests. This section will attempt to describe what exactly takes place between a healer and his or her client in an individual healing session and in a group public healing service.

---

narians – An Inquiry, Frankfurt: Peter Lang, 2003, 454.
[33] "Omere imposibility possible" is one of those popular choruses with which the "healers" confuse and deceive the local people.
[34] N. Ndiokwere, Search for Security, 1990.
[35] A. Umoren, Jesus and Miracle Healing Today, 2000, 48-74.

Many healers claim they are following the example of Jesus, who healed principally through the power of his word (cf. Mk 5:41-42; Lk 4:35-36); sometimes accompanied with a touch (Mk 1:31; 5:41; Matt 8:15); occasionally too using spittle (cf. Mk 7:33-34; 8:23); clay or washing with water (Jn 9:6-7); etc. The disciples later anointed the sick with oil (Mk 6:13). In a similar way, the healers make use of various elements - crucifix, holy water, candles, holy oil, medals, scapular, holy pictures and other blessed materials. These are common among Catholic healers. The Pentecostals are more sophisticated in their use of the bible, handkerchief, olive oil, apron, etc. In some healing centers, the clients take some of these elements home and are told to deep them like the handkerchief into their water used for drinking, cooking and bathing. Some Catholic priest healers have more recently introduced new phenomena into their healing methods. Some known as "Family Priests" (Fada Ezinauno) bury crucifixes, bags of salt, live animals in the ground, perform nocturnal rituals at river sides or grave yards, make sacrifices to pacify dead angry ancestors, encourage second burials, celebrate what they call black Mass at midnight with colored and specified number of candles. These practices appear superstitious and remind one of the old African Traditional Religion. They are practices that were associated more with African Independent Churches and their counterparts among the Pentecostal groups.

However, a typical healing session of an individual patient begins with a long consultation whereby the healer establishes a profound sense of personal relationship with his or her client. This is achieved through hypnotism in which the patient is made to fall into a deep, calm sleep or trance which induces control over him or her. The patient is told to relax and close the eyes; and literally he or she obeys. The healer then begins to pray with closed eyes, fisted and swinging arms and, pestering around the patient.

Mother Gacambi once narrated a session she had with Archbishop Emmanuel Milingo:

> *He just told me to sit on the armchair and he stood beside me and said something to this effect: 'Lord, when you were on earth the human bodies were subject to you, make this body be subject to me.' And then he put his hand on my head saying: 'Mama go to*

sleep.' I literally went to sleep. Peacefully, calmly and completely relaxed ... that kind of sleep whereby one is half conscious and half asleep ... I continued to hear the Archbishop ordering the various parts of the body 'Heart, in the Name of Jesus pump the blood to all parts of the body ... thanks be to God. Deo Gracias,' ... He went on to call the bones of the pelvis to go back to their place ... calling on the Name of Jesus involving the saints and the Blessed Virgin Mary ... I came to full consciousness when I heard the Archbishop say, Mama wake up, and with his hands on mine lifted me from the chair ... I realized the session had taken almost two hours ...[36]

This pattern described above is followed by virtually all the Nigerian healers, at least the popular and established ones in the Catholic circle, with minor differences. Prayer is the central and essential element in their method. Such prayer can sometimes be very intensive, leaving the healer extremely exhausted. The content of the prayer combines a direct calling on the name of God (several times), Christ and the saints with precise reference to that which is being prayed for. At some other times the healers use instruments like medicines of a sort (modern medicine or traditional herbs, etc.), holy water, water mixed with cod liver oil or palm kernel oil, a cup of tea, etc. Among the Pentecostals, something like a rod or staff is used reminiscent of the rod of Moses and Aaron. Some consider touching as important working instrument in their healing ministry. Consequently, they touch the ailing parts of the body, oftentimes indiscreetly anointing them, and sometimes undertaking to bathe their "clients with special water and oil."[37] Since most of the cases are often that of barrenness and young girls involved with the Queen of Water (Mamiwata), it is not surprising that one hears criticisms and complaints stimulated by this touching of women.

Many of the clients fall down during such sessions; others cry; and still others shake and tremble. This phenomenon of falling at the touch of the

---

[36] The Demarcations, 47, quoted by Adrian Hastings, African Catholicism: Essays in Discovery, London: SCM Press, 1989, 145.
[37] A. Echema, "Pastoral Administration of Sacraments and Sacramentals: Abuses," in M. Jiwike (ed.), The Challenges of the Pastoral Ministry in a Pluralistic Society, 2004, 50.

healer is often observed at the television and stadium healing sessions. Many of these fallings are claimed by some critics to be anticipated and pre-arranged in such a way that the patient falls into the arms of the attendants. As in the case of Archbishop Milingo, many healers speak in tongues (glossolalia) during their prayer sessions.

A typical public healing session among Catholic priest healers takes place within the Mass. It begins also with consultations, confessions, counseling, reconciling of warring groups or parties. While these are going on, the "prayer warriors" which usually are made up of mostly young illiterate girls are positioned at strategic corners of the praying ground or hall singing, beating of musical instruments and dancing. Music and dance play a very significant role in the public healing service. Then, the Mass begins as usual but with an elaborate penitential rite, during which water and salt are blessed and sprinkled or should one say poured on the congregation. Part of these are taken home as sacramentals. This is followed by the liturgy of the word. It is in the sermon that the healer exhibits all the charisms he possesses. The sermon is laced with choruses, bible quotations, speaking in tongues, gesticulations, and occasionally with dancing. A certain tone of voice is adopted, sometimes cajoling, commanding, and threatening. Some people normally fall down during the sermon. These are usually gathered together as special cases to be looked into at the end of the Mass. Such sermons can last for two hours or more. Then, the prayer of intercession follows which is often mixed up with testimonies and deliverances. People give account of what God has done for them – saving them from dangers or favors they have received – bursting intermittently into choruses and dancing. At the end of each testimony, there is prayer of thanksgiving and imposition of hands.

The next elaborate item is offertory. Those who have received favors or deliverance are expected to show appreciation and donate generously. A lot of time is allotted to offertory which sometimes could turn into a mini launching, presentation of gifts and donations of large sums of money to the "man of God."

The Eucharistic liturgy which comes next is in most cases simply to fulfill all righteousness because at this point both the "man of God" and the congregation are tired, what is understandable after almost four to five hours service. After Holy Communion another session is conducted for those who fell down during the sermon. This is called ministration. In addition, sacramentals are blessed. These range from scapular, crucifix, olive oil, rosary, handkerchief, holy pictures, bible, ring, writing materials (especially for those taking exams) to handsets and car keys. Everything is then covered with "the blood of Jesus" including the offertory proceeds, especially the money, the taxis and buses that will take worshippers home. The Pentecostal healing session follows this pattern except that they have no Eucharist. Many of them use water and olive oil. But the bible plays the most significant role in their healing prayer worship.

A closer examination at the healing techniques employed by some of the healers – whether Catholics or non-Catholics, Pentecostals or African Traditional Religionists – reveals a basic fact, namely, reliance on natural, psychic, African traditional religious and occult practices.[38] There are several natural means and exercises to improve health, like Yoga, Zen, Transcendental Meditation (TM), Silva Method, Reiki Positive Mental Attitude, which can be fostered through self-suggestion or auto-suggestion, Cathartic Method, Hypnotic Power, Logotherapy (Christotherapy), etc.[39] A little explanation of some of these techniques will be helpful.

a) Self-Suggestion (Auto-Suggestion)

This is a process whereby patients are induced into believing that they have been cured. For example, when one repeats helpful, positive self-affirmations like "Day by day in every respect I am getting better and better," or "I am healed," or "I am covered with the blood of Jesus," with frequency and emotion it is believed that in that way one can influence the subconscious mind. This is a process of Positive Mental Attitude (PMA). This explains the shouting and repetition of such phrases like "You are healed," or "shout alleluia" (at times repeated 10x at a stretch) which one

---

[38] Cf. A. I. Umoren, Jesus and Miracle Healing Today, 2000, 104; see also F. E. Ogbunu, Power to Cast out Demons, Makurdi: Onaivi Printing and Publishing Company, 1994, 79-92.
[39] I. da C. Souza, The Healing Ministry, Santa Cruz, Goa: New Age Printers, 1999, 30-35.

hears ad nauseam among Nigeria TV preachers and "healers." By shouting and repeating so frequently such positive self-affirmations, the patients begin to believe them.

b) Silva Method of Mind Control

The Mexican-American Jose Silva began to teach the Silva Mind Control Method in 1966. Today, more than 10 million people in over 180 countries are followers. It leads to professional success, happiness and maximum well-being. He found out that the mind operates on many different frequencies/levels. By attuning to the special frequency called ALPHA, a healing state is activated. If one can control one's brain waves, one can literally change one's life and that of those around.

Everybody is born with the capacity for intuitive thinking but education and society force us to use logic. As psychologists put it, we use the left hemisphere of the brain more than the right hemisphere. Meditation induces "calming, catharsis of tension, insight into the nature of the personal process and is often of considerable therapeutic value."[40] The method teaches one how to put forces at work to create an event one wishes to happen, improve one's memory, use one's intuitive mind while dreaming to solve problems and use one's imagination to kick bad habits. For instance, one could get healed of skin diseases or ward off pain from a recurring hernia.

The method can be used for different purposes. It helps one to view the world in a different perspective, without getting tensed while handling a situation. It can bring about remission of fever or bronchitis, or stem bleeding due to heart surgery, or make a person be free from a chronic headache, or cure viral encephalitis or be relaxed. It helps also in judging people better. It is a gradual progressive process - first, one is asked to set small goals. It improves the rapport with people, and increases self-confidence: "I feel I am going to be the winner" or "The Lord is going to do it again in my life." The technique emphasizes the primacy of the mind over matter, as the Roman adage says: "The mind supplants the matter" (Mens agitate molem). One can act upon one's intuition.

---

[40] Ibid.

It is clear that many of us are not tapping our potentials to its fullest capacity. For example, many of us cannot use our left hand or leg; instead of using all our teeth, we use them only on one side. With the Silva method, we can experience our infinite capabilities and learn to develop and use them for a better life. By using this scientific method, one can improve one's memory and help others in learning faster and better. It can help one to improve one's self image by rejecting thoughts of inferiority or guilt. One can enhance positive thinking, reasonable self-esteem, self-assertiveness and performance. Rhoda Lachar teaches the use of prayer to improve self: "Lord, help me to be what you want me to be." God is the "switch-board" for continuous conversion and self-improvement.[41]

c) Catharsis

This is the natural process of bringing into light what lies hidden in the subconscious mind. God allows the natural process of psychological healing by giving his supernatural light so that the hidden incidents may be brought out from the subconscious into light-the supernatural reinforces and accelerates the natural process of psychological healing.

d) Logotherapy

One finds meaning or fulfillment in discovering the deep meaning of life and giving meaning to life through creative activity. In other words, what matters is not what we expect from life, but rather what life expects from us. Life ultimately means taking the responsibility to find the right answers to its problems and to fulfill the tasks which it constantly sets for each individual.

Logotherapy was proposed and elaborated by Viktor Frankl.[42] He uses the device of paradoxical intention in curing phobic neurosis by intentionally trying to produce the neurotic symptoms (for example, fear of the mob, agoraphobia). The patient not only is unable to do so, but also changes his attitude towards his or her neurosis.

---

[41] See R. Lachar, You are Unlimited, quoted by P. McIntosch, "Faith is Powerful Medicine," in Reader's Digest, November 1999, 103-106.

[42] V. Frankl, The Doctor of the Soul: From Psychotherapy to Logotherapy, New York: World, 1973.

These are natural human methods which can be used to improve health and life. They could be used and through prayer be lifted to an extraordinary level. In the Christian context, Christ gives meaning to our life (Christo-therapy). Certain illnesses can be cured by such professional healing activities. Let us consider some of them briefly and how the therapy works.

Psychogenic Diseases
Psychosomatic or psycho-physiological diseases affect the body, but have their roots in anxiety, resentment or bitterness. These are genuine bodily ailments, where the physical discomfort is induced by emotional rather than organic factors. The patient may develop peptic ulcer, asthma, migraine, tension headache, rheumatoid arthritis, acne, cardio-vascular disorders. Cancer can be also stress-related disease. Alcoholism and smoking are the common signs of tension.

All these complications can be caused by four elements, namely, fear (of the dark, of high places, of falling, of loud noises, of snakes, of failure, of death), guilt (normal and abnormal), inferiority complex and misguided love (hate). These psychosomatic diseases can be cured through the ministry of prayer, for instance, arthritis related to pent-up anger can be dramatically cleared up by forgiveness/inner healing. But this is a real cure because from the medical viewpoint it is more difficult to cure stress-related diseases than purely bodily sickness. Prayer can also speed up the natural recuperative forces, for example, viral fever at a common level or cancer at a more difficult level. This is a common experience of priests whether "healers" or not when doctors refer certain patients to them. Bernard Häring shares a similar view:

> Very frequently in my experience, a psychotherapist has suggested at a certain point that the patient should see a priest to talk more explicitly on the spiritual dimension of the person's neurosis or to reach a higher point through the celebration of the Sacrament of Reconciliation and Healing.[43]

Godwin Ikeobi often gave statistics of such cases that were referred to him

---

[43] B. Häring, Healing and Revealing, Middlegreen, Slough: St. Paul Publications, 1984, 41.

by doctors.[44] Certainly, the power of God can quicken the natural healing process, for healing takes place through nature, God's creation.

1) Conversion Reaction in Clinical Psychology

There is another type of disease called "conversion reaction" in clinical psychology and psychiatry. Certain mental problems are converted into physical symptoms, for example, a person who has a strong need for attention and sympathy may develop paralysis or blindness. It may also lead to escapism whereby the patient escapes from difficult situations. This symptom is common among simple, credulous, feeble-minded people, who are easily suggestible. At the powerful suggestion of the preacher/healer, they will be "cured." Some of these "cures" may be of the type of "hysteric conversion reactions." These diseases are purely psychological and have no physical basis.

2) Spontaneous Remissions

There is a common phenomenon known as "spontaneous remissions" in diseases like schizophrenia and cancer. This may last for some time. For example, a terminal cancer patient may suddenly be "cured" of symptoms like pain. Then all of a sudden, the patient becomes seriously ill again and dies. Some of the alleged healings may be merely spontaneous remissions.

3) The "Placebo Effect" in Medicine

A person suffering, for example, from a splitting headache may be comforted by the physician's information that he or she will be given an injection of a new drug recently manufactured in the world. This news will humor and booster the patient, so that even if an injection of sterile water is given, the headache may be instantly "cured". Surely, this is not the effect of the new drug but of "faith" in the new drug and in the physician, who tried to exploit his or her patient's psychic behavior. A new hope in the patient may effect changes in the brain system (for example, production of the endorphin) and "heal" diseases.[45] Most of the people who are cured at the

---

[44] See G. Ikeobi, "Healing and Exorcism: The Nigerian Pastoral Experience," 1992, 60-61.
[45] Cf. The Mystery of Healing, Theological Research Centre, London: Quest, 1981, 39.

healing centers and services are patients with psychosomatic diseases. Solemn, pathetic preaching, group prayers, loud singing and praises, music and dancing, intercessions, touch by imposition of hands can facilitate the process of healing.

As Souza rightly emphasizes "these phenomena are not miracles. Most of them are based on psychological factors."[46] Souza is not alone in his verdict. Umoren is equally of the opinion that all that happens at healing services is not miracle. Some of them are "outright trickery and fakery." In his words: "Oftentimes what is termed a healing miracle is in reality not a healing miracle at all, but the effects of psychic, African traditional religious and occult beliefs and practices."[47] Nobody doubts or denies the reality of miracles. Indeed, miracles do happen every day. But not every cure or healing is a miracle. Even the Church that uses healing as one of the criteria for canonization is very cautious in declaring any phenomenon a miracle. For instance, between 1947 and 1988, among the 1,350 dossiers opened in connection with "alleged" healings at Lourdes, 56 cases were recognized by the Medical Bureau (only 47 of these were presented to the Medical Committee, for 9 occurred before 1947).[48]

It is not our intention to go into the phenomenon of miracle and the criteria for establishing its occurrence. It suffices to say that reports of healings are often exaggerated under the spell of enthusiasm. Miracle (from the Latin word miraculum, wonder) is an astounding, extraordinary event. What has occurred is a breach of the usual natural order. Nature on its own does not bring forth miracles; if they occur, the laws of nature must, by way of exception, have been suspended; and such a suspension can only be ascribed, directly or indirectly, to God, the Lord of the universe and of history.

In the same way, the healing techniques involving hypnotism, logotherapy, suggestion and auto-suggestion, etc. are natural, ordinary means of healing ailments and improving health. But when they aim at manipulating people's emotions to achieve some selfish ends, then they can no longer be justified.

---

[46] I. da C. Sousa, The Healing Ministry, 1999, 35.
[47] A. I. Umoren, Jesus and Miracle Healing Today, 2000, 104-108. See also R. Eya, "Healing and Exorcism: The Psychological Aspects," in C. U. Manus (ed.) et al, Healing and Exorcism: The Nigerian Pastoral Experience, 1992, 51.
[48] See I. da C. Souza, The Healing Ministry, 1999, 41.

Healers should not try to exploit the credulity of their clients. Furthermore, any practice or belief that rules out human freedom and responsibility is dehumanizing and regressive, and therefore, should be opposed and rejected. Such are the so called practices like vision, prophecy, speaking in tongues, dream, and so on which many healers, especially in Nigeria use to deceive people. Some of these processes of diagnosis are reminiscent of the oracles in African Traditional Religion. But in reality these phenomena resemble elements of parapsychology like hypnosis, clairvoyance and fortune telling.[49] Our people must be educated to know that belief in "paranormal" phenomena implies a negation of human freedom if they are taken in a fatalistic way. Such a possibility of predicting the future, with some degree of precision, suggests that the future is predetermined. Humanity is doomed to live it out passively. Such a belief and practice will foster a fatalist attitude to existence.[50]

Summary

Our attention in this chapter has been focused mainly on contextual issues. Anointing and the use of oil were first of all cultural customs before they were appropriated by Christ and eventually elevated to the level of a sacrament. Similarly, the ministry of healing belonged to the holistic mission of Jesus which he later entrusted to his Church. But it was the Pentecostals who popularized the phenomenon in the world and especially in Nigeria. Since its advent, healing has held a strong attraction to both healers and clients not only in the Pentecostal circles but also among the traditional mainline Churches including the Protestant and the Roman Catholic Churches. The ministers and the priests of these Churches have also succumbed to its appeals.

The analysis of the Nigerian context shows that certain factors are responsible for the influx of Christians to these ministries. Among others, two were singled out as the major ones on which all others depended, namely,

---

[49] H. E. Freeman has explained these phenomena in detail. See his Every Wind of Doctrine, Warsaw, Indiana: Faith Ministries and Publications, 1974, 99.

the persistent influence of the cultural religious world view and the scorching abject poverty and suffering of all kinds in the land.

The methods and techniques of the healers which are characterized by elements of parapsychology were considered. It was discovered that they make use of sacramentals like water, oil, candle, bible, apron, scapular, etc. Among the Catholic priest-healers, the Eucharist features prominently, while for the Pentecostals the bible is their most important instrument. Many, however, employ other dubious practices that remind one of the abandoned African Traditional Religion. Above all, they rely heavily on natural, psychic and occult methods like hypnotism, self-suggestion, Silva method of mind control, etc. These are purely natural means which can improve health and cure certain psychogenic diseases. But when these natural means are employed for selfish goals and are manipulated to deny the freedom and emotion of clients, they become something evil and fatal. Such beliefs and practices are dehumanizing and regressive insofar as they rule out human freedom and responsibility. We should, therefore, oppose, criticize and reject them. Illnesses could be cured by these natural means at the healing Churches but yet these are not miracles. In the chapter that follows, we shall examine in more detail the world view of the African as well as that of other cultures as it relates to sickness and healing.

---

[50] See I. da C. Souza, The Healing Ministry, 1999, 36.

Chapter Two
Survey of Various Attitudes towards Sickness and Healing

In this chapter we will consider sickness and healing from both religious and human points of view. The considerations will begin with a cursory reference to the attitude of the ancient Greek and that of Islamic culture. This will be followed with a detailed examination of the African world view on sickness and healing. Then the secularized attitude that was prevalent from the 16th century onwards as it evolved basically from the birth of modern sciences, particularly medicine will be discussed. Finally, we will look at some later insights on sickness and healing which will question the secularized attitude. The aim of this approach is to establish what these other cultures have in common with Christianity and perhaps to see how they will help in the understanding of the mission of the Church concerning human sickness and healing.

2.1 Pre-biblical Times and Sickness

For many centuries, humanity conceived sickness in a mythical way. In ancient Greek tragedy or the literature of the Roman world, it is evident that people considered sickness as a punishment meted out by the gods. The punishment was usually due to some form of disobedience (whether conscious or unconscious). For the Greeks, human pride (hubris) merited the punishment of the gods. However, these same gods who caused the illness could equally effect healing when appeased. In Islamic culture, there is very little literature on illness and healing. The idea of fate or destiny (moira in Greek) was prominent. In other words, sickness is accepted as coming from Allah and therefore, the attitude of resignation is encouraged. This agrees with Islamic view of Allah and its corresponding fatalism.

2.2 Sickness and Healing in African World View

The African world view is one of extraordinary harmony and coherence, where there is no strict demarcation between the sacred and the secular, the natural and the supernatural or the animate and the inanimate.[1] Such a harmonious and holistic outlook includes a complex interaction between God, some mysterious powers, the spirit world and the ancestors. Consequently, sickness is considered to be a sign of evil caused by the destruction of the equilibrium of the community. It is the reaction from the angry deities or displeased ancestors. It could also be caused by witches, sorcerers or the ubiquitous evil spirits. Thus, at the encounter of sickness, death (especially premature death) and other calamities, the first reaction of the African is "who did it and why?" which of the spirits or ancestors had been wronged and what human relationship had been strained?

Sickness is not just a physical condition but also a religious and spiritual matter. Thus,

> ... to deal with it people revert to religious practices. They use religion to find out who has been responsible for it or has sent it to the sick person. They use religion to prescribe the right cure, part of which is often the performance of certain rituals that the medicine man may specify. It is also necessary to take counter measures to make sure that the course of the disease is neutralized so that the person concerned will not suffer from the same disease again.[2]

This duty falls under the portfolio of the traditional diviner. Among the Igbo of Nigeria, there are three types of diviners or healers as they are called in some areas: "Dibia Afa" (diviner), "Dibia Aja" (priest), and "Dibia Ogwu" (medicine man/woman).

An individual may be diviner and priest or diviner and medicine

---

[1] A. Echema, Corporate Personality in Traditional Igbo Society and the Sacrament of Reconciliation, 1995, 4. However, the assertion does not mean that Africans are incapable of distinguishing between the sacred and the profane, the spiritual and the material or between the visible and the invisible.

[2] J. S. Mbiti, Introduction to African Religion, London: SPCK, 1975, 134.

man/woman at the same time.[3] The diviner is a "diagnostician" and a "diviner magician." The medicine man/woman on the other hand is a "physical and psychotherapist/spirit healer or a religious doctor."[4] When someone falls sick, the diviner (Dibia Afa) is consulted to examine the spiritual and the material factors involved. It is his/her duty to first diagnose and identify the source and cause of the illness and to prescribe the type of cure in the form of sacrifice to remedy the situation. After consultations, follow sacrifice and propitiation. This is the work of the diviner-priest (Dibia Aja). He makes sacrifices to the numerous spirits, some of which have no specific shrines. Such sacrifices are usually "joyless"[5] and made to evil spirits. Their aim is to drive away (ichu) evil or the devil believed to be responsible for the calamity or sickness, and thereby appease the malevolent spirits. One finds such sacrifices at road junctions and the border between villages. Immediately after sacrifices have been made, the medicine man/woman (Dibia Ogwu) sets out to bring about healing and cure. He or she does that through his/her herbs, roots, leaves, barks, seeds, liquids, juices, minerals, charcoal, powder, bones, plants, etc. In all circumstances no cure is carried out entirely by the medicine man/woman without consulting the diviner (Dibia Aja) and without the necessary sacrifices. In other words, physical healing is brought about by the medicine man/woman (Dibia Ogwu), while the symptom is taken care of by the diviner (Dibia Afa). This procedure in the cure of sickness is rooted in the belief of the African that "nothing is purely physical or merely spiritual or abstract. Things exist as combinations of elements."[6] Man is not exempted from this principle. That is why in critical moments like serious illness when the African says he or she is going to find out or consult; he or she is not only going to the laboratory, or to the psychiatrist or to the gynaecologist. He or she is more importantly going to find out the influence that is causing the undesirable events.[7] As Pius Kii rightly observes, "in the African situation, no avenue is left unexplored

---

[3] See A. B. Chukwuezi, Odenigbo, Ahuike: Ike Ogwu na Ike Ekpere, Owerri: Assumpta Press, 2004, 32.
[4] I. E. Metuh, African Religions in Western Conceptual Schemes: The Problem of Interpretation, Ibadan: Claverianum Press, 1985, 162.
[5] F. A. Arinze, Sacrifice in Ibo Religion, Ibadan: University Press, 1970, 60.
[6] D. I. Nwoga, "Nka na Nzere: The Focus of Igbo World View," 1984, 41.
[7] Ibid.

in the search for the possible sources of illness and suffering."[8] This is a holistic and integral approach to life in a world view in which the physical and the invisible world mutually interact.

The traditional "dibia" is a person of high caliber and charism who had the ability to grasp the personal problems and family history of the clients in relation to the departed members of their family. He is expected to have an extensive knowledge of overt and latent tensions existing in the prevailing relationships. In other words, he is "a person in true harmony with the spirits of nature."[9] The Igbo, for example, and many other ethnic groups in Africa have a deep faith and respect for the diviner or healer (witch-doctor) as he is called in some areas. They believe that his medicine has power to prevent the witches and other evil men or women from harming them. If one is attacked by witches the person looks for a witch-doctor who has more powerful medicine than the one who bewitched him or her. There are more than fifty different kinds of medicine among the Igbo to resort to when calamity strikes.

The considerations so far show that sickness was always caused by some thing external, a punishment from the angry or offended gods. In some cases also witches and sorcerers could be held responsible for illnesses and calamities. Therefore, a cure must be sought for. While in Islam, for example, resignation to the will of Allah is preferred to seeking for healing, in African Traditional Religion all possible avenues are explored to get healing. The Igbo of Nigeria, for instance will go to any length to obtain the desired cure when afflicted by sickness or evil spirits. This is as a result of their attachment to life; not just any type of life but a good and fulfilled life (Ezi Ndu).[10] This attitude, however, has been changing since the appearance of modern medicine.

---

[8] P. Kii, The Healing Ministry, 2004, 26.
[9] A. Echema, Corporate Personality in Traditional Igbo Society and the Sacrament of Reconciliation, 1995, 76; see also J. Healy & D. Sybertz, Towards an African Narrative Theology, 1996, 292.
[10] E. Milingo, The World in Between: Christian Healing and the Struggle for Spiritual

2.3 Secularized Notion of Sickness

Before the beginning of the 16th century, what is today known as the sciences of medicine, chemistry etc. were not sciences in the strict sense of the word; that is a discipline which bases itself on a purely rational explanation with careful observation and measurement. Medicine itself was a mixture of observable phenomenon, magic, superstition, and a blind (following) adherence to the methods and theories of the ancient Greeks. It was only after medicine liberated itself from these latter entanglements that it became a science proper, and was able to make great progress in the understanding and treatment of the human body. This development evolved gradually and can be regarded as a secularization of medicine.

Thus, modern times in contrast to the ancients see illness no longer as a punishment for sin or as the effect of the action of demons or evil spirits, at least among educated people. Since the beginning of the 16th century, sickness could be attributed to one of three possible causes; organic or congenital misconstruction, infection, or psycho-pathology or a weakening of an inner balance in the body. It is interesting to note that Christian attitude to suffering and evil in the world as we shall see shortly corresponds to the above secularized view. Christians believe that suffering and evil are ultimately the consequences of original sin, or the outcome of the sinfulness of the human condition. But in contrast to the ancients, Christians never say that someone's sickness is the direct result of a given action.

However, it is to be admitted that we live in a very secularized, sophisticated, and technological age. The world has become so complex that our actions do not always correspond with the rather enlightened, sophisticated and rational picture which we often paint of ourselves. For instance, the superstition with which we characterize "scientific" endeavors before the 16th century is still observable in today's society. In Africa, for example, it has been observed that belief in malevolent magic has not declined with either education or urbanization. Even wealthy and well-educated people including Christians in places like Nigeria resort to diviners and healers in times of trouble. As Wijsen reports about Sukuma Christians of East Africa:

Survival, New York: Orbis Books, 1984, 74-83.

> *Most Christians in the Geita Area have a firm belief in a mysterious power which can be manipulated by human beings in a beneficial or harmful way. Many Christians visit diviners and healers. Diviners are people who use a mysterious power for finding the cause of a person's misfortune. Healers use that same power for making curative and protective measures. Many Christians fear and take protective measures against sorcerers and witches who are believed to use mysterious powers for evil purposes.[11]*

The African case may not be a good example for the people are still struggling with their "two faiths" - one from their native-culture and the other from Christianity. Both faiths are said to be hanging rather "precariously in the convert's single mind."[12] In other words, the people do not as yet seem to have clearly understood the new and seem to be little unsure as to how or why they should completely abandon the old.[13] Thus, they allow the two faiths to exist together, resorting to each as occasion demands. Emeka Onwurah puts it this way:

> *Most Africans tend to uphold two faiths – they maintain the Christian faith when life is gay and happy, but hold to the indigenous faith when the fundamentals of life are at stake.[14]*

In the very words of *Instrumentum Laboris* of the 1994 African Synod:

> *Christianity remains for many Africans 'a stranger religion,' there being some part of their very selves and lives that stays outside the gospel this is the source of a certain double quality in living their beliefs, holding them divided between their faith in Jesus Christ and custom's traditional practices.[15]*

---

[11] Wijsen, There Is Only One God, 80, quoted by J. Healey & D. Sybertz, Towards an African Narrative Theology, 1996, 293.

[12] C. C. Okorocha, The Meaning of Religious Conversion in Africa, Avebury: Aldershot, 1987, 262.

[13] A. Echema, Corporate Personality in Traditional Igbo Society and the Sacrament of Reconciliation, 1995, 277.

[14] E. Onwurah, "The Quest, Means and Relevance of African Christian Theology," in African Christian Studies 3 (November 1988): 6.

[15] 1994 Special Assembly for Africa of the Synod of Bishops, *Instrumentum Laboris,* 53.

This dilemma of the African Christian has been dramatized in the words of a Zairean poet:

unhappy Christian:
Mass in the morning
Witchdoctor in the evening
Amulet in the pocket
Scapular around the neck.[16]

Godwin Ikeobi, however, has surprisingly referred to the experience of "Homeopathic Computerized Laboratory" which is capable of dictating "malevolent forces" in patients. As he puts it himself:

Before now, only human beings suspected the presence of evil spirits, now, it is science the computer, which states definitively that evil spirits are at work and declares with finality that the only remedy is spiritual healing ...[17]

This seems to be a new phenomenon in the area of science yet to be proved. All these go to show how complex and sophisticated the present modern world has become. One is at times confused which way to follow – the old traditional belief system or the new technological advancement.

Perhaps, a better example could be the rush of the Allied Powers after the World War II to hold all the German people responsible for the atrocities of the war in Europe, as the Nuremberg trials show. Is this not strikingly similar to the ancient Jewish notion of corporate responsibility, whereby the sin of an individual was not just a private matter affecting him/her alone but also the entire community? Apart from the progress made by science and the reappearance of superstition in our age, modernity has given new insights to the understanding of sickness and healing. A few of these developments will now be explored.

---

[16] Quoted in "Proposals for the African Synod," SEDOS Bulletin 1 (15 January 1992): 11.
[17] G. Ikeobi, "Healing and Exorcism: The Nigerian Pastoral Experience," 1992, 66.

2.4 Some Modern Insights on Sickness and Healing

New ideas and insights have been gained in recent times through modern research. Modern medicine has made tremendous progress and is no longer what it used to be a century ago. In this perspective, medicine is helped by other auxiliary sciences like psychology, sociology, and philosophy. It is discovering the holistic unity of the human person - a unity in which it is impossible to separate the body from the soul in the treatment of any of them. Yet this is precisely what "secularized medicine" first tried to do. This conception of the person as composed of two independent elements - body and soul - is fast disappearing. Even the radical Marxists who originally attempted to solve the body-soul relationship by eliminating the soul altogether are now abandoning their position.

2.4.1 Relationship between the Physical and Spiritual

Today sickness is no longer considered as a purely organic matter. There is a real deep relationship between the soul and the sickness of the body. This is becoming more evident through certain cures inexplicable in purely physical terms. Doctors now generally agree that a person who has a strong desire to live and to be cured often stands a better chance of surviving a serious illness than one who is resigned to death from the outset. An inner power (will-power) to fight for life can stimulate or even prevail over a sick body. A typical example is that of little Victor at the World Youths Day in Cologne. The six year old boy had suffered from cancer for two years. All medical treatment up till this time in point had not helped. But the boy had the greatest wish of meeting the Pope. This meeting eventually took place and the boy believed that now that he has received the "strongest blessing in the world" he will live. After three months of the event, the boy started recovering and responding effectively to treatment.[18] No one denies the good work of the doctors but along with that were the strong faith and the will-power to overcome the sickness. These according to the mother came

---

[18] This live story took place at the World Youths Day in Cologne Germany (August 18-21, 2005). See "Bild Zeitung," one of the most widely read daily News Papers in Germany, 5, 280/48, 30 November, 2005.

very strongly at the moment of the meeting with Pope Benedict XVI.

Another illustration is that of newly born infants. Research has shown that the feeling of affection which a newly born baby experiences from the close contact with the mother has a greater influence on the health of the baby than the most hygienic surroundings or the most nutritious food. Babies who are denied personal contact with the mother are more prone to rickets than a baby placed under the same hygienic and nutritional conditions, but with the presence of the mother assured. Similarly, children from broken homes without parents' affection have been known to suffer deprivation, depression and psychological weaknesses more than those who grew up under their parents' care.

2.4.2 The Role of Social Structures

Sociologists and psychologists confirm the importance of social structures in relation to good health; "demonic" structures, to use the sociological term, can destroy a human psyche and can endanger human health. The ghettos, slums and heaps of dustbins at most cities in Nigeria and elsewhere in Africa or other parts of the world and their effects on human health are familiar examples to us. Is there any wonder in many parts of Africa where almost all social infrastructures like electricity, roads, reliable hospitals, etc. are non-existent, that the people see demons every where? The bushes are so thick and the darkness so fearful that even the most courageous person could get frightened in certain parts of the continent. Fear itself is already a major cause of sickness or is itself a serious illness.

Abandoned projects and houses are a familiar feature in most cities of Africa. In Nigeria, for example, most of these uncompleted or abandoned houses are either used for healing homes, Pentecostal Churches or hide outs for all sorts of criminal activities ranging from armed robbery, sex or drug abuse, kidnapping and ritual meetings. All these are detrimental to good health.

2.4.3 The Practice of Faith-Healing

The presence and effects of the Pentecostal movement are undeniable. Their practice of faith-healing has added a new dimension to the understanding of illness and healing. Verifiable cures similar to the miracles in the Bible and throughout the history of Christianity are attested to in such groups. In our secularized and complex world, Pentecostalism has given some a new confidence, joy and security; and the last mentioned is believed by many to be the major reason why people flock to Pentecostal Churches, namely, the search for security.[19] Such people seem to be healthier or at least have a greater chance of recovering from their illness.

Inner-healing is the ever flowing of a spiritual experience into our affectivity, so that the individual experiences peace, joy, reconciliation and unity. This area appears restricted because oftentimes the experience is private and known only to the one who had the experience. Inner healing has to do with spiritual life and the encounter with God. However, inner healing is different from both physical and spiritual healings.[20] Physical healing occurs when an organic illness disappears and one sees God's intervention. God's healing may come about in various ways, and may begin with treatment by doctors and the effect of prescribed medicine as in the case of the little boy Victor mentioned earlier. The essence of physical healing is God's forgiveness which enables one to repent, to renounce sin, and to leave oneself open to a new life ruled by charity. According to Michael Scanlan, inner healing is the healing of the inner man. By "inner man" is meant the spheres of the intellect, the emotions and the will, generally called reason, heart and will.[21] Inner healing is thus, a healing of the psyche. It does not immediately refer to God and the God-oriented life but the organization of the intellect, the will, memory, and the emotional sensitivity. Generally speaking, inner healing could be said to be the healing of the heart, insofar as the heart is the place where the life of grace and the emotional sensitivity meet.

---

[19] Cf. N. Ndiokwere, Search for Security, 1990; see also J. Healey & D. Sybertz, Towards an African Narrative Theology, 1996, 293
[20] F. MacNutt, Healing, Notre Dame: Ave Maria Press, 1974, 163.
[21] M. Scanlan, Inner Healing, New York: Paulist Press, 1974.

Summary

At the end of our survey of the various attitudes of pre-biblical cultures towards sickness and healing, certain facts emerge. The presence of sickness has been a threat to humanity in all cultures that must be fought against. It is believed to be a punishment from the gods and to be cured these offended gods must be appeased. Among the Africans particularly, good health is coveted because life is the highest good. Therefore, any form of misfortune that threatens life, including sickness must be resisted with every available resource.

However, with the discovery of science of medicine, sickness is no longer seen in a mythical way, even though one sees traces of superstition still hanging around. This is more observable among Africans where "traditional medicine" experts are consulted at crisis moments. Despite this complexity, it is a fact that new insights have been gained on sickness since modern times. With the help of other auxiliary sciences, medicine is now moving towards considering the sick person as made up of body and soul, and not just body alone. Similarly, sickness is not seen as a purely organic matter. It affects other aspects of the person, psychic, social, emotional, moral, etc. Furthermore, social structures have been proved to have positive or negative effects on good health. Clean and healthy environment can prolong life by preventing diseases.

Finally, it is to be acknowledged that Pentecostalism and the practice of faith-healing have introduced a new understanding in the health circle. Many people have found joy, peace, security in these groups and thus are likely to be healthier and more resistant to diseases. In the chapter that follows, we shall turn our attention to the biblical understanding of sickness and healing. It will be interesting to know the similarities and dissimilarities between the pre-biblical and the biblical times.

Chapter Three
Biblical Insights into Sickness and Healing

The Church bases all its sacraments, one of which is that of the anointing of the sick on the Bible. All the present day healers appeal to the same Bible also for justification of their healing ministry. It will be necessary then to examine the scriptures, for they provide the canon for judging the Christian sacraments as well as the intentions, methods, and praxis of the healers. This is what this chapter proposes to demonstrate beginning with the Hebrew tradition. It will be followed with the New Testament outlook on sickness and healing. In other words, Christ's own attitude, which is the foundation of the anointing of the sick will be examined. The apostles whom their master gave the mandate to preach and to heal continued faithfully in the mission which eventually reached the early Christian communities. How these carried on with their care for the sick will conclude the chapter.

3.1 Sickness and Healing in the Hebrew Tradition

The Hebrew tradition traces sickness to a large extent to the destructive effects of sin. It sees both sickness and sin also as results of the action of evil forces on human beings. In the Book of Exodus (15:26), God made it clear what human beings ought to do in order to avoid sickness:

If you will listen attentively to the voice of the Lord your God, and do that which is right in his eyes and give heed to his commandments and keep all his statutes, I will put none of the diseases upon you which I put upon the Egyptians; for I am the Lord, your healer.

Also in Leviticus (15:1ff.), God gave the Israelites the injunctions which they are to observe and respect for them to remain unstained and healthy. Already at the beginning, the Law spelt out all the illnesses which Yahweh will bring down upon those who transgress his will:

Yahweh will strike you down with Egyptian boils, with swellings in

> the groin, with scurvy and the itch from which you will find no cure. Yahweh will strike you down with madness, blindness, destruction of mind, until you grope your way at noontide like a blind man groping in the dark, and your steps will lead you nowhere (Deut 28:27-28).

Those who disobey God, those who flout the laws of justice pay the price through falling sick as in the case of king Uziah who offended Yahweh and was struck with leprosy that later killed him (cf. 2 kgs 26:16-20). Sickness is thus seen as "a sign of God's visitation."[1] There are ample examples of such causal connection between sin and sickness throughout the Hebrew Bible. In Genesis (12:17), Pharaoh's household is struck down by severe plagues because he took Abraham's wife Sarah as his wife (cf. also Gen 20:18); the Egyptians suffered the plagues and the death of their first born because of their hardness of heart (Ex 9:8-10, 12:29). Miriam was afflicted with leprosy because of her conspiracy with Aaron against Moses (cf. Num 12:10); Gehazi suffered leprosy also because of his avarice (cf. 2 kgs 5:23-27), etc.

The same idea is expressed clearly in the Book of Psalms. Referring to early death as a punishment for sin, Psalm 51:14 says: "Save me from death, God my saviour, and my tongue will proclaim your righteousness." Psalm 6 sees the sick person's misfortune as a punishment for some hidden sin; in somewhat the same way that Job's friends viewed his calamity. Psalm 38:3 admits: "No soundness in my flesh now that you are angry, no health in my bones because of my sins" and "Some sick from their sins, made miserable by their own guilt and finding food repugnant, were nearly at death's door" (Ps 107: 17-18; see also Pss 22, 39, 88, 102, etc.). Similarly, the same ideas are objectified in the Book of Proverbs: "Do not think of yourself as wise, fear Yahweh and turn back on evil. It will be healing to your flesh and relief to your bones" (3:7-8).

---

[1] G. Ikeobi, "Spiritual Healing in the Nigeria Catholic Church" in Torch Magazine 88 (1988): 7.

The foregoing shows that all the sufferings and degradations of human beings have their origin in sin.[2] But there is an exception to this seeming rule. Job is a case in point. There is suffering which is experienced not by the unrighteous but by the righteous, in which case, "the normal cause and effect principle cannot be applied to the suffering of the just man."[3] Job protests against his unjust suffering and God eventually vindicates him. A new perspective on suffering, however, emerges with the "suffering servant of Yahweh" as found in the Book of Isaiah (52:53). This is suffering that is vicarious.[4] The innocent suffers and dies that others may be saved: "Surely he took up our infirmities, and carried our sorrows ... he was pierced for our transgressions, he was crushed for our iniquities ... Yahweh has laid on him the guilt of us all" (Is 53:4-6). The suffering servant preeminently depicts the person of Jesus who suffered and died that we may live. The new dimension in linking sin, sickness and suffering remained a truth, which Jesus later highlighted in his own suffering and dying, namely, that an individual's suffering may not necessarily be as a result of her/his own personal sin or of any other person's for that matter.

It is true that God is conceived as the sole source of both good and evil, of sickness as well as health. This Israelite thinking was to be vehemently contested by the Fathers of the Church. For the Fathers sickness, suffering, and death are traced to the original sin. They maintain that although, "God is the maker of all things, visible and invisible," he cannot be responsible for sickness, suffering and death. The argument of the Church Fathers is based on Genesis account which saw all that God made at the beginning to be wholly good (cf. 1:31). It was after the fall of Adam and Eve, that evil came into the world. This is the problem of evil which has occupied humanity many years before the birth of Christ. The interest here, however, is not in the classical problem of theodicy but on the Hebrew view on sickness and healing. It was after the exile that the Israelites started accepting

---

[2] Cf. L. Hamelin, Reconciliation in the Church: A Theological and Pastoral Essay on the Sacrament of Penance, trans. M. J. O'Connell, Minnesota: The Liturgical Press, 1980, 21.

[3] J. C. Ike, "Faith in God Amidst Suffering in the World," in R. Madu and A. Echema (eds.), Essays in Honour of Msgr. Alphonsus Aghaizu, Owerri: Assumpta Press, 2004, 141.

[4] Ibid, 143.

that sickness could be caused by demonic activities. Thus, the old outlook was gradually but inevitably annulled. However, since God does not glory in the death of a sinner, but wants his conversion to a new life, he undertakes every step to renovate the sinner's life. Consequently, in the midst of the stark reality of sin and its devastating effects, there was also evidence of the desire of a gracious God to heal humanity and restore it to wholeness.

In the same breath that ancient Hebrew saw sickness as punishment from God, so they conceived "God as one who exercised sovereignty over the whole creation, including man and his health."[5] They employed healing metaphors to describe Yahweh's absolute power over both the physical and the spiritual well-being of humanity. During Israel's difficult and long wandering in the desert, the people complained against the bitter water they got in Marah (cf. Ex 15:12-26). Moses pleaded with God. Yahweh provided them with sweet water and after that promised that he will not subject them to the same hardships as the Egyptians, for "I am the Lord your healer" (Ex 15:26). At this period in the history and religion of Israel, God revealed himself as the healer. The term "healer" (Rophe) became revered with awe so much that in subsequent history, no Jew adopted the title or claimed to be a healer.[6] Perhaps, that explains why actual healing was not popular with the ancient Jews, even though there were cases of evil machinations condemned in the Old Testament, especially in the Book of Job. If indeed, there were any such healers, their exploits were not recorded because of the fear that such practices which denied Yahweh of his almighty power over nature and the cosmos amounted to apostasy (2 kgs 1:4).[7]

There is, however, one notable case of healing narrated in Numbers (12:9-16) and attributed to Moses. Miriam and Aaron conspired to challenge the authority of Moses. Miriam was inflicted with Leprosy. Moses was begged to intercede with God to restore her health. On the belief that only God heals, Moses prayed to God in a loud voice: "Not this, O Lord! Heal her I pray." After seven days of seclusion, Miriam was fully restored to health. In the understanding of the text, Moses behest God to perform the healing and

---

[5] C. U. Manus, "Healing and Exorcism: The Scriptural Viewpoint" in C. U. Manus (ed.) et al, Healing and Exorcism: The Nigerian Experience, 1992, 87.

[6] Cf. Encyclopedia Judaica, vol 11, Jerusalem KPH, 1971, 1179.

[7] C. U. Manus, "Healing and Exorcism," 1992, 88.

Yahweh heard the request of his servant. There is a considerable attempt by the author to show that it was not Moses who healed Miriam but Yahweh. The tradition that Yahweh heals is well known in the period when the Psalms were composed. Ps 103:3-5 blesses Yahweh for healing diseases, and Ps 147:1 says: "It is he who heals the broken in spirit and binds up their wounds." There are other numerous references in the Psalms to the effect that Yahweh was the healer (cf. Pss 91, 41, 116, 121, etc).

There are other series of healing activities ascribed to the prophets Elijah and Elisha. These are recorded in the Book of Kings.

(i) Elijah's Revival of the Dead Boy (1 kgs 17:17-24)

The son of the woman of Zarephath falls sick and dies. The woman accuses Elijah, the man of God of bringing down God's wrath on her because of her sin. Elijah carries the corpse up to his upper room and lays it on his bed. He breathes three times upon the body of the child and prays: "O Lord my God, let the breath of life, I pray, return to the body of the child." After this ritual prayer, the child revives. The prophet returns the child to the mother downstairs. She recognizes Elijah as the man of God (his prophet-hood) and God's word as truth.

(ii) Elisha's Healing of the Dead Boy of the Shunamite Woman (2 kgs 4:8-37)

In a similar way, a young boy suddenly becomes ill from sunstroke while working in his parents' farm. He is rushed to the mother on whose laps he dies. The woman lays the corpse on Elisha's bed in the room the family reserved for the prophet and goes to call him. Elisha's servant Gehazi, arrives first with the prophet's wonder-working staff. He places the staff on the face of the corpse. The magic does not work. Upon the woman's insistence, Elisha comes along with her. He enters the room, prays to Yahweh and carries out a life transference healing rite seven times. The boy revives.

(iii) Elisha Heals Naaman, the Leper (2 kgs 5:1-19)

Naaman is the general officer commanding the valiant army of the king of Aram (Damascus in Syria). This officer has just won a resounding victory over the Israelites for his country. But he was leprous. The maid-servant, a captive from Israel advices him to go to the prophet in Samaria to be cured. Naaman's master, the king of Aram permits him to go and gives him a letter of recommendation to the king of Israel. The Israelite king reacts uncomfortably. Elisha overhears him and asks him to send over the man to him so that the Syrian prince "will know that there is a prophet in Israel" (v. 8c).

Elisha asks Naaman to go and bathe seven times in the River Jordan. He rejects the advice and goes away in anger. His servants dissuade him from returning home and convinced him to submit. He goes and dips himself in the river seven times as directed. He is cleansed.

(iv) The Healing of King Hezekiah (2 kgs 30:1-11/Is 38: 1-8)

This "prince of the people" has a mortal boil and is at the point of death. Isaiah, the prophet comes with a divine oracle and advices him to make his last will and prepare for death. The sick king prays fervently to God reminding him of his faithfulness and loyalty. Later, God sends back Isaiah to the king and asks him to say to him: "I will heal you, and on the third day you shall go up to the house of the Lord" (v. 5).

The prophet instructs his attendants to apply a fig-plaster; a type of shea-butter on the boil. The king is healed. In the Isaiahan version, king Hezekiah gives a thanksgiving in which, among other things, he praises God for restoring him and giving him back his life (v. 16).

Why this collection of healing in the Deuteronomic history? Why did the authors place them within prophetic circles? The heroes Moses and Joshua exude in their person divine authority. As charismatic leaders biblical tradition associates them with the possession of divine powers that were totally unthinkable in ancient Israel. The prophets Elijah and Elisha paralleled with Moses and Joshua respectively transmitted divine truths such that made the people revere them as divine men. They were recognized as media of divine revelation and bearers of oracles of salvation. Under Israel's strong belief that it is Yahweh who heals both spiritually and physically, and had sovereignty over the whole creation, "the orthodox Yahwist's chief means of healing was prayer and faith in God."[8] In this circumstance, the practice of exorcism by humans or any activities of a physician were completely avoided. For instance, in the one of the few cases where evil spirit is mentioned – the case of the mentally deranged Saul – the patient Saul is soothed with music from young David (cf. 1 Sam 16:14-23) and not by an exorcist or a physician. When there are doctors at all, they are regarded as healing instruments of Yahweh. Such is the paraenesis of the author of the Book of Ecclesiasticus written about 180 BC. Chapter 38 portrays the role of and the social standing of the doctor as well as the importance of prayer and faith in God who created medicine and the doctor.

The belief that God heals also prevailed in the time of Jesus. Jewish prayers, especially those used during the Second Temple period (Jesus' time) testify to that. The Eighteen Benedictions in its eight marcharism pleads:

Heal us, O lord our God from the pain of our hearts and bring healing for our afflictions. Blessed art thou who healest the sick of the people Israel.[9]

We shall now turn to the New Testament to consider Jesus' attitude to sickness and healing.

3.2 Sickness and Healing in the New Testament

The New Testament has its setting in the Graeco–Roman world of the first century. Jesus, the apostles, and the disciples were all from Palestine. By this time, Palestine had already had contact with Hellenism and Ancient Near East, where people believed that sickness was caused by demonic activities. In other words, in Rabbinic Judaism, unlike in the ancient Hebrew period, there was already widespread belief in demons. The Pharisees, especially the Scribes believed in the existence of the demons and the evil spirit. As Chris Manus shows:

---

[8] A. O. Igenoza, "Medicine and Healing in African Christianity: Biblical Critique," in AFER 30 (1988): 19; see also C. U. Manus, "Healing and Exorcism," 1992, 91.

[9] Cf. P. B. Harner, Understanding the Lord's Prayers, Philadelphia: Fortress Press, 1975, 123-125.

Rabbinic tradition held that the demons originated from the illicit sexual relation between fallen angels and women narrated in Gen 6:1-4. For people of that time in Palestine and elsewhere in the Ancient Orient, demons were said to "be very near and very real," and were believed to cause disasters, spiritual crises and miseries to human life.[10]

In the New Testament times, evil spirits were believed to have their abode often in human beings (cf. 1 Cor 12:2). It was further believed that these spirits caused sickness in human beings and made some mad.

Christianity, thus, developed in a world in which people recognized the practice of exorcism, healing and magic to expel, to appease and to control evil forces and demonic entities which were everywhere tormenting people. It was even known that some Rabbis were engaged in such practices.[11] The term "diamon" (demon) was used once and in Matt 8:31 where it appears only in the plural notation. Its diminutive form, "diamonion" is more frequently used, appearing 63 times in the New Testament. This preponderant use of the term suggests that Jesus and the early Christians shared the idea of their contemporaries to the effect that demons had power to cause harm and to do evil (cf. Lk 13:11, 16). It is against this background that one can appreciate Jesus' acts of healing which were an accomplishment of his proclamation (cf. Mk 1:39).

Healing is synonymous with Jesus' life and ministry. It is so central to the New Testament that Mark's gospel alone records over twenty individual acts of healing, so that roughly one–half of his gospel is devoted to healing narratives.[12] All the miracles of Jesus could be broadly divided into two categories, namely, nature miracles (for example, calming the see, etc.) and healing miracles.[13] Here the focus is more on the healing activities of Jesus. These are well noted in the synoptic tradition. Seven cases can be isolated:

---

[10] C. U. Manus, "Healing and Exorcism," 1992, 92; see also R. P. Martins, New Testament Foundations: A Guide for Christian Students, vol. 2, Acts–Revelation, Exeter, The Paternoster Press, 1978, 32.

[11] Cf. H. Bietenhard, "Diamonion, (demon)," in C. Brown (ed.), The New International Dictionary of New Testament Theology, Exeter: The Paternoster Press, 1975, 451.

[12] See C. W. Gusmer, And You Visited Me, 1990; cf. also P. Kii, The Healing Ministry, 2004, 39.

[13] See P. Kii, The Healing Ministry, 2004, 40-43.

1. Mk 1:29-31/Matt 8:14-15/Lk 4:38-39 – The healing of Peter's mother–in–law
2. Mk 1:40-45/Matt 8:1-4/Lk 5:12-16 – The cleansing of the leper
3. Mk 2:1-12/Matt 9:1-8/Lk 5:17-26 – The healing of the paralytic
4. Mk 5:21-43/Matt 9:18-26/Lk 8:40-56 – Jairus' daughter and the woman with a hemorrhage
5. Mk 7:31-37/Matt 15:29-31 – Jesus heals the deaf mute and many others
6. Mk 8:22-26 /- /- /- The healing of a blind man at Bethsaida
7. Mk 10:46-52/Matt 29:29-34/Lk 18:35-43 – The healing of Bartimaeus.

One of these healing works of Jesus will be considered in detail, in order to have a clearer picture of the whole episode.

The Healing of the Leper (Mark 1:40-45)

A Leper approached Jesus and kneeling before him begs him if he wills, to cleanse him of his leprosy. Moved by pity, Jesus stretched out his hand and touches him, saying, "I will, be clean." At these words, the man becomes healed instantly. Jesus sends him away immediately, charging him to say nothing to anyone but to go and show himself to the priest and to make an offering to God as the Law of Moses directs. The man goes away, but begins to talk freely about his cure, to the extent that it is difficult for Jesus to openly enter a town. Although, he remains in the outskirts, people come to him from every quarter.

It is not our intention to do an exegetical analysis of the text[14] but to underline certain theological and pastoral implications of this healing event that could apply to other healing activities of Jesus. Jesus is portrayed as the healer par excellence. According to C. Asthon:

Jesus healed all who came to him, including pagans. He healed people from demon possession, mental and emotional illness, epilepsy, leprosy, paralysis, fever, hemorrhage, blindness, deafness, dropsy, physical injury and sickness and remarkably, he raised three people from the dead. [15]

---

[14] For such an approach see for example, the work of A. I. Umoren, Jesus and Miracle Healing Today, 2000, 80-92.

[15] C. Asthon, Servant Spirit Serving Church quoted by P. Kii, The Healing Ministry, 2004, 49.

One of the reasons why Jesus embarked on this whole mission of healing is his deep compassion for the sick. The text under consideration makes it clear that "...he was moved with pity..." Jesus was hostile to whatever made human beings sick and brought destruction to them. Thus, his healing works were signs of the Kingdom proclaimed in the gospel as a new reign of peace and justice in which God will put an end to the ancient enemies of the human race: sin and evil, sickness and death. It was this motivation that made him even prepared to violate the tradition of the Sabbath. At least six of his healings were done on the Sabbath. In all this his aim was not to be hailed as a wonder worker but that those healed should see it as a sign of God's offer of deliverance and eternal salvation to human beings. Perhaps, that explains why the gospel generally avoided the conventional terms "miracle" or "wonder" in preference for the more modest "act of power" (dynamis) in the synoptics, "works" (terata) and "signs" (semeia) in John's gospel. This was necessary lest Jesus be misunderstood as a kind of thaumaturgical wonder worker.[16]

Already at the very beginning of his public life, Jesus declared his mission as that of healing, of liberation, and of salvation. Luke describes how Jesus himself conceived this mission. On coming to Nazareth, his own village, he went to the synagogue on the Sabbath as his custom was. As he opened the scroll that was given to him to read, he found where it was written:

The spirit of the lord has been given to me, for he has anointed me. He has sent me to bring the good news to the poor, to proclaim liberty to captives and to the blind new sight, to set the down trodden free, to proclaim the Lord's year of favor (Lk 4:16-22).

Jesus' healing ministry was thus, integral to the main reason of his coming into the world. As he himself says: In reply to Simon and those who followed him that "all were looking for him," he answered: "Let us go to other places, in the neighboring villages, so that I may also preach there for that is why I came ..." (Mk 1:37-39). In other words, Jesus' ministry of healing belongs to his holistic mission of proclamation. Almost all his healing works took place in the context of preaching the Good News. He did not

---

[16] Cf. C. W. Gusmer, And You Visited Me, 1990, 49.

embark on a healing galour nor did he need any fan-fare from those healed. On the contrary, Jesus was quick to send those healed away instantly and in most cases with strict charge not to tell anybody about what had happened (cf. Mk 1:40-45; Matt 8:2-4; Lk 5:12-16).

Jesus makes a radical departure from his Judaic contemporaries and indeed from the Old Testament as well as from the African world view by the way he viewed the relationship between sickness and sin. Surely, sin could lead to certain ailments or expose one to destructive forces of Satan. For instance, some people strongly believe that certain illnesses are directly associated with sin, at least humanly speaking: excess smoking and alcohol abuse could lead to stroke and cancer, sexual promiscuity could cause Aids, slander, perjury and pride could bring about leprosy, corruption may be responsible for blindness, and sex in the day time could cause epilepsy, etc.[17] Jesus, however, was against the identification of all sufferings of humanity with sin. He repudiated the idea that sickness was a punishment from an irate God who rains down chastisement upon disobedient children. Addressing those who came to tell him about the Galileans whose blood Pilate had mingled with their sacrifices, Jesus retorted:

Do you suppose these Galileans who suffered like that were greater sinners than any other Galileans? They were not, I tell you. No. but unless you repent you will all perish as they did or those eighteen on whom the tower of Siloam fell and killed them? Do you suppose that they were more guilty than all the other people living in Jerusalem? They were not, I tell you (Lk 18:2-5).

In a similar episode, when the disciples questioned him about the man born blind: "Master, who sinned that he was born blind? Himself or his parents?" Jesus replied: "Neither he nor his parents sinned ... (Jn 9:3). However, there are two instances where the relationship between personal sin and suffering are implied, namely, in the case of the paralytic (Mk 2:3) and that of the man at the pool of Bethzatha (Jn 5:14). In the former, forgiveness of sin preceded physical healing and in the latter Jesus warned the man

---

[17] Cf. C. Geißler, Was würde Jesus heute sagen? Die politische Botschaft des Evangeliums, Berlin: Berlin Verlag, 2004, 74; see also G. Mackrell, The Healing Miracles in Mark's Gospel, Slough: St. Paul's Publications, 1987, 25.

when he met him not to sin again lest something worse should befall him. As Morton correctly observes:

> *When he saw a need to speak of sin in connection with healing, he did not go on to say that this was the sole cause of the person's trouble. Jesus seemed to believe that a primary cause of sickness was a force of evil – loose in the world was hostile to God and his way. He believed that men were sometimes in the hands of this power, so that it exerted a baneful influence in their lives.*[18]

Jesus healed all kinds of diseases and infirmity that troubled people. He healed people physically, spiritually, emotionally and mentally. He did not inquire into peoples' moral life, whether they had repented or were in a state of grace before he healed them. He loved the sick and the feeble as they were and identified with them. His preoccupation was to liberate them from their misery.[19]

Perhaps, the central message of Jesus on human suffering was dramatically demonstrated in the example of his own suffering, death and resurrection. He could have avoided suffering and could certainly have come down from the cross, if he so wished, at least to demonstrate his power to the mocking bystanders (cf. Mk 15:32). But he did not; for he knew that his passion, death and resurrection will become the inexhaustible fountain of redemption and healing love for all generations. The scriptures could scarcely be more explicit on this point: "If any man would come after me, let him deny himself and take up his cross daily and follow me. For whoever would save his life will lose it; and whoever loses his life for my sake, he will save it" (Lk 9:23, 24). We shall come back to these themes later when Jesus' style of healing will be placed side by side with the present day healers. Meanwhile, the apostolic age will now be examined to find out its outlook on the sick and their care.

---

[18] K. Morton, Healing and Christianity quoted by P. Kii, The Healing Ministry, 2004, 47.
[19] See H. Geißler, Was würde Jesus heute sagen? 2004, 74.

3.3 Healing in the Apostolic Age

The attitude of Jesus towards the sick, the poor and the disabled was continued by the apostles in their own time. Healing which marked the ministry of their master characterized also their own mission and preaching. They were steadfast to the command of Jesus to preach the Good News and to heal the sick:

> *He called the twelve together and gave them power and authority over all devils and to cure diseases. And he sent them out to proclaim the kingdom of God and to heal (Lk 9:1-3; Matt 10:1-6; Mk 6:13).*

On another occasion,

> *... the Lord appointed seventy-two others and sent them ahead of him, in pairs, to all the towns and places he himself was to visit ... Whenever you go into a town where they make you welcome, eat what is set before you. Cure those in it who are sick and say "the kingdom of God is very near to you" (Lk 10:8-9).*

As it is evident from these accounts, the charge of Jesus was not merely doctrinal; it was full of power and authority to be exercised in the continuation of his total liberation of humanity from sin, suffering and sickness. Indeed, the apostles took these injunctions seriously and recorded a huge success in all their missions even as their Lord and Master was still with them (cf. Lk 10:18-20). The "explosive growth of Christianity in the first three centuries has been attributed by some Church historians to the fact that Christians healed the sick and cast out devils."[20] Towards the end of his earthly ministry, Jesus reiterated the great mandate to his apostles: "Go out to the whole world and proclaim the Good News" (Mk 16:16). He assured them that great signs will accompany them and among these signs include these:

> *...in my name they will cast out devils; they will have the gift of tongues; they will pick up snakes in their hands; and be unharmed, should they drink deadly poison, they will lay their*

---

[20] Cf. R. MacMullen, Christianize the Roman Empire: AD100-400, New Haven: Yale University Press, 1984, 13.

hands on the sick, who will recover (Mk 16:17-18).

These assurances were not empty promises as the events recorded in Luke's Acts show. Some of the miracles and healing performed by the apostles Peter and Paul include:

Acts 3:1-10 – Peter heals the cripple at the Beautiful Gate
Acts 9:32-35 – Peter heals Aeneas at Lydda
Acts 9:36-43 – The restoration of Tabitha, alias Dorcas
Acts 14:8-13 – Paul heals the cripple at Lystra
Acts 20:7-12 – The revival of Eutychus by Paul
Acts 28:7-10 – Paul's healing of Publius' father (of dysentery).

For a more graphic understanding, Peter's first healing act immediately after the Pentecost event will be considered.

Peter Heals the Cripple at the Beautiful Gate (Acts 3:1-10)

It is about 3.00pm. Peter and John are going to the temple to participate in the prayer of the Tamid sacrifice (Ex 29:39). A man who was lame from birth usually lies at the Beautiful Gate from where he asks for alms from those attending the temple prayers. Among those entering the temple this day are Peter and John. He begs for alms from them. Peter notices him and says to him: "Look at us." With the hope of receiving something he obeys him. Peter then tells him: "Silver and gold have I none, but what I have, that I give you. In the name of Jesus of Nazareth, walk!" (v. 6). Thereupon Peter takes him by the right hand and raises him up. Both his feet and ankles receive strength. He springs up, stands and walks. He enters the temple in the company of the apostles praising God. The people see him walking and singing praises to God. They are filled with wonder and amazement at the man's healing.

It needs to be stressed again that the interest here is not on exegetical exercise[21] but to dwell on the features that proved that what happened was a healing act and not a magic. The emphasis is on the theological and pastoral implications of the healing act. First of all, the healing miracle portrays the name of Jesus as one through whose representative Peter miracles

---

[21] For such elaborate exegesis see C. U. Manus, "Healing and Exorcism: The Scriptural Viewpoint," 1992, 97-99.

are to be wrought and recognize as superior to those of Jewish and Hellenistic parallels associated with Apollonius of Tyana, Asclepius at Epidaurus Vespasian at Alexandria and Serapis at Canobus, etc.[22] In other words, even in the time of Jesus and the apostolic era, magicians and wonder workers were in vogue. As if to dispel any doubts, the apostles were two; thus adhering to the rule of two witnesses (cf. Lk 4:20). The healed person is described as one with the infirmity from birth, stressing the fact that the illness has lasted quite a long period of time. This shows the enormousness of the healing act.

The Beautiful Gate of the temple is well known because of its decoration with bronze imported from Corinth as Josephus describes in his Wars (II 4 II, V1 98, 201-206, VI 293).[23] The imposing nature of this gate attracted many pilgrims and pious Jews going into the temple for prayers and ritual sessions. This is the reason why the beggar is brought daily to the gate, so that he could ask for alms. In the case of Peter, instead of receiving some money, the beggar is invited to "look at us." At that point Peter gave him what he had, namely, "the plenary power to heal in the name of Jesus."[24] From all evidence, it is clear that it was through the utterance of the name of Jesus that Peter cured the lame man. His ability to walk confirms the reality of his healing. People see and believe. Their reaction shows the reality of the miracle. In the words of Manus:

> *All the bystanders recognize in amazement that a miracle is wrought and consequently that they are overcome with Thambos (amazement), the sort of tremendum fascinans Rudulf Otto employs to express that awe which authentic religious beings feel in the presence of divine activity.*[25]

In all the healing activities of the apostles, whether that of Peter or Paul, the source of power of healing was not in doubt. All happened in the name of Jesus. In the case of Aaneans, Peter clearly tells him: "Jesus Christ cures you: get up and fold up your sleeping mat" (Acts 9:32-35). Paul himself

---

[22] Ibid; 98.
[23] Ibid.
[24] E. Haenchen, The Acts of the Apostles: A Commentary, Oxford: Blackwell, 1971, 200.
[25] C. U. Manus, "Healing and Exorcism," 1992, 99-100.

was cured of his blindness by Ananias who prayed for and laid hands on him (9:17). There were two cases of raisings from the dead: that of Dorcas (9:36-43) and the one of Eutychus (20:7-12).

Sometimes, many signs and wonders were worked among the people at the hands of the apostles that the sick were taken out into the streets and laid on beds and sleeping mats in the hope that at least the shadow of Peter might fall across some of them as he went (cf. 5:5-6).

> *And God did extraordinary miracles by the hands of Paul, so that handkerchiefs or aprons were carried away from his body to the sick, and diseases left them and the evil spirits came out of them (19:11-13).*

As we shall see later, many present-day healers have assumed this practice in a fundamentalist way and would claim that even their handkerchiefs could be taken to the sick who will recover. Although, healing was common in the apostolic communities, not every Christian possessed the gift. For Paul, there are "varieties of gifts." Certain people would be given a special gift of healing the sick by the same Spirit promised by Christ (cf. 1 Cor 12:9, 28, 30); others are given different gifts. But all these gifts are for the building up of the community. As time went on, and the various communities founded by the apostles and disciples started settling down, different ways of catering for their sick began to emerge. One such community was that of St. James.

3.4 Early Christian Community and its Care for the Sick

There are two passages in the New Testament that have to do with the religious use of oil in anointing the sick: Mark 6:13 and James 5:14-15. The passage in Mark belongs to the apostolic ministry of healing. But Mark is unique in his mention of anointing: "And they cast out many demons, and anointed with oil many that were sick and healed them" (6:13). Mark does not explicitly relate this anointing of the sick with either Jesus' own practice or with any specific command to his disciples. It is very likely to be a Palestinian custom and probably associated with exorcism. Initially, many

Roman Catholic commentators were reluctant to trace the origins of the sacrament of anointing to the apostolic ministry of healing. Their reason was that the principal goal of the sacrament was the spiritual cure of the sick person, not bodily healing. One notable exception was M. J. Lagrange, who felt that the rite described in Mark might well represent the "real origins of the sacrament."[26] The Council of Trent followed this line of thought when in 1551 it decreed:

> *This sacred anointing of the sick was instituted by Christ our Lord as a true and proper sacrament of the New Testament. It is alluded to indeed by Mark (6:13), but is recommended to the faithful and promulgated by James.*[27]

The attitude of the earliest Christian Communities to the sick, not only in charitable and therapeutic sense, but also in word and symbolic action, followed also in the example of Jesus himself. In the instructional document of the late first century circulated under the name of James "the brother of the Lord," the author speaks of prayer as one of the unifying themes applicable to three existential situations of Christians: suffering, joy, and sickness:

> *Is any one among you suffering? Let him pray. Is any cheerful? Let him sing praise. Is any among you sick? Let him call for the elders of the Church, and let them pray over him, anointing him with oil in the name the Lord and the prayer of faith will save the sick man, and the Lord will raise him up; and if he has committed sins, he will be forgiven. Therefore confess your sins to one another, and pray for one another, that you may be healed. The prayer of a righteous man has great power in its effects (James 5:13-16).*

James gives an insight into a Jewish-Christian community which bestored upon its experienced members official rank as well. He calls attention to the institutional character of the rite. It is not just elders in age that are rec-

---

[26] M. J. Lagrange, Evangile selon saint Marc quoted by C. W. Gusmer, And You Visited Me, 1992, 7.
[27] H. Denzinger and A. Schönmetzer (eds.), Enchiridion Symbolorum 1695, trans. J. Neuner and J. Dupuis, The Christian Faith, Westminster, Md: Christian Classics, rev. ed. 1983, 466.

ommended, or charismatics with their healing power. The healing power in this sense is an ecclesial power, ministered by elders who have been given an authority and a ministry in and to the local Church.

The elders anoint the sick person with oil and pray over him or her. This is an indication that in contrast to later generations, more attention is given to the prayer of faith than to the action of anointing with oil. As already noted the medicinal use of oil was well known in the ancient world. But the specification that the anointing is "in the name of the Lord," that is, by calling on his name which brings salvation, implies that this is not simply a medicinal remedy. In the words of Lawler, "oil is but the visible sign for the real, invisible healing power, which is both 'in the name of the Lord' and 'in the prayer of faith.'"[28] That power extends not only to spiritual healing, including the forgiveness of sins, but also to total, personal healing, including on occasion physical healing. The sick person is a whole person, and the hoped-for effect touches the health and salvation of the human person in a holistic sense, not just of either a body part or a soul part.[29] In view of the relationship in the Jewish mind between sin and bodily infirmity, the restoration could include both the healing from sin as well as from bodily affliction.

What is described in James is an action to be performed by elders, that is, ministers of the Church for the benefit of sick Christians. The rite consists of prayer of faith and an anointing with oil. The expectations from such a ministration are described in terms that refer to the future tense: "to save" (sozein), "to restore" or "to raise up" (egeirein) (v. 16). Nothing suggests that these verbs are to be interpreted in a purely eschatological spiritual sense, or that they refer to a future spiritual healing. On the contrary, neither do they seem to connote a purely bodily, medicinal result. As Poschmann points out:

> Both verbs, "sozein" and "egeirein," can in themselves signify bodily or spiritual healing. Actually, both are meant here, for, as James shows (cf. Mt 8:1ff = Healing of a leper, Lk 7:11ff = The raising of the young man of Naim; Mt 9:2 = Healing of the para-

---

[28] M. G. Lawler, Symbol and Sacraments: A Contemporary Sacramental Theology, 1987, 156.
[29] Ibid.

*lytic; and passim), bodily and spiritual recovery are closely connected. The "prayer of faith" will bring "salvation" to all; that is what is salutary for each one here and now, whether it be recovery or death in a state of grace.*30

Once again, we find a close relationship between bodily healing and forgiveness of sins. What is important here, however, is the association between the anointing of the sick with oil and the forgiveness of sins. The Epistle of James thus confirms that from the earliest Christian tradition, the anointing of the sick included a definite penitential aspect, specifically, that the anointing of the seriously ill entailed the forgiveness of all sins. Perhaps, it is important to mention here that the problem of the rite of anointing the sick started with this close association with "penance" together with the efforts to interpret James correctly. At one time, the tendency was to give a spiritual interpretation. This was compounded by the Vulgate – the Latin translation of the Bible by Jerome which used the term "salvo" (to save) to render both "sozein" (to save) and "egerirein" (to restore, to raise up). And at other times, some interpreted James purely from a physical cure. All these led to the origin of the practice of extreme unction which despite many reforms has plagued the rite of anointing the sick till this day.[31]

Summary

The discussion on the biblical insights into sickness and healing has underscored certain pertinent points. The Hebrew world saw everything as depending on divine causality. Sickness was no exception. It was conceived as a visitation of God on the unfaithful (Deut 28:21f, 27ff, 35). Beings superior to humans (but also dependent on God) could also be responsible for bringing sickness. These include Satan (Job 2:7), personified plagues (Ps 91:5f), etc. In the post-exilic Judaism the action of demons or evil spirits was emphasized. Thus, human religious intuition spontaneously establishes

---

[30] B. Poschmann, Penance and Anointing of the Sick, New York: Herder and Herder, 1964, 235.

a connection between sickness and sin. Biblical revelation does not contradict this view but tries to clarify the conditions under which this connection should be understood. The original intention of God was the happiness of humanity (Gen 2). Sickness, like all other human ills, contradicts this basic intention. Sickness entered the world only as a consequence of sin (cf. Gen 3:16-19) and thus, is one of the signs of God's wrath against a sinful world (cf. Ex 9:1-12). But all sickness is not caused by the personal sins of the sick person. The case of Job as we saw or that of Tobit (12:13) are exceptions. When sickness strikes righteous people, it can represent a test of one's fidelity. In the suffering Just One, the Servant of Yahweh, it serves to atone for the faults of sinners (Is 53:4ff).

If God sends sickness to his people, then it is he who will also bring about cure. It was God who smites and who cures (Deut 32:39; cf. Hos 6:1). God is the preeminent doctor (Ex 15:26). Medical practices and exorcisms were rare but by no means non-existent. The prophets like Elijah, Elisha or even Moses who practiced healing did so insofar as they were seen as media of divine communication, as spokesmen and representatives of God. The work of the doctor and his medicine is praised because he is seen as the healing instrument of God.

The belief that God heals also prevailed in the time of Jesus. The eschatological promises of the time when there will be no more sick people (Is 35:5ff), no more suffering or tears (Is 25:8, 65:19) found their fulfillment in Jesus. It is against this background that Jesus launched his total mission of preaching and healing. Later he commissioned his disciples to continue in his footsteps with authority and signs which accompanied their mission. With the earliest Christian communities, new interpretations and adaptations started to emerge. These reached their climax with the Epistle of James; where the rite of anointing the sick with oil began to take shape with its entanglements, sometimes with penance and other times with deathbed anointing. All that happened from the Patristic Church to Vatican II had their roots in the later early Christian communities. That whole history of the Church's conception of the Anointing of the Sick will be the preoccupation of the next chapter.

---

[31] Cf. F. MacNutt, Healing, 1974, 255.

Chapter Four
Historical Review of the Church's Attitude to Sickness and Healing

The Church's concern for the sick is symbolized by the sacrament of the anointing of the sick. This sacrament can, and in fact did change throughout its long history. At the very beginning, it was known as the sacrament of the sick and later was called the sacrament of the dying. At some other time, the sacrament was understood to be for those at the point of death and at another that of those beginning to be in danger of death. A further step in the journey required the sacrament to embrace all the infirm, even though they do not begin to be in danger of death. The purpose of this chapter will be to examine these stages of development. The previous chapter analyzed the data of Christian experience from the biblical perspective. This present one will trace the ecclesial tradition.

For the sake of convenience, we shall outline the historical developments in the following order: Patristic Church followed by the Carolingian renaissance. Then, the Scholastic period which opens the door for reform of the Council of Trent will be discussed. Finally, the ecumenical development will conclude the chapter. It goes without saying that the division of history into two, three or more periods is an artificial one. The result is usually a gross oversimplification. However, the division reveals a definite change and development that needs to be examined, in order to draw from it practical, as well as doctrinal consequences.

4.1 The Patristic Church (4th – 8th Centuries)

Healing in the name of Jesus continued to be the common experience of Christians even in the time of the Fathers. Although, they wrote very little about the healing ministry in comparison to the early Church, what they left behind is enough to confirm that healing was "simply an accepted part of the ordinary Christian experirnce."[1] Among the Church Fathers who left

---

[1] P. Chibuko, "HIV/AIDS and the Healing Mission of the Church Today: Reversing

credible testimony of healing include Augustine of Hippo (AD 354-430); Origen (AD 185-254); Tertullian (AD 160-230); Irenaeus (AD 130-202); Justin (AD 100-165); etc.

It is noteworthy that Augustine in his early writing did not mention anywhere the custom of anointing the sick with oil. He even expressed the opinion that the age of healing as it occurred in the time of the apostles was over. However, after several years of pastoral experience as bishop of Hippo, he retracted his earlier views and testified that in his own diocese alone, in a period of two years nearly seventy well attested miracles of healing had taken place.[2]

Origen acknowledges that healing prayers said in the name of Jesus could cause a total healing in a person's life. Even the Greek and the Barbarians who accepted Jesus Christ and invoked his name in prayer also shared in the gift of healing.[3] Tertullian in one of his letters notes that some Roman officials who publicly opposed Christians were privately seeking prayers for healing from them. He gives an example of the secretary of a certain gentleman, who was cured of his suffering from falling sickness caused by demons. Not only distinguished officials but also common people including a certain little boy were all beneficiaries of healing from either of devils or their sickness. Tertullian specifically mentions the use of holy oil in the cure of ailments.[4]

For Irenaeus, healing belongs to Christians as a natural activity which channels the creative power of God to the sick through prayers. He shows how Christians have been able to give sight to the blind, hearing to the deaf, put all demons to flight, the infirm, the lame or those paralyzed or disturbed in other parts of the body have been cured. Others who contracted some bodily illnesses or have had some kind of accident have been restored back to good health. He urges the Church to make good use of its innate gift of healing, which in certain cases raised even the dead to life. Irenaeus makes a pertinent point when he says that the Church has uncountable gifts

---

the Stigma of the Scourge," in BTS 25 (2005): 52.

[2] See Augustine, City of God, XXII, 8, trans. G. Walsh and D. Honan, New York: Fathers of the Church, 1954.

[3] Cf. Origen, Against Celsus, in The Ante Nicene Literature after Irenaeus, vol. 2, Christian Classics, Maryland, Westminster, 1986, 43-98, I, 46, 67.

which it received from God, in the name of Jesus Christ, and which it exercises every day for the benefits of the Gentiles, neither practicing deception upon any, nor taking any reward from them. For as it has received freely from God, freely also it ministers to others.[5] This remark from Irenaeus is of topical interest in the Nigerian healing experience today.

In the sixth chapter of his second apology to the Roman Senate, Justin confirms that many demoniacs everywhere in the world including Rome were exorcised by many Christians in the name of Jesus Christ who was crucified under Pontius Pilate. Moreover, Christians were still curing those under demonic possession and dispelling the demons who had taken possession of people, even when they could not be cured by all the other exorcists, and exploiters of incantations and drugs.[6]

Apart from the above mentioned Fathers of the Church, there are many others like Cyprian, Gregory the Great, Gregory of Tours, etc. All of them agree that healing played a prominent role in their ministry of proclamation among the pagans. They believed strongly that healing is wrought by calling on the name of Jesus Christ. For the Fathers, God continues to heal his suffering sons and daughters through the power of Christ, mediated in the Church. There were various means of bringing about cure: exorcism or deliverance from demonic attacks and possessions, special prayers of healing, the use of holy oil, veneration of relics of saints and martyrs, (Augustine, Gregory of Tours), through contact or exchange of pleasantries with the newly baptized at Easter Vigil (Augustine), by direct physical contact with the tombs of saints and martyrs, and visits to the shrines of holy ones. However, many of them caution against "exploiters of incantations and drugs" (Justin Martyr), against "deception" and "taking of reward" (Irenaeus) and above all they remind sick Christians to seek joy in suffering. In the words of Gregory the Great: "the sick are to be admonished that they feel themselves to be the sons and daughters of God in that the scourge

---

[4] Cf. Tertullian, To Scapula 4, in The Ante Nicene Literature after Irenaeus, 251–317.
[5] Irenaeus, Discourse on Healing, in Against Heresies, 11, 6.2, 31.2, 32.4-5, vol. 1, Christian Classics, Maryland, Westminster 1986, 287-313.
[6] Justin Martyr, Apologia 2, To the Roman Senate, 6, in Johannes Quasten, Patrology, The Beginnings of Patristic Literature: From the Apostles' Creed to Irenaeus, vol. 1, Christian Classics, 1986, 196-219.

of discipline chastises them."[7] These are words that need to be heard over and over again in the world today, not only in Nigeria, perhaps even more in Europe and America.

In addition to the Church Fathers, accounts of healing abound in hagiographical texts. The first patristic text to provide clear and informative evidence with reference to James and the actual practice of anointing the sick with oil is Pope Innocent's celebrated letter to Decentius, bishop of Gubbio. This letter, dating from the year 417 contains authoritative explanation of how to carry out in practice the prescriptions of James 5:14. The document appears to have been designed to answer two specific questions: who is the recipient of anointing and who the minister is. In answer to the first question, Innocent specifies that the faithful who are sick are eligible to receive anointing with the holy oil of chrism, blessed by the bishop, and which not only priests, but all Christians may use for anointing for their own needs or those of their family members.[8] Answering the second question, concerning the minister, Innocent replies:

... if the bishop either can, or deems it proper that he should, visit someone in person, surely he whose office it is to prepare the chrism can both bless and anoint with chrism. But he cannot pour it on penitents, since it is a kind of sacrament. And how can it be deemed proper to grant one Kind of sacrament to those who are denied the rest of the sacraments?[9]

From this passage it will seem that anointing of the sick was already an established custom at Rome. The preparation of oil was reserved to the bishop. The anointing with oil could be done by the people, by presbyters, or by the bishop himself. Being a "kind of sacrament" (genus sacramenti), it is not to be given to penitents and catechumens, but only to the faithful in good standing.

Just as Innocent represents the tradition of the Church in Rome (West), so also Caesarius of Arles (d. 543) reflects the custom of the Church in Gaul

---

[7] Gregory the Great, On the Pastoral Care of the Sick, quoted in Jesus Alvarez Gomez, The Care of the Sick in the History of the Church, in Dolentium Hominum, 31, 1996, 45.

[8] Cf. P. F. Palmer, Sacraments and Forgiveness: Sources of Christian Theology II, Westminster, Md.: Newman Press, 1955, 283.

(East). Caesarius exhorts the faithful not to have recourse to pagan superstitious practices in times of sickness:

How much more correct and salutary it would be to hurry to the Church to receive the body and blood of Christ, and with oil that is blessed to anoint in all faith themselves and their dear ones; for according to what James the Apostle says, not only would they receive health of body, but also the remission of sins ...[10]

Caesarius encourages not only lay anointing presumably at home, but also anointing in the Church by priests assisted by deacons. Repeatedly, patristic documents continue to exhort people not to rely on the incantations of sorcerers among pagans. Instead of resorting to magical rites of healing, they should hurry to the Church to receive Christian healing rites of the Eucharist and oil of anointing which assure one of healing of body and remission of sins. Of particular interest is the perennial phenomenon that healing practices can easily become part of a people's religion, at times bordering on magical superstition.

In the seventh century, Eligius, bishop of Noyon in Southern France, almost repeated the exhortation of Caesarius, urging his faithful to trust in the Eucharist and the blessed oil of the Church rather than in magical remedies. He gives prominence to lay anointing with oil blessed by the bishop.[11] Also from the Church of England in the eighth century comes the testimony of Venerable Bede (d. 735). Commenting on the Epistle of James, he allows the laity the use of consecrated oil. Appealing to the authority of Innocent, he makes the forgiveness of sins unambiguously dependent on confession to a priest. Bede insists that anointing is a sacrament of the sick. He judges that it is clear that the custom of anointing the sick was handed on to the holy Church by the apostles themselves; thus those who are possessed or sick are anointed with oil consecrated by pontifical blessing.

As one can see, these documents are wanting in unequivocal clarity. They do not sufficiently distinguish sacramental from private anointing of the

---

[9] P. F. Palmer, Sacraments and Forgiveness, 284.
[10] Sermon 279, 5; PL 39, 2273, quoted in P. F. Palmer, Sacraments and Forgiveness, 285.
[11] Cf. On the Correctness of Catholic Conduct 5 (PL 40, 1172f), quoted by P. F. Palmer, Sacrament and Forgiveness, 286.

sick or they unite the rite for the sick with penance. All these are understandable because up to this time there was no clear concept of a sacrament clearly differentiating individual sacraments from each other and from non-sacramental actions.

Other important documents of the period under review relating to the anointing of the sick include the blessing of oil found in the Apostolic Tradition of Hippolytus of Rome (c. 215). This text contains the petition that this oil "... may give strength to all that taste of it and health to all that use it."[12] Another liturgical text from the Eastern Church is the Prayer Book of Serapion (c. 350) bishop of Thmuis Egypt. In its formulary of prayer provision is made for the blessing of bread and water. However, the second prayer of the Euchologion also stresses the spiritual effect of the blessed oil; which is to be "a means of grace and goodness and the remission of sins, a medicament of life and salvation, unto health and soundness of soul and body and spirit, unto perfect well-being."[13] As Gusmer rightly comments:

> *Perfect well-being* are the words that best summarize the purpose of this anointing. Its comprehensiveness aims at a wholeness that includes the removal of every disease and sickness, the exorcistic casting out of demons and unclean spirits, and a means of grace and remission of sins.[14]

More frequently are also accounts and recommendations of private anointing with oil blessed by the bishop. Suplicius Severus, for example, relates that the wife of a noble man named Avitus asked St Martin of Tours to bless "as is the custom" a vessel of oil intended as a remedy for sickness.[15] In a similar way, St. Genevieve was known to anoint with blessed oil the sick for whom she cared. One day as she needed the oil and found the vessel empty; she was panic stricken "because there was no bishop within reach to bless the oil."[16] It is very likely that the rite of simple blessing of oil as found in the *Rituale Romanum of 1614* has its origin from this earlier practice.

---

[12] G. Dix (ed.), The Apostolic Tradition, London: SPCK, 1968, V, 10.
[13] P. F. Palmer, Sacraments and Forgiveness, 280.
[14] C. W. Gusmer, And You Visited Me, 1990, 13.
[15] C. W. Gusmer, And You Visited Me, 1990, 18.
[16] C. W. Gusmer; And You Visited Me, 1990, 18.

In summary then, among the earlier Church Fathers, very few like Tertullian mentioned the use of blessed oil in the healing of sickness. From the third and fourth centuries, however, with the early liturgical formularies of prayer for the blessing of oil of the sick and other patristic and hagiographical texts more specific mention is made. In fact, most of the texts, speak more about the blessing and application of oil in the event of a member of the community falling ill.

For them what is more necessary is that the oil of sick must be blessed by the bishop. Hence several verbs were used to describe this oil: "blessed oil," "holy oil," "sacred oil," "consecrated oil," "prepared oil." A primordial importance was attached to the blessing of the oil which placed it in the category of a "sacrament" (Innocent). However, care must be taken here not to understand sacrament in its more technical sense of the seven sacraments as this did not evolve until around the twelfth and thirteenth centuries. The efficacy of the oil is related to its blessing. Thus, what is more important for the Fathers is the consecration of the oil by the bishop and not the issue of who applied it. While the preparation and blessing of the oil is strictly reserved for the bishop, the application of it is not restricted only to the ordained ministers. Lay or private anointing is encouraged. Innocent and Bede though distinguish two types of unction, lay and presbyteral, no great difference between the two is made.

Furthermore, it is only the blessing of the oil that is liturgically organized before the middle of the eighth century. Its application occurred in varying ways. External usage is most frequent, usually by application to the ailing member of the body. Internal usage is also practiced, namely, by drinking the oil. Sometimes, the imposition of hands accompanied the anointing; more often before the ninth century, the laying on of hands is performed independently of the anointing.

Another important development of the period is the restriction of anointing only to the baptized, and among them according to Innocent, only to those who are not liable to the public penitential discipline. A later sacramental theology would say that anointing is a sacrament for the living. The corporeal or bodily effects of anointing receive particular emphasis. There is nowhere anointing of the sick appears to be a preparatory rite for death. There is also no mention of "unction in extremis" before the ninth century. However, after that transitional period it occurs very frequently. One of the reasons is that most people were content with the more convenient form of a domestic religious remedy whereby they anointed themselves and members of their family when they were sick. Priests were, therefore, only summoned, if at all, in cases of grave sickness. Similarly, from the fourth century onwards, penance was also for the most part only received in time of sickness. As we have already seen, anointing was refused to penitents in accordance with the decretal of Innocent. It will also not be true to think that the expected results of anointing the sick will be

> *Simply bodily healing but a deeper wholeness: strength, forgiveness of sins, vivification, protection of body, mind, and spirit. In other words, what is involved is the entire somatic realm of salvation for a sick person battling with demonic power while reaching out to the indwelling of the Holy Spirit and the powers of Christ.*[17]

Finally, all the Fathers of the Church and the prayers of blessing see the practice of anointing in direct relation to the prescription of James 5:14-16. It is thus James who sort of promulgated the rite and its practice since the early days of the Church.

4.2 The Carolingian Renaissance (8th - 9th Centuries)

This period in the anointing of the sick is characterized by a number of reforms. The reform measures were prompted by the Irish and English missionaries in Northern Europe. Among the goals of these reforms are the renewal of priestly ministry and the abandonment of the practice of lay anointing. A document called The Statuta Bonifatii, probably originating from a Burgundian Synod (800–840) required that priests on journeys should always carry the holy oil along with them as well as the Eucharist.

---

[17] A. Knauber, Pastoral Theology of the Anointing of the Sick, Collegeville, Minnesota: The Liturgical Press, 1975, 16-17.

Particularly remarkable, in view of the earlier approved practice, is their prohibition under pain of deposition of delivering blessed oil to non-priests for use as a remedy or for any other purpose. The reason given is that it is genus sacramenti (in the category of sacrament).[18] Canon 48 of the Council of Chalon II (813) insists that anointing is to be administered only by the ordained, for such remedy "which heals the weaknesses of soul and body, is not to be lightly regarded."[19]

Other local Synods held at Aachen (836) and Mainz (847) also enacted laws that supported the practice of presbyteral anointing. Chapter 8 of the Council of Pavia (850) associates this growing custom more closely with other rites for the dying, namely, deathbed reconciliation and viaticum. This strong affiliation is the result of certain developments in the sacrament of penance. During the first eight or nine centuries of the Christian era, penance became increasingly severe and excessively rigorous. A penitent, for instance, even after reconciliation is prohibited from holding public offices, engagement in military service, or marital intercourse. Other penances imposed include starvation diets, entrance into a monastery or convent, etc. Given this state of affairs, it is only natural that people loathed this sacrament and chose to postpone it until towards the end of their lives.[20]

Furthermore, there is an explicit connection between the anointing of the sick and the forgiveness of sins in the Epistle of James:

> *Is any among you sick? Let him call the elders of the Church, and let them pray over him, anointing him with oil in the name of the Lord; and the prayer of faith will save the sick man, and the Lord will raise him up; and if he committed sins, he will be forgiven (5:14-15).*

Since people were putting off the practice of their penances until the later part of their lives, and also the fact that anointing of the sick carried with it the forgiveness of sins, for which it seems that no penance is necessary, it is easy to understand how the anointing of the sick was also postponed until

---

[18] PL 89, 821, 823.
[19] Mansi XIV, 104, quoted by P. F. Palmer, Sacrament and Forgiveness, 290-291.
[20] Cf. A. Echema, Corporate Personality in Traditional Igbo Society and the Sacrament of Reconciliation, 1995, 163-4

the later part of one's life; that is, to a point of very near death. In effect, it became not the life giving or curing sacrament that it was during the time of Caesarius, but an immediate preparation for death, whence the name Extreme Unction (*extrema unctio*).

Extreme unction in this way became a part of a larger liturgical ceremony, involving 1) confession by the sick person; 2) absolution; 3) viaticum; 4) finally, the last anointing. Thus, considered in all aspects, extreme unction was really the last thing. The close linkage between anointing and penance transferred the primary emphasis of anointing to the forgiveness of sins. It became an immediate preparation for death and for the final judgment. This understanding has colored the classical form and meaning of the sacrament until the recent revision after Vatican II. The former rite called for the anointing of the five senses, reflecting the idea that it is through our body that we have sinned, and thus that it is our body which must be purified and prepared for the final judgment. The anointing was accompanied by a prayer that God be merciful and forgive all sins committed through the eyes, tongue, sense of touch, etc. In the judgment of Poschmann, this is how "anointing became more and more a sacrament of the dying, although this corresponded neither to its nature as a remedy against sickness nor to the directives of the Church, which even in the early Middle Ages required a serious but by no means a hopeless sickness as a condition for its administration.[21]

To sum up, the two major factors in the transition of the practice of anointing in the 9th century are the rise of an organized ritual for anointing increasingly entrusted to the priests, and the association of the anointing ritual with deathbed reconciliation of penitents. Consequently, anointing in the Middle Ages is marked by two characteristics that color the sacrament to this day: a spiritualizing tendency whereby much emphasis is placed on remission of sins, thus confusing the effects of deathbed penance and anointing; and the designation of the rite as a sacrament of the dying, a characteristic which evolved from the unfortunate association of the sacrament with deathbed penance and viaticum.[22] By the end of the twelfth cen-

---

[21] B. Poschmann, Penance and the Anointing of the Sick, 1964, 246.
[22] C. W. Gusmer, And You Visited Me, 1990, 25-6.

tury, anointing had become even more "extreme unction" with the original order of sacraments changing from penance, anointing, viaticum, to penance, viaticum, anointing.[23]

Perhaps, one final point that needs to be mentioned is the widespread neglect of the sacrament in the Middle Ages. Apart from the extreme rigors which discouraged people from availing themselves of the sacrament, laziness and indifference often kept priests from visiting the sick and the faithful from troubling about the sacrament. Matters degenerated when the custom of remunerating the priest for his services developed and what was at first a free-will offering soon became a considerable burden for poorer people. Significant of this situation is the admonition frequently addressed to priests that they should require not only the rich but also the poor to receive anointing.[24] This is a sad commentary of pastoral care and thus calls for purification of the sacrament, not only of its strong penitential overtones but also its pastoral abuses.

4.3 The Scholastic Period (12th Century)

Although, the original order of administering the sacrament had changed from penance, anointing, viaticum to penance, viaticum, anointing, "no one spoke of 'extreme unction' until Peter Lombard (d. 1160) first used it in the middle of the 12th century."[25] This gradual change in pastoral practice and liturgy, which started in the 8th and 9th centuries led to a change in the theological reflection on anointing during the Scholastic era. The Scholastics simply commented on the practice and liturgy of unction as they experienced it in their age, namely, that anointing of the sick was an extreme unction of the dying. They generally neglected the patristic and liturgical documents of the earlier period. In their systematic development of sacramental theology, they viewed unction as a preparation for the passage from

---

[23] P. Murray "The Liturgical History of Extreme Unction," in Studies in Pastoral Theology, vol. II, Dublin, 1963, 28-30.

[24] B. Poschmann, Penance and the Anointing of the Sick, 1964, 243-4; see also Peter Browe, "Die letzte Ölung in der abendländischen Kirche des Mittelalters," in Zeitschrift für Katholische Theologie 55 (1931): 515-61.

this life to the next, and considered its effect not as a means of restoring health but as a way of preparing the soul for the beatific vision. The argument of the Scholastics is that sacraments are means of grace, and grace is a supernatural perfection. Consequently, a physical effect, which is the recovery of health cannot be an effect of the sacrament.

However, a controversy ensued between the Dominican school of Albert the Great and Thomas Aquinas, and the Franciscan school of Bonaventure and Dun Scotus. Both schools agreed that the principal effect of the sacrament was the remission of sins. The Franciscans believed that the effect of unction is the forgiveness of venial sins while the Dominicans claimed that it is for the remission of the remnants (reliquiae) of sin which impeded the soul's passage to glory. According to Aquinas, the principal effect of unction is the spiritual cure of those "failings which render a man spiritually sick, with the result that he has not that perfect strength needed for leading a life of grace and glory. Now this failing is nothing else but debility of sorts, which is left as the result of actual or original sin."[26] However, they all agree that this sacrament for the dying prepares the soul for heaven. Both Albert and Thomas held that the recipient of anointing must be in "a state of departure." For Albert, the extreme (last) unction has become the last (extreme) sacrament; for Thomas, anointing is the Church's last remedy.

Bonaventure and Scotus on the other hand went as far as demanding that the very imminence of death was necessary for the reception of unction. Bonaventure insisted it be given only "where danger of death is imminent" and only to those "who are as it were in transit to another state."[27] Dun Scotus (d. 1308) completed this development of anointing from a rite for the sick to a sacrament of the dying when he stated that it "is to be given only to such as a sick person who no longer capable of sinning and who is in danger of death."[28] Put in another way, the proper time for receiving the sacrament is in extremis, in the agony of death, because the recipient is no

---

[25] F. MacNutt, Healing, 1974, 256.
[26] Supplement to Summa Theologica, q. 30, a. 1; P. F. Palmer, "The Purpose of Anointing the Sick: A Reappraisal," in Theological Studies 19 (1958): 333.
[27] P. F. Palmer, "The Purpose of Anointing the Sick," 334.
[28] P. F. Palmer, "The Purpose of Anointing the Sick," 335.

longer in the position to sin again and thus cannot negate the effect of the sacrament.

The Reunion Council of Florence, in its Decree for anointing the Armenians (1439) provides a fitting summary of the Scholastic teaching on extreme unction:

> *The fifth sacrament is extreme unction. Its matter is olive oil blessed by the bishop. This sacrament may not be given except to a sick person whose life is feared for. He is to be anointed on those parts: on the eyes on account of sight, on the ears on account of hearing, on the nostrils on account of smelling, on the mouth on account of taste and speech, on the hands on account of touch, on the feet on account of movement, on loins on account of the lust seated there ... The minister of this sacrament is the priest. The effect is the healing of the mind and as far as it is good for the soul, of the body as well ...*[29]

4.4 Council of Trent to Vatican II

The above was the state in which the Reformers saw "extreme unction" and thus they rejected it as a sacrament. As Martin Luther wrote in his Babylonian Captivity (1520), "James spoke of charismatic cure, not of unction, which though good, is not a sacrament."[30] For the Reformers, faith was all that counted, and so unction was good insofar as it could be a means of stimulating faith in forgiveness. However, there is evidence of a letter written by Luther in the last year of his life and in it he advices a pastor how to minister to the sick. Luther suggests a home visitation with two or three good men involving common prayer and the laying on of hands, which is to be carried out three times a day together with public prayers in the Church.[31] John Calvin on his part held that anointing pertained to a miraculous gift of healing that accompanied the first preaching of the Gospel, a

---

[29] Denzinger-Schönmetzer, 1324; J. Neuner and J. Dupuis, The Christian Faith, 1983, 430.
[30] P. F. Palmer, Sacraments and Forgiveness, 1959, 298.
[31] Quoted by C. W. Gusmer, And You Visited Me, 1990, 33.

gift not communicated to subsequent generations. Even if the precept of anointing did pertain to the present age, the Roman practice with the superstitious blessing of oil and anointing of "half-dead carcasses" according to Calvin was an abuse of the anointing encouraged by James.[32]

These were some of the issues that the Council of Trent (1551) addressed itself. The Council Fathers devoted three chapters to extreme unction: the institution of extreme unction, the effect of the sacrament, and the minister and time of administration.[33] Of more dogmatic significance are the four canons.[34] First, extreme unction is a sacrament instituted by Christ and announced by James. Second, it has an enduring salvific meaning in terms of conferring grace, remitting sins and comforting the sick. Third, the rite and practice of the sacrament correspond with the scriptural precedent in James. Fourth, the proper minister of anointing is an ordained priest.

It is particularly noteworthy that, though Trent was heavily dependent on the Scholastic terminology the Council refused to canonize the Scholastic approach. The Council was primarily concerned with reasserting the proper sacramentality of unction as one of the seven sacraments. There are at least three indications that the Council Fathers wished to avoid a definition of anointing as a sacrament exclusively for the dying. For instance, the original draft stated that extreme unction is to be administered "only (*dumtaxat*) to those who are in their final struggle and have come to grips with death and are about to go forth to the Lord." The final wording was amended to read: "This anointing is to be used for the sick, but especially (*praesertim*) for those who are dangerously ill as to seem at the point of departing this life."[35] Furthermore, the canons of Trent say nothing concrete about the function of anointing as a sacrament of the dying or the degree of sickness: three times the term sick (*infirmi*) not dying (*moribundi*) is used to describe the subject of the anointing. Finally, the benefits of anointing are described as the strengthening of the entire human person in time of sickness through

---

[32] J. Calvini & O. Selecta (eds.), Peter Barth and Wm. Niesel, vol. 5, Munich: Chr. Kaiser, 2nd rev. ed. 1962, 452-55.
[33] Denzinger-Schönmetzer, 1695-1999; J. Neuner and J. Dupuis, The Christian Faith, 441-43.
[34] Denzinger-Schönmetzer, 1716-1919; J. Neuner and J. Dupuis, The Christian Faith, 446-47.
[35] Denzinger-Schönmetzer, 1698.

the grace of the Holy Spirit with resulting spiritual, psychological, and physical effects.[36]

In spite of Trent's attempt to present the sacrament of anointing as a sacrament of the sick, both post-Tridentine theory and practice continued to portray and administer it as a sacrament of the dying. Thus, the stage was ripe for the reforms of Vatican II. In addition to preferring the name "anointing of the sick" to "extreme unction" and encouraging that the time of ministration be the beginning of the danger of death from sickness or old age, the Council, in its *Constitution on the Sacred Liturgy,* made two further statements: First, paragraph 74 restores the original sequence of reconciliation (penance), anointing, and viaticum:

> *In addition to the separate rites for Anointing of the Sick and for Viaticum, a continuous rite shall be prepared in which a sick man is anointed after he had made his confession and before he receives Viaticum.*[37]

The position of viaticum, and not unction as a sacrament for the dying was thereby emphasized. Second, paragraph 75 contains recommendations for adapting the anointing and prayers of the rite itself:

> *The number of the anointing is to be adapted to the occasion, and the prayers which belong to the rite of Anointing are to be revised so as to correspond to the varying conditions of the sick who receive the sacrament.*[38]

4.5 Ecumenical Convergence

It is surprising how close the practice of anointing of the sick in other Christian communities is with the tradition of the Roman Catholic Church. Both the Eastern Orthodox and the member Churches of the Anglican Communion have ritual services for anointing the sick. Almost all the Eastern Churches anoint the sick with oil, except the Armenians and Nestorians, where the rite has fallen into disuse, and the Ethiopian Church where it is

---

[36] Denzinger-Schönmetzer, 1696.
[37] Vatican II, Constitution on the Sacred Liturgy, 22.
[38] Vatican II, Constitution on the Sacred Liturgy, 22.

rarely celebrated.[39] The tradition of anointing is based on the Eastern Euchologion, and the Prayer Book of bishop Serapion of Thmuis in Egypt (4th c.)

The service is elaborate and a public ceremony; when possible performed by seven priests, at least a deacon, together with a choir and congregation. Other elaborations include seven readings, seven prayers, and seven anointing of the sick person in the form of a cross on the brow, the nostrils, the checks, the lips, the breast, and the hands. The prayers are addressed to the Father as "Physician of soul and bodies," who sent his Son to heal every infirmity and to deliver us from death. The petition to heal the body and soul is made through the intercession of Mary, the angels, the cross, and the saints, particularly, those associated with healing. This service for anointing is variously called "prayer oil" (*euchelaion*), "holy oil," "holy unction," and "rite of the lamp" stressing physical and mental healing as well as the spiritual benefits, especially the remission of sins. But the ritual is not the last rites, and does not mention any extreme cases. Anointing could be used as a penitential rite on Holy Thursday, in which case it is open to all the faithful.[40] *The First Book of Common Prayer* of 1549 retained an order for anointing in its office of visitation of the sick. Although the rite of anointing the sick was deleted in the 1552 *Prayer Book*, there were high Church reform movements in the 18th and 19th centuries advocating the revival of anointing.[41] Today, with the rise of an active healing ministry, anointing of the sick together with the laying on of hands is practiced in most of the member Churches of the Anglican Communion.

The liturgical reforms of the American Episcopal Church contain a four-part service entitled "The Ministration to the Sick and Suffering": the ministry of the word, confession and absolution, anointing or the laying on of hands, and communion of the sick. The order for anointing provides a form for blessing the oil by a bishop or priest. In case of necessity, a deacon or lay person, using oil blessed by a bishop, may perform the anointing. Also

---

[39] C. W. Gusmer, And You Visited Me, 1990, 37.
[40] See B. Groen, "The Anointing of the Sick in the Greek Orthodox Church" in Concilium 2 (1991): 50-59.
[41] Cf. C. W. Gusmer, "Anointing of the Sick in the Church of England," in Worship 45 (1971): 262-72.

included in the Ministration to the Sick are prayers for the sick adapted to various occasions – recovery from illness, sick child, before an operation, doctors and nurses, etc. as well as prayers for use by the sick themselves. A more recent publication, *The Book of Occasional Services*, has further enriched the Episcopal Church with a very hopeful and consoling public service of healing.[42] A most recent ecumenical development has taken place within the Lutheran Synods in North America, namely, the inclusion of the laying on of hands and the anointing of the sick in the *Occasional Services: A Companion to the Lutheran Book of Worship* (1982). It contains two services: a "Service of the Word for Healing" presented in a corporate setting and a simplified order for the home or hospital.[43]

Finally, anointing of the sick has been restored though optional to the United Church of Christ and the Presbyterian Church. The United Church of *Christ's Book of Worship* (1986) provides an "Order for Healing for Use with an Individual" and an "Order of Healing for Congregational Use." Both orders include scriptural reading, confession (individual or corporate) of sin with pardon, intercessory prayer, anointing and/or laying on of hands. Provision is also made for a prayer of thanksgiving to be said over the oil.[44]

The Presbyterian Holy Baptism and Services for the Renewal of Baptism contains a "Renewal of Baptism for the Sick and the Dying." After the renewal of baptismal promises, the minister lays hands on each person. According to the rubrics, "the sign of the cross may be marked on the forehead of each person being ministered to, using oil prepared for this purpose," accompanied by an appropriate prayer.[45]

---

[42] The Book of Occasional Services, New York: Church Hymnal Corporation, 1979, 147-154.
[43] Occasional Services: A Companion to the Lutheran Book of Worship, Minneapolis, Augsburg, 1982; see especially 94 and 101.
[44] Book of Worship, United Church of Christ, 1986, 296-320.
[45] Holy Baptism and Services for the Renewal of Baptism; Supplemental Liturgical Resource 2, Philadelphia: Westminster Press, 1985, 92-93.

Summary

Our historical review has shown the journey of the anointing of the sick; a journey that was so uneven and complicated.

In the Patristic era, the Fathers of the Church made use of anointing and healing in their apostolate. Some of them who earlier thought that the phenomenon of healing had ended with the age of the apostles later changed their mind. Augustine, for example, witnessed several healings in his own diocese. Other testimonies to the tradition of anointing were gathered from liturgical sources and hagiographical texts. Primordial importance was attached to the blessing of the oil by the bishop. However, its administration was most likely done in a more informal way, by either presbyters or by any baptized Christian. The oil could be applied externally or taken internally. In all events, the expected results were a wholeness of body, mind, and spirit. In no way was anointing regarded as a rite for the dying.

With the Carolingian renaissance, however, a shift which began to appear in the seventh century transformed anointing from a rite for the sick into a sacrament for the dying. The context for the development was a Carolingian reform that brought about a change in pastoral practice and liturgy. The reform started with a renewal of priestly ministry which led to the prohibition of anointing by lay people and restricted it exclusively to the ordained. A further step was the development of a ritual for the presbyteral administration of the blessed oil. Finally, the newly created rite of anointing was inserted after deathbed reconciliation in such a way that it became ultimately the extreme unction, the last rites in one's life time. The change in pastoral practice meant a change in the theological reflection on anointing. The Schoolmen commenting on the practice of unction in their day viewed it as a preparation for the glory of the beatific vision. Like all seven sacraments, unction bestows a spiritual grace which is conferred *ex opere operato*. Generally, they taught that the spiritual effect of unction was the remission of sins: either venial sins (Franciscan school) or the remnants of sin (Dominican school).

The Council of Trent, though heavily dependent on the terminology of the Schoolmen, rejected their theology of anointing as a sacrament for the dying. The Council Fathers maintained that unction conveyed the grace of the Holy Spirit with its multiple spiritual, psychological, and physical benefits. Thus, the stage was set for the reforms of the Second Vatican Council which recovered the original intention of anointing, namely, for the seriously ill.

Chapter Five
The Revised Rites for the Sick

When the original draft of the Constitution on the Sacred Liturgy was presented to the bishops of the Second Vatican Council on October 22, 1962, the section on unction raised objections. Some bishops called for a change of name from extreme unction to anointing of the sick. They declared that the sacrament was per se not the sacrament of the dying but of the grievously ill, and thus, should be administered at the beginning of a serious illness. The initial schema also provided for the repetition of the sacrament during the same illness.[1]

The final version of the Constitution promulgated on December 4, 1963, clearly stated the name and nature of the sacrament in these words:

"Extreme unction," which may also and more fittingly be called 'anointing of the sick,' is not the sacrament of those only who are at the point of death. Hence, as soon as any one of the faithful begins to be in danger of death from sickness or old age, the fitting time for him to receive this sacrament has certainly already arrived (SC 73).[2]

This definitive version does not provide for a possible repetition of the administration of the sacrament within the same sickness. However, there was a suggestion that a continuous rite be prepared according to which the sick person is anointed after confessing and before the reception of viaticum.[3] In 1972, the Roman Congregation for Divine Worship promulgated the revised order for the pastoral care and anointing of the sick, the *Ordo unctionis infirmorum eorumque pastoralis curae*. This was accompanied by the Apostolic Constitution *Sacram unctionem infirmorum* of Paul VI dated November 30, 1972. All these reinforced the views of the Liturgy Constitution.

---

[1] Acta Synodia S. Concili: Oecumenici Vaticani II, I, Pars II, Vatican City: Typis Polyglottis Vaticanis, 1970, 285.
[2] Austin Flannery (ed.), The Documents of Vatican II, New York: American Press, 1966, 161. See also 75.
[3] Vatican II, Constitution on the Liturgy, 74.

In March 1974, the approved translation of the Rite of Anointing and Pastoral Care of the Sick, prepared by the International Committee on English in the Liturgy (ICEL), appeared in book form. A striking feature of the new rite is its overall pastoral thrust, as the title indicates. The designation "extreme unction" and the reference to the life-threatening nature of the sickness are avoided, though at the same time - in an ambiguous way - the corresponding statements of the Council of Trent are repeated. Furthermore, the new ritual emphasizes the solemn character of the anointing of the sick and thus, provides for communal celebrations for anointing of large numbers of relatively young people. This admits of variation in the rite as carried out in a sickroom with family and friends and as celebrated in a parochial or diocesan liturgy. There are specifications of "Offices and Ministries" which elaborate on the earlier sacramental categories of priest/minister and subject/recipient.[4]

Another general characteristic of the new revised rite is the clearer distinction between rites for the sick (Part I) and rites for the dying (Part II). The ritual begins with the normal Ministry to the Sick (chapter 1), Visits to the Sick, and continues in the subsequent three chapters: Visits to a Sick Child (chapter 2), Communion of the Sick (chapter 3), and Anointing of the Sick (chapter 4). At the background of the introduction to the revised rites are certain special questions, which the rite of anointing tried to provide answers; at the same time, however, it raised new problems as well. All these will constitute the bulk of this chapter.

5.1 Pastoral Care of the Sick

In order to appreciate fully the pastoral enrichment of the new ritual, a little comparison with the Rituale Romanum of 1614 will be helpful. Already the formal title VI, Extreme Unction was replaced with the Visitation and Care of the Sick as Chapter IV of the post-Tridentine ritual. Let us briefly summarize the contents of the Rituale Romanum of 1614.

---

[4] Nos 32-37. These expand the ministries, which were already mentioned in the General Introduction.

The document enjoins the parish priest to be available to the sick parishioners. It is expected, that he will be informed of their sickness. There should be a register of the sick in the parish. If he is incapacitated, he may delegate other priests and lay faithful to assist him in this ministry. He ought to visit the sick with the spirit of a true pastor. The fact of the obligation to provide charity and help to the poor and destitute through arms and special collections not withstanding, the parish priest's primary concern is the spiritual good of the sick. He is expected to approach the sick with a sense of mission, with a spiritual understanding of sickness and the value of redemptive suffering. He is to lead the sick person gradually to the sacrament of penance. He has the obligation to warn against treatment or remedies that are normally against the faith. When signs of the danger of death appear, nothing should obscure the salvation of the soul or delay Holy Communion. If the sick person is not yet ready to confess his or her sins, the priest is to exhort the person continually by appealing to divine mercy and by public and private prayers. The priest is to provide the correct remedy to temptations and any false ideas the sick person may have. Nonverbal symbols such as the images of the Blessed Virgin Mary, the Saints are important as well as the use of other sacramentals like the holy water, the rosary, etc. The priest is to recite prayers with the sick: versicles from Psalms, the Lord's Prayer, the Hail Mary, and the Creed. He may read the passion of the Lord, lives of the Saints, or speak of the joys of heaven. The sick person should be consoled with the knowledge that the priest and parishioners are praying for him or her. The priest is to encourage the ailing Christian to settle his or her temporal affairs by making a will. If the patient recovers, he or she should use the occasion of the illness as a starting point for a better life by first of all going to the Church to give thanks to God and to receive communion.[5]

The Rituale Romanum of 1614 also provided a detailed office for visiting the sick. The introduction included the greeting of peace, the sprinkling of the room, one of the four penitential Psalms or Psalm 90, versicles and responses, three collects, the blessing, and sprinkling of the sick with holy

---

[5] Rituale Romanum VI, De sacramento extremae unctionis, cap. IV De visitatione et cura infirmorum, 1-17.

water. There are five alternative formats of the liturgy of the word from which the priest could choose. The basic pattern is a psalm, followed by a gospel reading, and conclusion with a prayer. The suggested psalms are Psalms 6, 15, 19, 85, and 90. The Gospel pericopes are Matt 8:5-13 (centurion's servant), Mk 16:14-18 (missionary mandate), Lk 4:38-40 (Peter's mother-in-law and the healing of the sick), Jn 5:1-14 (pool at Bethzatha), and Jn 1:1-14 (prologue). The fifth and concluding format consists of the laying on of hands, a final blessing and sprinkling with holy water.[6]

In sum, the Rituale Romanum of 1614 is pastorally rich in its provisions for visiting and caring for the sick. A keen pastoral sensitivity runs through the directives given to the priest on how to minister to the needs of the sick. Sacramental confession and preparation for the life to come are strongly emphasized. However, the possibility of recovery is not excluded since the restored person is encouraged to see his or her recovery as an occasion of conversion and so is to give thanks to God in the Church, a provision retained in the Pastoral Care of the Sick (no. 40c). The liturgical services for visitation of the sick, although lengthy when fully celebrated, are very scriptural in content, with emphasis on nonverbal communication with the infirm such as sprinkling with holy water, laying on of hands and so on. They are moreover designed to touch the religious affections of the sick by disposing them to trust in the Lord, who is their Savior and Healer.

The new rite in its introduction to Part 1, Pastoral Care of the Sick, makes a subtle shift in the ecclesiology of pastoral ministry. Unlike the Rituale Romanum of 1614 where the care of the sick was almost exclusively the priest's responsibility, number 43 of the new rite expands the ministry of the sick to include the entire Christian community:

"This ministry is the common responsibility of all Christians, who should visit the sick, remember them in prayer, and celebrate the sacraments with them."

The sick are also to be remembered in the prayer of the faithful at Sunday Masses, as well as during morning and evening prayer of the Liturgy of the Hours.

Number 44 highlights the facilitating and animating role of the priest

---

[6] Rituale Romanum, 18-26.

within the Body of Christ in the ministry of the sick. In preparing the sick for the sacraments of penance, the Eucharist, and the anointing, the priest is admonished to engage the sick person with his or her family in praying together. The priest is assisted by deacons and "other ministers of the Eucharist" (acolytes and extraordinary ministers of the Eucharist), terms which "are used advisedly" throughout the rite. For instance, there are services at which these ministers may preside: Visits to the Sick, Visits to a Sick Child, and Communion of the Sick - three of the four ministrations treated in Part 1. This is another instance of the expansion of ministries called for by the "Offices and Ministries for the Sick."

Number 45 speaks of the adaptation of pastoral care of the sick to the nature and duration of the illness. A short duration type of illness probably with the view to recovery of health calls for "a more intensive ministry," whereas a long-term illness with the possibility of ending in death requires a "more intensive ministry."

The Introduction continues with more specific admonition concerning particular ministrations taken up in the subsequent individual chapters: Visits to the Sick, Visits to a Sick Child, Communion of the Sick, and Anointing of the Sick.

5.2 Visits to the Sick (Chapter 1)

According to number 46:
> *Those who visit the sick should help them to pray, sharing with them the word of God proclaimed in the assembly from which their sickness has separated them. As the occasion permits, prayer drawn from the psalms or from other prayers or litanies may be added to the word of God. Care should be taken to prepare for a future visit during which the sick will receive the Eucharist.*

The prayers adopted in this chapter for visiting the sick follow the common pattern of reading, response, prayer, and blessing.

Reading includes Acts 3:1-10: "In the name of Jesus and the power of his Church, there is salvation-even liberation from sickness" or Acts 8:14-17:

"Jesus fulfils the prophetic figure of the Servant of God taking upon himself and relieving the suffering of God's people."

For Response, either Psalm 102 or Psalm 27 is used. The Lord's Prayer and Concluding Prayer (3 options) are recited; followed by Blessing (2 options). The order is flexible. The minister has the liberty to add some comments in order to explain the scripture. The blessing concludes with the laying on of hands by the priest. The other ministers may trace the sign of the cross on the forehead of the sick. The sick person could join in planning the visit by suggesting his or her favorite scriptural pericopes, prayers, and hymns, etc; he or she should be encouraged to pray privately.

Lest this model format of prayer become monotonous, three other sources for prayer material are suggested: 1) sources contained in Part III of the rite, Readings, Responses, and Verses from Sacred Scripture; 2) the readings from the Lectionary, especially on Sundays; 3) psalms-many of which are so appropriate to use with the sick, litanies, and other devotional forms. This second set of the sources afford the minister a variety of readings to choose from especially in the case of a long duration of illness. He could even reach out to the readings of the Sunday Eucharistic assembly.

Number 56 urges the minister to encourage the sick person to offer his or her sufferings in union with Christ and to join in prayer for the Church and the world. The intentions for such prayers could include "for peace in the world; for a deepening of the life of the Spirit in the local Church; for the pope and the bishops; for people suffering in a particular disaster."

We must admit the valuable help which a structured service for visiting the sick provides. As we have seen, the old Rituale Romanum did. In this perspective, Gusmer rightly observes:

> *Although a handy and flexible format may often be helpful, especially when several people are gathered around the sickbed, there may be occasions when a less formal and more spontaneous manner of prayer would be desirable.*[7]

This observation is very true of the African, who is said to love lengthy prayers. When these are well thought out and adequately constructed without repetitions, such prayers could be efficacious; they could touch the af-

---

[7] C. W. Gusmer, And You Visited Me, 1990, 59.

fection of the sick person, especially if they are adapted to the nature, circumstance and age of the sick person. The example of the movement for Charismatic renewal and the Pentecostals in this area could be emulated. For such ministrations to be effective, the minister needs to understand the condition of the sick person.

5.3 Visits to a Sick Child (Chapter 2)

The rite of visitation of sick children follows the same pattern of prayer as that of the sick generally, except that a greater sense of informality is anticipated. The minister is to establish "a friendly and easy relationship with the child" (no. 63) in order to win confidence, especially where the child does not already know the minister. The minister should also help sick children to appreciate their special place in the eyes of God, and to understand that "they can offer their sufferings for the salvation of the world" (no. 64).

The following readings are specially chosen for children:

Mark 9:33-37: "Jesus proposes the child as the ideal of those, who would enter the kingdom."

Mark 10:13-16: "Jesus welcomes the children and lays hands on them."

Mark 5:21-23, 35-43: "Jesus raises the daughter of Jairus and gives her back to her parents."

Mark 9:14-27: "Jesus cures a boy and gives him back to his father."

Luke 7:11-15: "Jesus raises a young man, the only son of his mother, and gives him back to her."

John 4:46-53: "Jesus gives his second sign by healing an official's son."

Other stories narrating Jesus' healing ministry may also be used; it is recommended that the children's version of the bible be used so as to facilitate this proclamation.

The Responsory is short and repeated:
> Jesus, come to me.
>> - Jesus, come to me.

Jesus, put your hand on me.
- Jesus, put your hand on me.
Jesus, bless me.
- Jesus, bless me.

After the Lord's Prayer, the Concluding Prayer (two alternatives are provided) follows:
God of love,
ever caring,
ever strong,
stand by us in our time of need.

Watch over your child N. who is sick,
look after him or her in every danger,
and grant him/her your healing and peace
We ask this in the name of Jesus the Lord. Amen (no. 69A).

In addition to the laying on of hands (priest) and the signing of the cross (ministers), others present may be invited to trace the sign of the cross on the forehead when this would appear to be opportune. The child should be given holy communion regularly if already a communicant; and could even be anointed if possible. In case of serious illness in a child who has not yet been fully initiated, the priest should discuss with the parents as well as with the child the possibility of celebrating any or all of the sacraments of Christian Initiation (baptism, confirmation, first communion).

By way of commentary, one fact needs to be stressed. In preparing for the visitation of the sick, whether adults or children, the knowledge of the condition of the sick person is very important. The minister should take this information into account when arranging the rite, in choosing the readings and prayers, etc. This will help the minister to adapt the rite to the situation of the sick; in other words, it will determine if the ceremony will be long or short, formal or more spontaneous. Furthermore, in all dealings with the sick, all pastoral care must be done for individual persons and not in the abstract categories of sickness.[8] One must differentiate between a social conversation and a pastoral visit. Pastoral conversation centers on the person, helping the sick to share himself or herself. Unlike the social conversation where discussions can go to any length and theme, pastoral visit aims at uplifting the faith of the sick. It is meant to help the sick person to accept suffering in human life as sharing in the Paschal Mystery of Christ. Above all, the minister must have the virtue of listening. A good listener disposes the patients to unburden themselves and to tell their story.[9] It is helpful especially in the case of sick children to give them certain souvenirs such as children's bible, rosary, holy pictures, crucifix, etc.

5.4 Communion of the Sick (Chapter 3)

The Introduction to Part 1, Pastoral Care of the Sick, had earlier made it clear that the most important visits to the sick are those in which sacramental communion is received. It also gives a crucial ecclesial reason why:

Because the sick are prevented from celebrating the Eucharist with the rest of the community, the most important visits are those during which they receive Holy Communion. In receiving the body and blood of Christ, the sick are united sacramentally to the Lord and are reunited with the Eucharistic community from which illness has separated them (no. 51).[10]

It goes on to provide two rites: an elaborate one in the form of a liturgy of the word, and a shorter service for emergency, taking into account the environmental situation of the health care institutions.

Priests are to give the sick and aged "every opportunity to receive the Eucharist frequently, even daily, especially during the Easter season" (no. 72). Those who assist the sick may also be communicated. To ensure that the priest and infirm are adequately catered for, a sufficient number of ex-

---

[8] J. Onyenemegam, Pastoral Care of the Sick in Igbo Community-Nigeria, Rome: Typo-Lithografia, 1985, 54.
[9] C. W. Gusmer, And You Visited Me, 1990, 62.
[10] Cf. N. Mitchell, Cult and Controversy: The Worship of the Eucharist Outside Mass, Collegeville, Minnesota: The Liturgical Press, 1990, 112-116.

traordinary ministers of communion should be informed and adequately trained. They should meet with the priest, who is the coordinator and instructor of this ministry regularly in order to plan the service.

There is a mutual link between the community's Eucharistic celebration, especially on the Lord's Day, and the communion of the sick. Thus, the sick are to be remembered in the prayer of the faithful as well as by taking communion to them from the parish Eucharistic celebration. This aspect of the to the sick, namely, "the reception of communion is not only a privilege but also a sign of support and concern shown by the Christian community for its members who are ill" (no. 73).

The Eucharistic ministers could leave the assembly during communion in order to visit the sick. They could take along with them a copy of the parish bulletin and share with the sick and the aged some of the highlights of the homily. Ordinarily the usual guidelines promoting reverence are to be observed. "The communion minister should wear attire appropriate to this ministry" (no. 72).

The sacrament is carried in a pyx or "small closed container." A table covered with linen cloth is to be prepared, together with lighted candles, and where customary, a vessel of holy water. Sick people who cannot take solid food may receive communion under the form of wine. As much as possible the ceremony should be made lively as the rite admonishes: "Care should be taken to make the occasion special and joyful" (no. 74). The priest is to give opportunity for the sacrament of penance and, when possible,[11] occasionally celebrate Mass in the home of the sick together with their families and friends.

5.4.1 Communion in Ordinary Circumstances

The Rituale Romanum of 1614 mixed the communion of the sick together with viaticum, so much that none of them was accurately perceived.[12] The

---

[11] This possibility is not to be interpreted arbitrarily. The rite is clear on the matter and says: "The Ordinary determines the conditions and requirements for such celebrations" (no. 77).

[12] The English Ritual even lumped the two ministrations together: "The Rite for the Administration of Viaticum and Communion of the Sick."

new rite gives the communion of the sick its own and separate liturgical format.

Structure of the Rite

Introductory Rites	Greeting
	Sprinkling with Holy Water
	Penitential Rite
Liturgy of the Word	Reading
	Response
	General Intercessions
Liturgy of Holy Communion	The Lord's Prayer
	Communion
	Silent Prayer
	Prayer after Communion
Concluding Prayer	Blessing

Structurally, this format of the rite of communion of the sick is the same for all ministers - priests, deacons or extraordinary Eucharistic ministers, except where the sick requires sacramental confession. Four different kinds of greeting are provided. The sprinkling of holy water, though, optional plays a very symbolic role of reminding the sick and all participants of their baptism. This is equally in keeping with the use of holy water in other liturgical revisions, such as at Mass, and at funerals. Two antiphons are equally available to accompany the sprinkling. This rite of sprinkling holy water is reserved for the priest or deacon only. In my opinion, the extraordinary ministers of communion could sprinkle themselves as well as the sick as it is ordinarily and normally done in every Catholic family. Most Catholic homes reserve holy water and use it regularly. The penitential rite follows the order of Mass if there is no sacramental confession.

The inclusion of the liturgy of the word has restored the traditional sequence: word-action. It has equally ensured that sacramental encounters are not only signs of grace, but also signs of lively faith.[13] All the biblical passages are drawn from John's gospel. However, extra scriptural readings can

---

[13] Cf. C. W. Gusmer, And You Visited Me, 1990, 64.

be selected from the rich treasure of Part III, Readings, Responses, and Verses from Sacred Scripture, as well as from the Lectionary. A brief period of silence may be observed after the scriptural reading followed by a brief explanation by the minister. The liturgy of the word is concluded by general intercessions. No specific model is given; thus allowing the minister a good opportunity to formulate prayer points for the specific needs of the sick.

The liturgy of Holy Communion corresponds to the revised order of Mass, beginning with the Lord's Prayer and concluding with a prayer after communion. All the given options for the prayer after communion speak to the effects of the Eucharist: "you have called us to share the one bread and the one cup ..." "we thank you for the nourishment you give us through your holy gift ..." "may the body and blood of Christ your Son be ... a lasting remedy for body and soul ..." (no. 90). Priests and deacons conclude the rite with one or two solemn blessings provided, or by making a sign of the cross with the Blessed Sacrament if any remains; other ministers conclude by making the sign of the cross on themselves while saying a simple blessing such as "May the almighty and merciful God bless and protect us, the Father, and the Son, + and the Holy Spirit. Amen."

5.4.2 Communion in a Hospital or Institution

The rite may begin in the Church, the hospital chapel, or the first sickroom to be visited. Additional ministers of communion could assist with the distribution especially when there are many communicants. Other elements may be absorbed from the full rite of communion when it is more convenient; otherwise the simple rite may be used. The structure of the rite is very simple:

Introductory Rite	Antiphon
Liturgy of Holy Communion	Greeting
	The Lord's Prayer
	Communion
Concluding Prayer	

The rite starts with a choice of one of three Eucharistic antiphons (Thomas Aquinas' Sacrum convivium, and two others). A candle bearer may accompany the minister. The liturgy of Holy Communion takes place in each individual room. If the full rite is celebrated, scripture readings and the Lord's Prayer are encouraged whenever possible. The minister then shows the Eucharistic bread to those present with either of the following words:

This is the Lamb of God
who takes away the sins of the world.
Happy are those who hunger and thirst,
for they shall be satisfied (no. 95A).
        Or
This is the bread of life,
Taste and see that the Lord is good (no. 95B).

The concluding prayer is said in the Church, hospital chapel, or the last sickroom visited. Unlike the fuller rite, there is no final blessing. The proper time and manner of communion in a hospital or institution has long been a pastoral concern. The best time would seem to be when the hospital is least busy and the sick is most likely to be in the room. For a harmonious fulfillment of the ministration to the sick there should be an agreement between the minister, the nursing personnel and the doctors. "Every effort" according to Gusmer "should be made to see that this 'sacred medicine' of the sacrament of the Lord's body and blood is communicated in an atmosphere of faith and prayer."[14] And Gusmer goes further to say that the general rule is to maintain a sense of reverence – "reverence for the sacrament and reverence for the sick person whose Eucharistic communion will draw him or her ever more deeply into the body of Christ."[15]

---

[14] C. W. Gusmer, And You Visited Me, 1990, 66.
[15] C. W. Gusmer, And You Visited Me, 1990, 66.

5.5 Anointing of the Sick (Chapter 4)

Three major features characterize the reforms of the rite of anointing, namely, its clear designation as a sacrament of the sick, the change in the central sacramental sign, and its new liturgical shape.

Sacrament of the Sick

Number 97 of the rite states unambiguously: "The sacrament of anointing is the proper sacrament for those Christians whose health is seriously impaired by sickness or old age." The ritual completely avoids the terms "extreme unction" or "last rites." This is a welcome development, because in accordance with James (5:14-15), the recipient is mentioned. However, the name is deficient in the sense that it does not bring out clearly the prayer of faith to which James subordinates the anointing. In this perspective, the term "prayer oil" (euchelaion) as this rite is mostly called in the Greek Orthodox Church seems more appropriate, for it refers to the key elements of the celebration: prayer and oil. But again the recipient is not mentioned. The suggestion of J. Feiner: "prayer of anointing the sick and infirm with oil"[16] as the name of the sacrament seems to be the most accurate.

The recipient of the sacrament is a sick person "whose health is seriously impaired by sickness or old age" (no. 8). The faithful are to be anointed as soon as their illness is prudently judged to be serious. The elimination of the designation "extreme unction" and the reference to the life-threatening nature of the illness is a great advancement from the compromise of Vatican II's Constitution on the Sacred Liturgy (no. 73).[17] This advancement with regard to the name of the sacrament and the condition for its reception go to show the remarkable recovery of the primitive tradition in the evolution, which characterized the history of the sacrament of the sick and infirm. This evolution continues.

---

[16] J. Feiner, "Die Krankheit und das Sakrament des Salbungsgebetes," in Mysterium Salutis V, 494-550.

[17] Although, SC 73 was a compromise between the Council of Trent and the earlier draft of the Liturgy Constitution, it at least opened the door to a fuller restoration of the primitive meaning of the rite as a sacrament for the sick.

Sacramental Sign

The approved matter for valid celebration of the sacrament of anointing is olive oil. However, the rite follows the directive of Paul VI in his Apostolic Constitution, who aware of the pastoral needs and the difficulty involved in obtaining the olive oil, allows the use of "another kind of oil provided it is obtainable from plants, and similar to olive oil."[18] The ancient prayer of blessing, the Emitte from the Gelasian and Gregorian sacramentaries, is substantially the same, except for the removal of the reference to the anointing of "priests, kings, prophets, and martyrs," which originated from Hippolytus in the third century. As we have already seen, the bishop ordinarily blesses the oil of the sick at the Chrism Mass with solemn prayers. In cases of necessity, however, the rite makes provision for the oil to be blessed by a priest, but only during the administration of the sacrament. One such occasion may be during a communal anointing when additional blessed oil is needed. Despite the fact that the oil is already blessed, the rite retains the revised Roman Emitte as well as a litanaic prayer of thanksgiving to be said over the blessed oil.

In the Rituale Romanum of 1614, the procedure of anointing presented a one-sided penitential understanding of extreme unction. The prayer that accompanied anointing says: "May the Lord forgive you by this holy anointing and his most loving mercy whatever sins you have committed by the use of your sight (hearing, smell, taste, power of speech, touch)."[19] The anointing of the feet could be omitted, probably to avoid the old practice when even the loins were anointed as the seat of lust. A single anointing was enough in cases of necessity.

In the Apostolic Constitution Sacrum unctionem infirmorum, that accompanied the 1972 rite, Pope Paul VI introduced changes in both the liturgical action and in the liturgical word. The number of anointing is reduced to two, on the forehead and on the hands. The liturgical word is divided in such a way that the first part accompanies the anointing of the forehead and the second part is said while the hands are anointed. This is a great im-

---

[18] Paul VI, Apostolic Constitution Sacra unctionem infirmorum, (30 November 1972); see also The Rites, volume 1, 20.
[19] The Rite for Administering the Sacrament of the Anointing of the Sick, English Rituale, 220-235.

provement from the earlier one-sided penitential understanding whereby the senses were associated with sinful actions. The rite provides for additional parts of the body to be anointed, especially the area of pain or injury, without however repeating the prayer (nos. 24 and 124). This provision is not new; it dates back to the ninth century.

Even more significant is the change in the liturgical word, namely, the prayer which accompanies anointing as the form of the sacrament. This prayer brings out the rich theological meaning of the sacrament. The prayer originated from three sources: the Rituale Romanum of 1614, the Council of Trent, and the Epistle of James (5:14-15). The opening words "Through this holy anointing may the Lord in his love and mercy" come from the Rituale Romanum. "Help you with the grace of the holy spirit" are taken over from the Council of Trent. The second part of the prayer is drawn from James' injunction: "save you," "raise you up," and "frees you from sin." The original ICEL translation of the Latin reads thus:

Through this holy anointing and his great love for you
May the Lord help you by the power of His Holy Spirit. (Amen.)

May the Lord who freed you from sin heal you and extend his saving grace to you. (Amen.)[20]

This text raised a lot of controversy and was eventually rejected by Rome. The conflict centered more on the English translation of the latin allevare in the typical edition: "extend his saving grace to you." Although all the three: Vulgate, Trent, and Vatican II use alleviare for "alleviate," "console," or "comfort," many manuscripts have allevare, "to raise up," which is more accurate Latin for the Greek egerein. The final English translation of the liturgical word is thus more accurate and most satisfying:

Through this holy anointing,
may the Lord in his love and mercy help you
with the grace of the Holy Spirit. (Amen.)

May the Lord who frees you from sin
save you and raise you up. (Amen.) (no. 25).[21]

---

[20] Rites for the Sick, 25.

Liturgical Shape
Another innovation of the new rite is in the area of the liturgical shape of the celebration. It emphasizes the solemn character of the anointing of the sick and therefore also provides for communal celebrations. In fact, three of such provisions are made to meet varying pastoral circumstances, namely, Anointing outside Mass, Anointing during Mass, and Anointing in a Hospital or Institution.

Anointing outside Mass
The new rite conforms to the basic pattern for all sacramental celebrations and thus includes the introductory rites, proclamation of the word, sacramental action, and conclusion.

Introductory Rites	Greeting
	Sprinkling with Holy Water
	Instruction
	Penitential Rite
Liturgy of the Word	Reading
	Response
Liturgy of Anointing	Litany
	Laying on of Hands
	Prayer over the Oil
	Anointing
Prayer after Anointing	The Lord's Prayer
Liturgy of Holy Communion	Communion
	Silent Prayer
	Prayer after Communion
Concluding Rite	Blessing

The preliminary rites begin with greeting those present especially the sick person and enquiring about the state of his or her condition. This is very important more so when the minister had not earlier gotten this information, in order to know which of the rites - the fuller or the shorter form to

---

[21] C. W. Gusmer, And You Visited Me, 1990, 70.

adapt to the state of the sick person (cf. no. 40a). The greeting can be done alongside the optional sprinkling with holy water. The rite of sprinkling with the accompanying word reminds us of our baptism and recalls Christ who by his passion, death and resurrection redeemed humankind. Anointing is the celebration of the Paschal Mystery which for all Christians starts with baptism. A new antiphon is provided for the rite of sprinkling:

The Lord is our shepherd
And leads us to streams of living water (no. 116a).

The opening instruction (address) emphasizes the need for the sacrament of healing by referring to the scriptural basis of the sacrament in James (5:14-15). The penitential rite follows as at Mass. If the sick person had not earlier gone to confession and wishes now to do so, the general penitential rite could be suspended. The priest hears his or her confession while those present leave the room. However, it is recommended that an opportunity be provided for the sick person to confess his or her sins on another convenient time to avoid unnecessary rush and unfavorable situation. The readings for the liturgy of the word may be drawn from the scriptural resources of Part III, or a passage from one of the synoptic gospels may be read:

Matthew 11:25-30: "Childlike confidence in the goodness of God will bring us the 'rest' that only Jesus can give."

Mark 2:1-2: "Much more important than the health of our bodies is the peace and consolation of the presence of Jesus who can forgive us our sins and reconcile us with God."

Luke 7:19-23: "The healing hand of Christ is a sign of the presence of God; that same hand is extended to us in this sacrament now, to console and strengthen us."

As Manfred Probst rightly observes, the reading should help the sick person to experience the powerful and encouraging presence of God as presented by the community of the Church. For this reason, the readings should be chosen with consideration for the faith and life situation of the sick person. If, for example, the sick person finds it difficult to accept his or her situation, then a reading from the Book of Job may be appropriate than one chosen from the pericope of the miracle of healing from the New Testament. At times a reading from the Old Testament might be better than one from the New. Indeed, the choice of readings from the Old Testament seems very limited and oftentimes does not seem to be suitable. Thus, Probst suggests a number of extra readings from the Old Testament:

Tobit 13:2-9 (Prayer of Praise)
Job 19:23-27a (Fixed Confidence in God)
Job 33:15-28 (Sickness as Warning from God)
Ecclesiasticus 2:1-18 (Test and Pleasure)
Ecclesiasticus 18:1-14 (Fear of God)
Isaiah 49:8-16 (Consolation for God's Servant)
Isaiah 55:6-12a (Searching for God)
Isaiah 57:15-21 (Consolation for the Humble)
Lamentations 3:18-26 (The Everlasting Mercy of God)
Ezekiel 34:11-15 (The Lord as the Good Shepherd).[22]

According to E. Walter, three categories of situation of the sick could be distinguished in ministering to them:

Those who (more or less) have no faith
Those who have faith
Those who live besides their faith.

If the minister considers these different situations of faith of the sick as criteria in choosing the readings, he could select for those in the first group readings with a viewpoint on "invitation to faith," for example, 1 Cor 1:18-25, Jn 3:14-18.

For the second group, readings with perspectives on "thanksgiving to God for the gift of faith" will seem appropriate, for example, Rom 5:1-5, Lk 17:11-19.

For the third group, readings which deal with "a call to the renewal of faith" will certainly be adequate, for example, 1 Jn 5:1-12; Matt 6:25-34.[23]

The response is a brief period of silence or a brief explanation of the reading. The inclusion of scripture is one of the welcoming enrichments of the rite of anointing; something completely lacking in the Rituale Romanum of

---

[22] M. Probst, "Die Elemente und Zeichen in der Feier der Krankensalbung," in M. Probst und K. Richter (Hrsg.), Heilssorge für die Kranke, Freiburg: Herder, 1975, 95.

[23] E. Walter, "Lebendige Seelsorge" 23 (1972): 360, quoted by M. Probst, "Die Elemente und Zeichen in der Feier der Krankensalbung," 1975, 95.

1614. The purpose of the readings is to show that "through the sacrament of anointing the Church supports the sick in their struggle against illness and continues Christ's messianic work of healing" (no. 98).

The celebration of the sacrament consists of three principal actions: the prayer of faith, the laying on of hands, and the anointing with oil. "This rite signifies the grace of the sacrament and confers it" (no. 5). The prayer of faith as suggested by James (5:14-15) is made by the whole Church, represented at least by the priest, family members, friends, and others. This prayer of faith is concentrated in the litany of intercessions. Quoting Thomas Aquinas, the rite states:

The sick person will be saved by personal faith and the faith of the Church, which looks back to the death and resurrection of Christ, the source of the Sacrament's power, and looks ahead to the future kingdom that is pledged in the sacraments (no. 7).[24]

The litany begins with intercessions for the relief and comfort of the sick, for all those dedicated to their care and concludes with a petition that provides a transition to the laying on of hands. The laying on of hands is a happy development, for it restores the original symbol of prayers over the sick.[25] This biblical gesture with which Christ healed the sick is a sign of both a blessing for health and strength and invocation of the Holy Spirit. It could also serve as a sign of solidarity especially in the case of a seriously ill person or one who has almost lost consciousness.

After the blessing or thanksgiving prayer over the oil, the priest anoints the forehead and hands, and when opportune other parts of the body, while saying the prescribed prayer of faith. The gesture of anointing the sick with oil signifies healing, strengthening, and the presence of the Holy Spirit. The anointing may also be concelebrated in one of two forms: either one priest says the prayers and anoints while the others take the various parts and join in the laying on of hands, or in large congregations, each priest may lay hands on some of the sick and anoint them.

A choice of six prayers is available for use after the anointing. These are adapted to the condition of the sick person. Two are of a general nature the

---

[24] T. Aquinas, In 4 Sententiarum, d. 1, q. 1. a, 4, quaestiuncula 3.
[25] See A. Knauber, 4 "Gottesdienst" 7 (1973): 28.

other four are for extreme or terminal illness, advanced age, before surgery, for a child and for a young person. When anointing is combined with Eucharistic communion, the same order as in the case of Communion of the Sick is followed. The final blessing which concludes the anointing service assures the sick person of God's help and presence. Three solemn blessings are given from which the minister could choose and adapt to the condition of the patient.

Anointing outside Mass is usually considered to be the ordinary or normal mode of celebration. The rite is further adapted to meet the other pastoral situations, such as Anointing within Mass, where in view of the usually larger congregation, the normative rite would be expanded and elaborated; and Anointing in a Hospital or Institution, where for practical reasons the rite may have to be simplified and abbreviated.

Anointing within Mass

The rite of anointing within Mass takes place in a Church, or in another suitable place in the home of the sick person or in the hospital. It is especially appropriate for bigger gatherings of a diocese, parish, society for the sick, or pilgrimage, where communal anointings are given with full participation. An opportunity for the sacrament of reconciliation should be provided beforehand. The priest usually puts on white vestments apart from the sacred seasons of Advent and Lent. The readings are normally chosen from the Lectionary (para. 871-875) or Part III. The Mass for the Sick is not permitted during the Easter Triduum and on most Solemnities. On other important liturgical days (Sundays of Advent, Lent, Easter Season, Solemnities, Ash Wednesday, Weekdays of Holy Week), one of the readings from the Mass for the Sick and the special form of final blessing may be substituted.

The Structure of Anointing within Mass
Introductory Rites

Greeting	Reception of the Sick
	Penitential Rite
	Opening Prayer
Liturgy of the Word	
Liturgy of Anointing	Litany
	Laying on of Hands
	Prayer over the Oil
	Anointing
	Prayer after Anointing
Liturgy of the Eucharist	
Concluding Rites	Blessing
	Dismissal

Of special note in the Anointing within Mass is the rite of reception of the sick:

> We have come together to celebrate the sacraments of anointing and eucharist. Christ is always present when we gather in his name; today we welcome him especially as physician and healer. We pray that the sick may be restored to health by the gift of his mercy and made whole in his fullness (no. 135A).

The anointing follows the liturgy of the word just as in all the other revised rites for sacraments celebrated within Mass. The rite provides two orations each as options for the opening prayer, prayer over the gifts, and prayer after communion and a preface and inserts for Eucharistic Prayers I, II, and III. The insert for Eucharistic Prayer III reads:

> Hear especially the prayers of those who ask for healing
> in the name of your Son,
> that they may never cease to praise you
> for the wonders of your power (no. 145).

In the African context where music and dance play a curative role, these could be maximally employed at such Masses, especially at the Entrance,

Offertory, and Dismissal. The penitential rite could include the blessing and sprinkling of holy water. However, care should be taken that so many symbols are not brought together in one single ritualistic celebration.

Anointing in a Hospital or Institution

The rite in its pastoral introduction to this form of anointing makes it clear in which circumstances this liturgy is to be celebrated. "It is intended for those occasions when only the priest and sick person are present and the complete rite cannot be celebrated" (no. 149). The priest is supposed to enquire beforehand about the physical and spiritual condition of the patient in order to adapt the celebration to his or her needs; when possible involving the sick person in the planning. Should the sick person request to go to confession, it is preferable that this be done on a previous occasion. If it is necessary, this may take place during the introductory rites. Again except in case of urgency, the priest may postpone anointing a sick person to a more convenient and conducive atmosphere. Such unhealthy circumstances include emergency room or casualty ward of a hospital. There should be a continued pastoral care whereby frequent opportunity for communion is to be provided.

The structure of the rite is as follows:

Introductory Rites	Greeting
	Instruction
Liturgy of Anointing	Laying on of Hands
	Anointing
	The Lord's Prayer
	Prayer after Anointing
Concluding Rite	Blessing

There are notable omissions in this ritual which include the liturgy of the word and the blessing and thanksgiving over the oil. However, the instructional prayer contains the Jacobean prescription for anointing. This adaptation serves the pastoral need in circumstances where the fuller rite may not be celebrated.

5.6 Important Questions Concerning Anointing

As already indicated earlier in this chapter, there are certain questions which underlined the background to the introduction of the new rite. Some of those questions concern the actual subject of anointing. Who is really the recipient of anointing? Must the illness always be physical? What about serious psychological, nervous and mental disorders? Who is the proper minister of anointing of the sick? Should sick children before the age of reason be anointed? What prevents the reception of the sacrament from time to time during the same sickness? These questions will be taken in turns to see how the new rite attempted their solution.

5.6.1 Who is the Recipient of Anointing?

The revised rite for the sick successfully avoided those misleading terms like "extreme unction" and "last rites." The introductory section of the Recipients of the Anointing of the Sick describes the subjects or recipients of anointing as a Christian, "whose health is seriously impaired by sickness or old age." This is an important breakthrough, for the retention of the restrictive condition "danger of death" could only undermine the true meaning of this sacrament of the sick and lead to its continued abuse as a kind of religious verdict of death. This development in comparison with the Constitution on the Sacred Liturgy and even the earlier ICEL translation of the initial draft revision of anointing represents a considerable evolution in doctrine and practice since the teaching of the Second Vatican Council. Moreover, the sacrament may now be repeated during various stages in a progressive illness.

Anointing may be administered to a patient who is going in for surgery on account of a dangerous illness. However, it would seem a trivialization of the sacrament to anoint those who are to undergo routine or cosmetic surgery, though some have died during such operations. Elderly people may be anointed if they are in a weakened condition, although no dangerous illness may be in view. Old age is indeed a condition for receiving the sacrament, since long years can constitute an intrinsic threat to life. Children who are seriously ill are also to be anointed if they have sufficient "use of reason" to be comforted by the sacrament. The earlier restriction of anointing of the sick to those who had attained the use of reason was in part attributable to the medieval penitential understanding of the sacrament, a phenomenon which actually necessitated the revision of the central prayer or form of anointing. It is to be noted that the phrase "use of reason" is distinct from the more technical "age of reason" which is generally demanded as a criterion for first communion. "Use of reason" seems to have less to do with chronological age than with a child who is alert enough to know in a natural way that something good is happening: the healing Christ is reaching out to touch the child. Gusmer spots a theological inconsistency here. Sacraments are not only signs of grace but also signs of faith. But they are not intended only for the rational and alert. The Western Church we know baptizes infants. The theological justification of infant baptism is that the children are baptized on account of the faith of the Church universal, and that of their parents. What then could be said about the vicarious faith of the sick child's parents?

Practical praxis in some areas however is already making tremendous progress to go beyond these somewhat restrictive provisions.[26] As if to buttress the above argument, the new rite permits the anointing of sick people who have lapsed into unconsciousness or have lost the use of reason, especially if as Christians they would have requested it were they in control of their faculties. One hears such request often from the children and relatives of people in such conditions. Although, priests are enjoined to celebrate the sacrament "while the sick person is capable of active participation" (no. 99, also no. 13), it is all the same a wise and compassionate advice to anoint such people. It has been known that people who recover from coma were able to comprehend everything that was said to them, although they were incapable of responding in a tangible way. Dead persons are not to be anointed. Number 15 is very direct on this point. The priest is to "pray for them asking that God forgive their sins and graciously receive them into the Kingdom." Only in cases of doubt whether the sick person has actually died is the priest to administer the sacrament. If it is ascertained that the

---

[26] C. W. Gusmer, And You Visited Me, 1990, 84.

sick person is dead, the family becomes the immediate pastoral care, not the deceased. The inclusion of the ritual of Prayers for the Dead (chapter 7) is a pastoral help in these emotionally packed situations.

5.6.2 For Sickness other than Physical?

An answer to this question, the possibility of anointing the mentally or emotionally ill finds expression in number 53 of Pastoral Care:

> Some types of mental sickness are now classified as serious. Those who are Judged to have serious mental illness and who would be strengthened by the sacrament may be anointed. The anointing may be repeated in accordance with the conditions for other kinds of serious illness.

It is understandable that a person who is mentally ill and at the same time judged to be seriously sick (physically) may be anointed. This is a holistic approach towards the sacrament. As long as the sacrament would be a comfort to the psychologically or mentally ill, it could be administered to them. Furthermore, insofar as many of such mental and psychological aberrations are sometimes associated with an earlier faculty process of religious socialization, the judgment as to the comfort derived by such patients might well be made in consultation with the medical personnel entrusted with their care.

It may also be asked in this connection whether non-Roman Catholic Christians may be anointed. The answer to this question is given in the Directory Concerning Ecumenical Matters. Here the same principles laid down for admission to the Holy Communion applies: in danger of death or in urgent need (during persecution, in prisons), no minister of the person's own denomination, a spontaneous request for the anointing, a faith in harmony with the sacrament, and avoidance of scandal.[27] These are exceptional circumstances which from time to time confront Catholic hospital chaplains.[28]

---

[27] Directory Concerning Ecumenical Matters: Part 1, Ad Totam Ecclesiam, May 14, 1967, 55; see also canon 844 of the New Code of Canon Law.

[28] I was faced with similar circumstances on three occasions during my one year ministry as chaplain of the Heart of Jesus Hospital Dernbach, Germany (25.10.2005-30.09.2006).

In view of the increasing frequency of communal anointing a question often arises, namely, whether everyone may be anointed indiscriminately out of a sense of solidarity with the sick or for other reasons.

Furthermore, what is to be said of communal services inviting everyone over 65 to partake of the sacrament? Pastoral Care gives a clear indication of the mind of the Church in this matter when speaking of anointing of the sick with a large congregation:

> *In particular, the practice of indiscriminately anointing numbers of people on these occasions simply because they are ill or have reached advanced age is to be avoided. Only those whose health is seriously impaired by sickness or old age are proper subjects for the sacrament (nos. 108 and 99).*

This practice which is gaining ground in many parts of Nigeria but also found in Europe and America smacks of abuse of the sacrament. Indeed, no other sacrament is so indiscriminately celebrated; not baptism, confirmation, first Holy Communion, penance, marriage or holy orders. Why then anointing of the sick? I think there are ample ways and means of caring for the sick and showing them solidarity other than trivializing both the sacrament of anointing and serious illness. Gusmer puts it beautifully thus:

> *The practice of indiscriminate anointing could undercut the whole reform of the sacrament by trivializing serious sickness and reducing the anointing to the level of the blessing of throats on the feast of St. Blasé.* [29]

A careful pastoral ministry to the sick will usually dictate who should be anointed, how often to anoint, or whether some other sacramental ministration is called for. However, it is not the medical condition of the sick person that is the most important determinant whether to celebrate the sacrament of anointing or not. It is rather the sick person's spiritual and religious condition that is determinative. In severe illness or advanced old age death casts its shadow forward. The sick person sees the foundation of his or her world shaken. Men and women react with anxiety, hopelessness and despair or with impatience and rebellion. Anointing is meant to address this crisis situation and provide tangible help, so that with strength, patience

---

[29] C. W. Gusmer, And You Visited Me, 1990, 87.

and trust they may withstand the crisis of their illness, the decay of life and the threat of death.[30]

5.6.3 Repetition of the Sacrament

May the sacrament be repeated from time to time within the same illness? To answer this question, the new rite adopts a more liberal approach just like in most other questions. For the sacrament to be repeated within the same illness, two conditions are stipulated:

a. when the sick person recovers after being anointed and, at a later time, becomes sick again;

b. when during the same illness the condition of the sick person becomes more serious (no. 102, also no. 9).

According to the earlier legislation, the sick person could be re-anointed only if one recovered and then once again grew grievously ill. But now it is a matter of pastoral discretion to judge how often a person may be anointed during the progressive stages of an illness.

5.6.4 The Proper Minister of the Sacrament

The question concerning the proper minister in the anointing of the sick has become more acute with the restoration of the permanent deacon whose important responsibilities include ministering to the sick. It is becoming increasingly difficult to explain why extraordinary Eucharistic ministers and pastoral workers may provide support and counsel in faith but not its consummation in the sacrament. The present discipline of the Roman Catholic Church is clear. The teaching of the Council of Trent is restated in the revised rite: "The priest is the only proper minister of anointing of the sick" (no. 16).[31] The choice of the term priest (sacerdos) means that both bishops and presbyters are all included. But how does one understand the term "priest" or "presbyter" in reference to James (5: 14-15) who teaches that the presbyteroi are not charismatic healers, but rather officeholders in

---

[30] G. Greshake, "The Anointing of the Sick: The Oscillation of the Church between Physical and Spiritual Healing," in Concilium 5 (1998): 86-87.

[31] Cf. Council of Trent, 1551: DS, 1697; 1719; CIC, canon 1003.

the primitive Church? Surely, there were charismatic healers at the time such as are described in 1 Corinthians 12. As already seen, the tradition of the first 800 years made frequent reference to James but there were varying interpretations. More attention was given to blessing the oil by the bishop than to the prayer over the sick or even the actual anointing. Thus, there was no apparent distinction between the anointing by the presbyters or by the lay people. The restriction of anointing only to the ordained started with the Carolingian turning point.

Even with the Council of Trent, it must be said that only a cursory attention was paid to the question of the minister. The Council was more a reaction to the Reformers who maintained that the minister could be any baptized member of the priesthood of all the faithful. When Trent discussed extreme unction in 1547 and 1551, its primary concerns centered on the sacramentality of extreme unction and the defense of the Roman practice of anointing the dying. In other words, the anathemas of the Tridentine canons may not necessarily imply defined doctrine. The anathemas which concerned heretical positions were understood by Trent in a wider sense as they appear to be today. At that time, they included doctrinal error, or simply disobedience to Church authorities.

John Ziegler and Paul Palmer have argued convincingly for the extension of the sacramental ministry of anointing. After examining canon 4 of Trent, Ziegler concludes that it is no longer "a necessary obstacle to the Church's appointment of someone other than the priest as a minister of the sacramental anointing of the sick."[32] For Paul Palmer, "proper minister" according to Trent may not mean that only the ordained priest has the sacramental power to anoint. On the contrary, it could be interpreted that the priest alone is the ex officio or ordinary minister of the sacrament of the sick.[33] There is, however, a precedent for the extension of sacramental ministry. In the early Church, the initiation rites were presided over by a bishop; today even a non-Christian may validly baptize in a case of necessity when he or she has the right intention of doing what the Church does. The recent reforms of the rites of initiation have gone further to provide another radical extension of

---

[32] J. J. Ziegler, Let them Anoint the Sick, Collegeville: The Liturgical Press, 1987, 25.
[33] P. F. Palmer, "Who Can Anoint the Sick?" Worship 48 (1974): 81-92.

ministry. In order to preserve the sacramental unity of Baptism, Confirmation, and Holy Communion, the priest may confirm when initiating an adult or a child of catechetical age, or when receiving baptized Christians into full communion.[34] But there is nowhere the celebration of penance (reconciliation) was mentioned.

This evidence shows that it is possible to extend the ministry of anointing the sick not only to deacons but also even to the non-ordained. The reforms of Vatican II urge the earlier and more frequent reception of the sacrament of anointing with the hope of making it more available to the sick. With the shortage of priests in many parts of the Catholic world, especially in Europe, this hope may never be realized. That means that many sick people will be deprived of the sacrament of anointing, though, they are really in dire need of this sacrament, its misconceived purpose notwithstanding. It is this situation which makes the suggestion of Zieger and Palmer worth considering, namely, that not only deacons but also lay people who care for the sick could be designated special ministers of the sacrament of anointing.[35]

In this era of ecumenism, we could follow the example of the Anglican Communion as represented by the American Episcopal Church which permits its deacons and lay persons to anoint in emergency situation using oil blessed by either a bishop or priest. Indeed, there are no binding doctrinal arguments that prohibit the extension of anointing at least to deacons, should the Church for pastoral reasons choose to do so. But empowering the deacon to anoint does not solve many pastoral problems when the sick Christian is first of all in need of sacramental absolution. This is where the major problem lies. Empowerment of the deacon as a minister of sacramental reconciliation finds no support in the tradition and would constitute a more radical reform. In any case with the Vatican Instruction on the Collaboration of Non-Ordained Faithful in the Priestly Ministry (15 August 1997), the official leeway is very restricted. We make our own the illuminating words of Gusmer:

> *... an unhealthy sacramental concentration or "privatization" of the sacrament should be avoided at all costs. Sacraments cannot replace*

---

[34] Rite of Confirmation, 7.
[35] P. F. Palmer, "Who Can Anoint the Sick?" 92; J. Ziegler, Let them Anoint the Sick, 153.

pastoral care. Anointing is only one sacrament of the sick, together with the Eucharist, the sacrament of sacraments, and the sacramental action of the laying on of hands.[36]

5.7 New Problems Raised by the Revised Rite

As we have already noted, although the revised rites for the sick answered previously unresolved questions and prepared the way for proper implementation, they also raised new problems. Two of such problems would be the ministry to the dying and to the afflicted, and the relationship between sacramental and charismatic healing.

5.7.1 Anointing as a Sacrament for the Dying

The revised rites for the sick make it clear that the fifth sacrament is for the sick and not for the dying. Thus, it encourages ministers to celebrate the sacrament as early as possible. Regarding the strange practice of anointing the apparent dead, the rite is very explicit: "When a priest has been called to attend to those who are already dead, he should not administer the sacrament of anointing. Instead, he should pray for them, asking that God forgive their sins and graciously receive them into the kingdom. But if the priest is doubtful whether the sick person is dead, he is to confer the sacrament, using the rite given in no. 269" (no. 15).[37]

But what constitutes physical death, one may ask? Some people still maintain the opinion common in earlier theology manuals, that conditional anointing may be administered up to one hour after apparent death, or even two to three hours if the person was in full rigor at the time of demise. Some others insist that once the doctor has already confirmed a person dead, the anointing is not to be given. The obsession of making sure that all the departed whatever the circumstances of their death, somehow receive the "last rites" is a misunderstanding of the nature of religious ritual. Such

---

[36] C. W. Gusmer, And You Visited Me, 1990, 82.
[37] No. 269 referred to in the quotation deals with anointing in emergency situations or the so called conditional anointing. See also CIC, canon 1005.

a mistaken opinion operates under a misguided assumption that God is bound and restricted in his saving grace by the very sacraments he himself has created.

In correctly asserting that anointing is a sacrament for the sick, one must nonetheless be careful neither to minimize the reality of death nor to obscure the Christian meaning of death as a special consummation of the Paschal Mystery. Such a perversion could only be liturgically counterproductive, theologically misleading and pastorally a surrender to a contemporary death denying culture.[38] In this perspective, one observes that the religious ministrations to dying Christians provided in the revised rites for the sick deserve a high profile. The choice of prayers, litanies, responses, psalms, and scriptural readings given do not seem to be enough. This area needs further enrichment.[39] "Viaticum" (chapter 3) literally meaning "food for the journey," is the Eucharist given to a dying Christian. In view of advanced scientific medical techniques which can prolong life beyond the stage when a terminal patient can consume solid food, the revised rites recommend an earlier administration of viaticum, when the dying Christian is still capable of participating to some extent: for example, at the preferred celebration within Mass, the renewal of the baptismal profession of faith, the sign of peace, and communion under both kinds. Here lies the problem. The priest in one celebration administers the sacraments of reconciliation (penance), anointing and viaticum to the dying and goes away. Scarcely does he go back to the sick person afterwards. But the duty of the minister to the dying does not end with the giving of the sacraments.

One of the most important discoveries in the recent studies is that a dying person passes through attitudinal "stages" in "coming to grips" with the reality of death. Elisabeth Kübler-Ross[40] provides one of the best analysis comprising five stages a dying person passes through:

1) The stage of "denial." This stage, one of "temporary defense," is an almost instinctive reaction to what is initially grasped as an impossible

---

[38] Cf. V. Guroian, Life's Living toward Dying, Grand Rapids, Michigan: William B. Eardmans Publishing Co; 1996, 1-8.
[39] K. Richter, "Die Heilssorge in Todesgefahr," in M. Probst and K. Richter (Hrsg.), Heilssorge für die Kranken, 1975, 111.
[40] E. Kübler-Ross, On Death and Dying, New York: Macmillan Publishing Co; 1969,

occurrence. The predominant reaction is "No, not me! It cannot be true." Quite often, at this stage, the sick person will try to conceal his or her distress. This reaction occurs when the patient first learns of his/her impending death.

2) The stage of "progressive acceptance." This second stage begins, however, with feelings of anger, rage, envy, and resentment, as the sick person rebels against the thought of death. He or she reacts often aggressively to any least provocation, against any available target, for example, the nurse who failed to carry out some procedure, the doctor who did not diagnose the illness properly some years past, etc. This reaction is normal, for the "will to live," or the so-called "instinct of self-preservation" does not disappear with the onset of a terminal illness. It is during this period that the question of the ultimate "meaning" of life arises in the mind of the sick person.

3) Perhaps, the most interesting stage is the third; the stage of bargaining or negotiating. This is a stage wherein the terminally ill person tries to "console" him/herself by exchanging certain behavior for feelings of comfort, painlessness, etc. The thought processes of the sick person operate on the slim hope that some sort of "right behavior" might result in an end to the situation of terminal illness. It is actually a kind of campaign to postpone the inevitable, to put off the relentless and inexorable arrival of death. It is interesting to note that most "bargains" are "made" with God; that is, usually a promise of a strict religious life in exchange for health. The dying seeks at this point an extension of life. The mood of the sick person usually changes often and radically during this period as gradually he/she realizes that none of the "bargains" is going to "work."

4) The next stage is "depression." This is the stage that seems familiar to most people, but it is by no means the first reaction to terminal illness. It is a time of preparation for the final separation from everyone and everything the sick person loves – family, friends, possessions, and the world. The important thing here is that he or she must "work through" grief and fears for the future; so it follows that the most effective type of

pastoral ministry at this point might be the ministry of "listening" as the patient allows fears to surface and to dissipate.

5) The final stage before death is that of "acceptance." At this point, the patient is reconciled with his or her own self, with family and friends, and with the world. The patient at last accepts his or her lot, namely, death. Death is faced with trust and calm. Here too, the best ministry involves "presence": the living must be at the side of the dying person in silent companionship, rather than in verbal communion. In this stage, something of the social "attachment" of the sick person to his or her surroundings revives: the sick person learns to be "human" and now lives his or her situation, willing it. He or she is now ready and no more afraid to die. It would be fitting if viaticum could be coordinated to correspond to this stage, even when the patient lingers on for several days afterwards.

The "Rite of the Sacraments to those near Death" (chapter 4) is a more accurate rendering of what has commonly been called the "continuous rites" and should be used precisely as the occasion – an emergency situation, for example – may demand. The order is as follows: penance with the apostolic blessing, anointing and viaticum. "Confirmation of a Person in Danger of Death" (chapter 5) should take place at a service distinct from the anointing of the sick, so as to avoid confusion regarding the symbolism of oil. In case of necessity the chrismation, the ritual completion of Christian Initiation, may be performed by virtually any priest.

The rich and consoling "Rites for the Commendation of the Dying" (chapter 6) merit special attention. Consisting of prayers, litanies, aspirations, psalms and scriptural readings, the service is designed to prepare the dying Christian for ultimate conformation or assimilation with the crucified and risen Lord, as well to comfort his or her family with a renewed faith in the paschal character of Christian death. The freely chosen prayers and readings are to be adapted to the situation and recited in a quiet, reassuring tone of voice with alternating periods of silence.

Insofar as touch is usually the last sense to die, it is appropriate that the rite suggest the nonverbal symbolic action of the signing of the cross on the forehead of the dying Christian. In addition to this baptismal reminder, many would want to clasp the hand of a loved one in this critical moment of passage to a new life. When a priest or a deacon is unable to be present at the time of death, the office of commendation is to be conducted by a lay faithful. The concluding prayers of the commendation may also be helpful in consoling the family of a Christian who has already expired when anointing would not be suitable.[41]

5.7.2 Sacramental and Charismatic Healing

Another new problem raised by the revised rites for the sick is the issue of the relationship between sacramental and charismatic healing. As we have already seen, the Acts of the Apostles are full of instances of charismatic healing. There is also strong evidence of a flourishing charismatic ministry in the early Church, as attested to by Quadratus (c. 125), and many of the Church Fathers (cf. chapter 3). Some have attributed the declining of explicit charismatic healing activity to the rejection of the enthusiastic Montanist Movement of the Spirit in the second century; others locate the waning of charisms in a loss of spiritual vitality resulting from the conversion of Constantine and the advent of the cultural synthesis known as Christendom.[42]

Nonetheless, traces of charismatic healing continued in the lives of saints and worthies such as Martin Luther (d. 1546), Philip Neri (d. 1595), George Fox (d. 1691), John Wesley (d. 1791), Pastor Blumhardt (d. 1880), and Father John of Kronstadt (d. 1908). In the Roman Catholic Church, charismatic healing is found in shrines dedicated to the memory of the saints, for example, Mary of Lourdes, Fatima, and in the provision for verifiable healings required in the canonization process. As we also mentioned earlier, although, charismatic healing has always been recognized, at least theoreti-

---

[41] See J. L. Topolewski, "Death in the Family: A Model of Ministry," in The Drew Gateway 47 (1976-77): 72-84;
cf. also J. Onyenemegam, Pastoral Care of the Sick in Igbo Community-Nigeria, 1985, 90-101.

[42] On the ever abiding charism of healing in the Church see J. V. Taylor, The Go-Between God: The Holy Spirit and the Christian Mission, 1972, 198-222; see also P. Kii, The Healing Ministry, 2004, 76-79.

cally, only in this century through the efforts of Pentecostal and neo-Pentecostal communities has this gift of the Spirit been more fully restored. Indeed, charismatic and sacramental healings have many similarities. Both are situated within the community of the Church, although a healer with a special charism or a presiding liturgical celebrant may play a greater role in the service. Both employ similar gestures: the laying on of hands, the sense of touch conceived as a way of bestowing or realizing the power of the Holy Spirit. They are both charismatic and liturgical, first and foremost a prayer: prayer of petition (charismatic "soaking prayer," sacramental "litany of intercession") and prayer of praise and thanksgiving.[43] Despite these common grounds, there is as Thomas Tally notes:

> ... *an increasing blurring of the distinction between the Church's liturgical address to affliction and the charism of thaumaturgy, the effecting of miraculous cures, and with that blurring of distinction, a serious confusion regarding the whole nature of sacramental realities.*[44]

The basis for distinction lies in their different specific thrust and emphasis. It must be said that the Church embraces both charism and sacrament. The sacramental may appear to mirror more the visible, tangible, incarnational side of the Church, whereas the charismatic reflects more the invisible, intangible, pneumatological aspect of the Church. Too great a split must be avoided, however, for both come from God and should be animated by the Spirit of Jesus. Both sacramental and charismatic "healing" must be part of the charitable ministry to the sick as carried out every day in hospitals, homes, and parishes by those who actively care for and visit the sick; otherwise the liturgical rites will be reduced to mechanistic magic, and charismatic healing to thaumaturgic charlatanism. It follows, then, that charismatic healing falls into the charismatic dimension while sacramental healing - in particular, the anointing of the sick – belongs to the Church's liturgy on behalf of the sick.

Another area of distinction refers to expectations that are sought from charismatic and sacramental healing. Again both involve expectant faith: dis-

---

[43] C. W. Gusmer, And You Visited Me, 1990, 156-157.
[44] T. Talley, "Healing: Sacrament or Charism?" Worship 46 (1972): 520. See also K. Rahner, The Dynamic Element in the Church, Freiburg: Herder, 1964, 42-83.

cernment of the Spirit should also be applied in order to discover what the praying community and the sick person can realistically expect. Sacramental and liturgical realities are always realizable within the scope of a deeper spiritual level. That is why we do the theology of the liturgy a lot of harm by extravagant claims of extrinsic effects. Too many communities have been brought to despair by discovering that in spite of the introduction of the Kiss of Peace in the Mass, they still do not love one another. Worse still is the experience of those who have been told that sacraments and prayer in true faith would remove a malignant tumor. Unfortunately, they have learned from its continued growth the insufficiency of their faith, and thus have died in despair. This is because liturgy was confused with charism. In general, charismatic healing intends a cure, be this physical, psychological (healing of the memories), or spiritual (healing from sinful habits such as drug, alcohol, or sexual abuse). Sacramental healing would seem to be less directly concerned with physical or emotional cures, but rather aims at a deeper spiritual conformation with Christ through the healing power of the Paschal Mystery.[45]

It needs to be said that the exaggerated claims sometimes made for charismatic healing today are out of proportion with its traditional significance. That is why it is important to discern which spirit is at work in the service for the sick. Gusmer has suggested such "principles of discernment." For me, four of such principles are very important:

1. Is there a sense of cooperation with the medical profession?
2. Is there a proper emphasis on the worship of God and service of neighbor, rather than a narrowly selfish therapeutic attitude which delights in the 'miraculous'?
3. Are healings, whenever and wherever they occur, signs pointing to a deepened faith and conversion in which the beneficiaries become changed or transformed persons?

---

[45] See C. W. Gusmer, And You Visited Me, 1990, 159; for details on charismatic healing see F. MacNutt, Healing, 1974. See also R. Laurentin, Catholic Pentecostalism, Garden City, New York: Doubleday, 1977, 100-131.

4. Is the approach imbued with the central mystery of Christian faith, the passion, death, and resurrection of Jesus Christ and our participation in this saving paschal event?[46]

In the final analysis, the tension between the sacrament of anointing and charismatic healing does not deny their close relationship. Their difference is not one of ultimate end. Both proclaim and reveal Christ and the power of his resurrection over all disorder. Both are instruments of God, and means of manifesting his glory. Thus, both should vitalize each other in interaction. However, it needs to be pointed out that the healing ministry is neither an extension of the sacrament of anointing of the sick nor is it part of this sacrament. On the contrary, the sacrament of anointing of the sick is rather a part of the healing ministry of the Church. Healing is God's sovereign power that is revealed in the situation of his people; and thus it is a moment of distinctive and decisive profession of faith. It is the ambitious, self-seeking, gallery playing and self-proclaimed healers who have given the healing ministry a bad name. Indeed, healing belongs to the Church's overall pastoral ministry.

Summary

One of the major features of the revised rites for the anointing of the sick is its liberal approach to almost all the issues concerning the sick, the ministers and all those who take care of the sick. All the liturgical rites for the sick are squarely situated within the pastoral ministry of the Church to the sick. In order to appreciate the enormity of the new rite we placed it side by side with the Rituale Romanum of 1614. Unlike the Rituale Romanum, the new rite expanded the ministry of the sick to include the whole Christian community. It is no longer the exclusive responsibility of the ordained. Every baptized Christian has the duty to minister to the sick members of the Church. The new rite provides very rich pastoral patterns for visiting the sick generally and then a sick child. It designed rituals for bringing holy

---

[46] C. W. Gusmer, And You Visited Me, 1990, 159. See also "Healing: Charism and Sacrament," in Church 2 (1986): 16-22 from the same author.

Eucharist to the sick in ordinary circumstances and in a hospital or institution. All these rites are richly provided with ample prayers, responses, litanies, scriptural readings and psalms. A lot of freedom and initiative is allowed the minister to adapt or adjust to the condition of the sick person as well as the situation or environment of celebration.

There is then the rite of anointing the sick, which is characterized by three major features, namely, what is specifically a sacrament of the sick; its sacramental sign, and its new liturgical shape. Here great innovations are made, for example, olive oil remains the approved matter of the sacrament. But where it is difficult to obtain, another vegetable oil similar to olive could be allowed. Anointing now could be celebrated privately or communally; it could be given within or outside Mass. In all these the sick person remains the centre and subject of all that is done. He or she is to be involved in the planning of such celebrations.

Certain important questions emerged which actually formed the background to the introduction of the new rite. In the attempt to provide solutions to the questions, the new rite raised other issues. For instance, while anointing remains the sacrament of the sick, the dying is not to be neglected. They are to be accompanied and assisted till their final breath. This could be a long process as Kubler-Ross' analysis showed and the most important period when the dying need our solidarity and assistance.

Another crucial issue is the relationship between sacramental anointing and charismatic healing. This is one of the most contemporary and controversial topics among Christians. It is contemporary because of the current concern in the Churches for healing, especially among Pentecostal and Charismatic groups, and the crisis of sacraments in general, and the anointing of the sick in particular. The revised Roman Catholic Rite of Anointing and Pastoral Care of the Sick is actually an attempt to salvage a sacrament that is perhaps the least understood among all the other sacraments. The theme of anointing and charismatic healing is controversial because of the many theologically complex issues involved, for example, the mystery of suffering and evil in the world, the meaning of the healing activity of Jesus, the abiding place of healing in the mission of the Christian Church, etc. In the next chapter we shall consider some of these issues from their theological dimension.

Chapter Six
Theological Meaning of Sickness and Healing

We now have sufficient evidence to delineate the ritual meanings of the anointing of the sick and charismatic healing. From the testimony of the New Testament, Jesus did not anoint any person; even in the text of Mark (6:13), it is not Jesus who does the anointing. Similarly, in the Epistle of James (5:14-15) which is usually taken as grundschrift for the sacrament of unction, the author does not present the elders as anointing with oil following the personal example of Jesus, nor does he present anointing as an action commanded by Jesus. The anointing is done simply in the name of Jesus. But how are we to understand the anointing of the sick as a sacrament today? It is clear that there is no evidence that it was instituted by Jesus (without prejudice to the affirmation of the Council of Trent). Yet the early Church experienced the presence of Christ in life situations of sickness and brokenness, thus leading to the use of the symbolism of anointing.

God is, however, present in the world through the Church (primarily, though by no means exclusively). Wherever the Church expresses itself in the final and radical meaningfulness of being the visibility of God's salvation, of being the living and creative presence of God in our lives, that is where a sacrament is. It is in this sense that one can connect the sacraments with the Church. It needs to be emphasized that care should be taken not to read into James (5:14-15) and Mark (6:13) meanings which might not be there.

The Church draws its sacramental tradition concerning Anointing of the Sick from these texts, especially James, as well as from Innocent I, Caesarius of Arles and from Trent. But the real origin of this sacrament and indeed all the sacraments is that Christ instituted the saving community, the Church as the first form of his kingdom. The Church is the "visible, efficacious sign" of God's salvation for the whole world.[1] In this more general reality of the Church, the sacraments are applications of the salvation presented by the Church to the recipient in his or her individuality, as a member of the holy community in God and Jesus Christ.

---
[1] B. Häring, Healing and Revealing, 1984, 33.

Of the charism of healing there is, in fact, little to be said systematically, for it is not a systematic phenomenon. Perhaps, what needs to be noted is that while charisms such as healing may be found in those who are ordained, they cannot be restricted to them, nor can it be shown that any rite of ordination confers them. On the other hand, charism and those who exercise them remain under the authority of the Church for proper spiritual guidance. Justin Ukpong confirms this point when he writes:

The impression one gets from reading Paul's first letter to the Corinthians chapters 12-14 is that the Corinthian Church, like the Nigerian Church today, was alive with the activity of the Holy Spirit manifested through many charisms. That Paul intruded to give instruction on the ordering of these charisms given by the Spirit clearly indicates that the exercise of charisms remain subjected to ecclesiastical authority (cf. 1 John 4:6).[2]

With these preliminary theological clarifications, we will now consider other equally important anthropological and theological issues as they relate to sickness and healing.

6.1 Dualism of Body–Spirit

What does it mean to be seriously ill? Sickness represents a crisis situation in the life of the person who is ill. There is crisis of communication with oneself, with fellow human beings, with the Church and finally with God himself.

With regard to oneself, the sick person experiences a crisis in his or her life. His or her situation seems to come to an endpoint: it can get worse; it can also get better. He or she hovers between life and death. The crisis of the sick person is a personal crisis. He or she is from the illness totally affected and touched. In such a situation, one experiences total helplessness, weakness, and limitations of life. One is sick in his or her whole existence.

---

[2] J. S. Ukpong, "Charisms and Church Authority: A New Testament Perspective," in Authority and Charism in the Nigerian Church (Proceedings of the 8th National Theological Conference held at the National Missionary Seminary of St. Paul, Gwagwalada, Abuja, April 13-16, 1993), 26.

Such a person is in danger of failing, giving up or doubting. Many patients express their situation thus: "I am now good for nothing." "I don't worth anything any more." In these words lies the fear that people, relatives and acquaintances might loose interest in him or her or that he or she may be forgotten and abandoned. The sick person in such a crisis situation feels standing at the railway station alone, having missed all the trains. This personal crisis of the sick person could be called identity crisis, for he or she stands in danger of loosing his or her personality, and self-confidence or at least self-worth.

The crisis of the sick person is also a crisis of communication with others within his or her environment. This is caused by the fact that the sick can no longer consciously plan and execute his or her personal affairs. Everything is completely beyond his or her control. He or she is helped to eat, to bath, and to bed; when anything is needed, the nurses or those who take care of the sick must be called. One feels like a child again. This situation of crisis worsens if the sick leaves home and is delivered in a hospital. Immediately this happens, the world of the sick collapses. Perhaps he or she is confined in bed. At that point his or her world comes to an end. Now and again new and strange people continue to come in and go out: doctors, nurses, trainees, those taking care of the sick, etc. The same is with tests of all kinds: x-ray, heart, intestine, etc. Meanwhile the patient feels so wretched and miserable that the fear in his or her heart continues to rise. He or she is in reality a patient, a sufferer. The painful situation of the sick comes out clearly in a modern free translation of Psalm 38. One reads among other things:

Lord, I am now lying here, and my fate is determined by the doctors ... They give the command – I obey like a child ... To my questions, they give no answer. They whisper among themselves in their technical language. From the first day, I am handled like a fool ... I am like a deaf, who does not hear any tone. I live like a dumb, who does not open his mouth. My mouth has no longer any ready answer. The question dies at my tongue. I am powerless like one utterly crushed; I call for help. Who will really help me ...?[3]

---

[3] U. Seidel-D. Zils, Psalmen der Hoffnung, Driewer, Essen: Schriftenmissions-Verlag,

Certainly a person in such a situation needs help to be able to sort out his or her feelings which swing between hope and resignation; to cope with his relationship with the surroundings and to give meaning to life and death. In short, the patient needs support lest he or she should lose bearings and identity beneath the overwhelming mass of new impressions that pour over him or her.[4]

The crisis of the sick person is naturally also a religious crisis. This is experienced often by Christians who have been active in their parishes and now feel forgotten and forsaken. Such a person is mad with God. He or she suffers from the contradictions of being, from the apparent meaninglessness of life, and from the darkening of his or her faith. The patient notices how the days are approaching, the inner power getting exhausted and the way out to God getting closed. The poverty of his or her heart is expressed in the following remarks: "Why me?" – "Why have I merited this?" – "I always fulfilled my duty as a Christian, and now God allows me to suffer." – "I can no longer trust in the love and justice of God." And God keeps quiet. The worst and most dangerous thing that can happen to the sick is that he or she can no longer place his/her darkness, misfortune, and sadness in relation with God. This leads the patient into a bigger fear. God's forsakenness can come over him/her like in the case of Jesus' experience on the cross, who though, still united with God, exclaimed: "My God, my God, why hast thou forsaken me?" (Matt 27:46). It is in such a crisis situation that the presence of the Church through its ministers and faithful is most needed; not so much to administer any institutionalized rite or another sacrament. No! What is needed at this point is empathy, understanding and human consolation.

In this way the Church can help the sick and dying to accept their plight by uniting their will fully with the will of their Saviour; for the final challenge to the dying is to put their soul into the hands of the Crucified: "If we have died with him, we shall live with him. If we hold firm, then we shall reign with him" (2 Tim 2:11). Thus, the final achievement of the Christian is to plunge his or her suffering into the suffering of Christ. Perhaps the most

---

Gladbeck/Verlag Hans, 1973, 61. Translation is mein.

[4] Cf. J. Onyenemegam, Pastoral Care of the Sick in Igbo Community-Nigeria, 1985, 92-93.

important statement of Vatican II on anointing and the pastoral care of the sick may be found in the paragraph II of the Constitution on the Church:

> *By the sacred anointing of the sick and the prayer of the priests the whole Church commends those who are ill to the suffering and glorified Lord that he may raise them up and save them (cf. Jas 5:14-16). And indeed she exhorts them to contribute to the good of the people of God by freely uniting themselves to the passion and death of Christ (cf. Rom 8:17; Col 1:24; 2 Tim 2:11-12; 1 Pet 4:13).*[5]

Pope John Paul II makes the same point when in his *Apostolic Letter Salvifici Doloris* he writes:

> *By bringing redemption through suffering, Christ has elevated human suffering to the level of redemption ... Therefore, in his suffering man can become a sharer of Christ's redeeming suffering (no. 19).*

Serious illness presents a temptation to one's faith in God and the Church. It is an ambivalent situation, for the growth and holiness or else regression and possible despair. The revised rites for the sick capture this liminal predicament thus:

> *Those who are seriously ill need the special help of God's grace in this time of anxiety, lest they be broken in spirit and, under the pressure of temptation, perhaps weakened in their faith (no. 5).*

In sum when one is seriously sick, the condition ushers in a crisis that affects one's entire well-being. Such a devastating state calls for a holistic Christian anthropology of the human person as a psychosomatic unity rather than the old Cartesian or Hellenistic dualism which speaks easily of "pastors of souls," thinking only or one-sidedly of "souls" and salvation in heaven. Today Christian thought still labours under such dualism: a kind of disincarnate spiritualism. For example, we speak of bodily and spiritual effects of anointing, as if the human composite could be divided into two distinct parts. On the other hand there is a strong and sometimes equally one-sided reaction against this verticalism and dualism. Some seem to see only the horizontal dimension of human well-being.[6]

---

[5] A. Flannery (ed.), Vatican Council II: The Conciliar and post-Conciliar Documents, New York: Costello, 1975, 362.

[6] B. Häring, Healing and Revealing, 1984, 33.

Against this dualism is the more balanced approach of the biblical anthropology which views the human person as an animated body. The Book of Psalms, for example, - the prayer book of the Bible - vividly depicts the existential plight of the sick. Psalm 6 says:

> Be gracious to me, O Lord, for I am languishing; O Lord, heal me, for my bones are troubled. My soul is solely troubled. But thou O Lord-how long?

In a similar tone of anguish, Psalm 22 complains:

> I am poured out like water, and all my bones are out of joint; my heart is like wax, It is melted within my breast; my strength is dried up like a potsherd and my tongue cleaves to my jaws; thou dost lay me in the dust of death.[7]

Contemporary theology also moves in the same direction. In the contemporary anthropology of Karl Rahner the human person is a spirit in the world, an incarnate spirit.[8]

Some insights have also been gained from an examination of human wholeness from the perspective of depth psychology. Indeed, more exploration is needed into the psychogenesis of sickness, including certain types of cancer especially prevalent among people living under stress-filled conditions. Now and again it has been said that the wholeness and health of persons depend to a certain degree on the health of the society and culture within which people live: the healthiness of the life-style, public opinion, public life and family life. In cases of such illness emanating from unhealthy conditions, and "repressive environment," cure cannot be achieved without the person involved becoming healthier from within. This holistic approach to illness was the secret of Godwin Ikeobi's success in his healing ministry.[9] The principle which is known as "individuation" in C. G. Jung's depth psychology consists of a synthesis of the conscious and unconscious personalities. If the unconscious can be a source of illness, it can also be a source of healing which results when the contents of the unconscious are

---

[7] See also Psalms 26, 28, 32, 38, 49, 51, 69, 88, and 102.
[8] K. Rahner, On the Theology of Death, Questiones Disputatae 2, New York: Herder, 1961, 24-34.
[9] Cf. G. Ikeobi, "Healing and Exorcism: The Nigerian Pastoral Experience," 1992, esp. 62-65. See also John A. Sanford, Healing and Wholeness, New York: Paulist,

made conscious. In other words, most people's psychological difficulties have spiritual roots and the most important need in the therapeutic cure is for a sense of meaning and purpose in life, that is, a positive outlook.

The above process is gained from logotherapy as we have already seen in chapter one. According to this view, health has much to do with discovering the deep meaning of life, and giving meaning to life through creative activity, harmonious social relationships, and by finally giving meaning to suffering. In such cases, healing will be brought about, above all, through the discovery and implantation of meaning in a fully human perspective.[10]

Insights from depth psychology have also been applied to charismatic healing techniques such as the "healing of the memories" to discern how both nature and grace work together. Such approaches to sickness can bring about cures or healings without one resorting immediately to the notion of miracles. All these new insights are a caution against a one-sided approach to illness. They call for the setting of priorities right without indulging in dichotomy. For instance, in the first 800 years of anointing, physical healing was at times overplayed, and the Scholastic period could recognize only the spiritual effects of the sacrament. It is important to always remember that illness is a very real phenomenon that confronts the total human person. Therefore, we need today a theology of healing which includes anointing and regards the sacrament as affecting the whole person.

6.2 Repentance and Healing

The classical teaching is that illness, suffering and death originated in the sin of Adam and Eve and spread to all of humankind, since as Paul says all have sinned (Rom 5:12). Furthermore, Paul teaches that "the wages of sin is death" (Rom 6:23) and "the sting of death is sin" (1 Cor 15:56). Thus, the Fathers of the Church are unanimous in relating illness, infirmities, suffering, corruption and death to ancestral sin. For them the source of all these as well as if all the evils that now affect human nature is to be sought

---

1977.
[10] Cf. V. Frankl, The Doctor of the Soul: From Psychotherapy to Logotherapy, 1973.

solely in the misuse of personal will by the first human being and in the sin which he committed in paradise.[11]

This mystery is deeply and profoundly embedded in human personal and social reality and is not subject to scientific or empirical verification. Yet both daily experience and modern medical science say something about it. As we have already seen, there are statistical correlations between overeating (gluttony) and heart disease, sexual promiscuity and dangerous sexually transmitted diseases, and excessive drinking and liver disease, to mention but a few. We have also seen how the stresses generated by various kinds of deception, vengefulness, and manipulation in the workplace and in the home can lead to a whole range of life-threatening illnesses. Vigen Guroian rightly points out that "where the vices rule, death draws near."[12]

However, no description of the Christian vision of the origin, nature, and course of death is complete without the element of the doctrine and practice of penance (reconciliation). The first words of Jesus' teaching are: "Repent, for the Kingdom of heaven is at hand" (Matt 4:17). Some have suggested that Jesus' command echoes God the Father's desire for repentance following Adam and Eve's disobedience and eventual fall. The Armenian Teaching of Saint Gregory reasons that immediately after they ate the forbidden fruit, God gave Adam and Eve one last chance to repent and to reverse the course of corruptible death. A key biblical passage is Genesis (3:9-10): "But the Lord God called to the man and said to him, "Where are you?" And he said, "I heard the sound of thee in the garden, and I was afraid, because I was naked; and I hid myself." The teaching interprets this passage to mean that "(God) wished by being somewhat indulgent to capture him (Adam), that the gentleness of God might lead them to repentance." Instead, the couple made excuses for themselves. "Then he (God) set judgement, passed sentence, which they paid and returned to dust (Gen 3:19); for the judgement of God is true over those who work evil."[13]

---

[11] J. C. Larchet, "Illness, Suffering and Death as Related to Ancestral Sin," in Concilium 5 (1998): 49.
[12] V. Guroian, Life's Living toward Dying, Grand Rapids: William B. Eerdmans, 1996, 43-44.
[13] The Teaching of Saint Gregory: An Early Armenian Cathechism, trans. R.W. Thomson, Cambridge: Harvard University Press, 1970, 51-52.

It is easy to understand the speculation of the author of the Cathechism. The Genesis story indicates that God expels the first couple from the Garden and from proximity to the Tree of life only after he speaks to them this last time. And only then does Adam blame Eve for what he has done and Eve blame the serpent for what she has done (Gen 3:12-13) - excuses and deceptions that seal God's judgement and invite corruptible death. However, God did not abandon humanity to its doom. He still provided his prophets to prepare a kind of medicine of cure for the pain of the illness, namely, to remove and extirpate the scandal of death and destroy it forever. The last prophet is Christ, who cured our sickness unto death, defeating death itself by his own righteous sacrifice on the cross.[14]

Thus, death remains the outworking of sin in the human being, but it has also been transformed by Christ into the revelation of true life. In the Old Testament, the Hebrew word for "salvation" derives from yasha, which means "to save from danger." God delivers us from all dangers and evil especially that of sickness and from death itself. In the New Testament, the Greek sozo comes from saos, meaning "healthy." Penance (reconciliation) is for the sin that attaches to all "flesh" and makes this flesh subject to corruptible death; penance issues from the belief that God desires to heal our infirmities and make us whole.

The acts of repenting and asking God for forgiveness and healing are related to a profound understanding not only of death but of healing that encompasses the whole human being – spiritual, psychological and physical. The Byzantine rite of anointing gives a holistic interpretation of healing to the Epistle of James. Anointing with oil for them symbolizes the prayer, penance, forgiveness of sin, healing, and salvation that the passage in James mentions. Anointment indicates the deep connection between sickness and the mystery of God's redemptive purpose. It is not a substitute for medical care, but it reveals the telos of medicine nonetheless. The story of the Good Samaritan from the Gospel of Luke (10:25-38) introduces anointing, offering the assurance that even in the face of sickness and death God does not forget or abandon us, because his love is like that of the Samaritan, only stronger.

---

[14] Cf. V. Guroian, Life's Living toward Dying, 1996, 53.

If indeed, some mysterious relationship exists between sin and sickness, it follows correlatively that reconciliation and healing often go together. The close relationship between penance and anointing has been historically further intensified by the association of anointing with deathbed reconciliation during the Middle Ages. All the rites for the sick and dying - communion, anointing, viaticum, continuous rites in exceptional circumstances (penance, anointing, viaticum) - make provision for the sacrament of penance (reconciliation), when desirable or necessary. The Rite for Reconciliation of Individual Penitents is included as an appendix in Pastoral Care of the Sick.

Some people in a therapeutic and utilitarian climate (including some of the healers, especially in the Pentecostal circles) object to the exceptional attention that is given to sin and penance in many Christian rites. According to them references to sin and penance are insensitive and inappropriate in a programme of care for terminally ill or dying patients. It is true that overemphasis on sin and guilt is not helpful in the process of cure. As Guroian observes, "Condescension and punitive impulses can turn what is supposed to be healing into another form of torment for the afflicted."[15] There are among the clergy and laity who are motivated either by an inflexible orthodoxy or other reasons to assume the divine prerogative of judgement and thus add to the suffering of countless afflicted by reminding them incessantly of their sins and failures. It is on account of this wrong approach to sin and penance which tends to be humiliating, towards masochistic behaviour and psychologically unhealthy that Martin Luther criticized and rejected confession as that "which tormented more than it consoled."[16]

But these abuses of a penitential theology do not discredit the profound and practical wisdom of the Church when it places repentance and forgiveness at the centre of its ministry to the sick and dying. This emphasis makes perfect sense in the light of the Gospels and indeed the whole of Scripture. It is a common experience of pastors and chaplains to the sick that the burden of

---

[15] V. Guroian, Life's Living toward Dying, 1996, 84.
[16] For a discussion on this, see A. Echema, Corporate Personality in Tradition Igbo Society and the Sacrament of Reconciliation, 1995, 199-201; also his article on The Sacrament of Reconciliation: Implications of the New Term," in JIT 4 (1997): 32-44.

personal guilt frequently weighs heavily on the mind of a sick or dying person. In such circumstances the mistakes that a person has made or the wrongs and injustice he has committed over a life time can suddenly return to haunt him or her in devastating ways. Many sick persons have at such conditions sent for priests and sought reconciliation. The Byzantine Rite of Holy Unction contains several psalms and prayers that invite sick persons to review their lives penitently. One of such prayers recalls and invokes repentance and divine judgement and forgiveness. It equally recalls great sinners of the Bible who were forgiven by God or were accepted by Christ because they repented:

We thank thee, O Lord our God, who art good and lovest mankind, the Physician of our souls and bodies .... Who didst justify the Publican by thy word, and didst accept the Thief at the last confession; who takest away the sins of the world, and wast nailed to the Cross.[17]

Many people believe that reconciliation is the most important thing for the dying irrespective of whether or not the person is religious or secular. Moreover, there is a difference between curing and healing. A person can be healed even at the point of dying. Even when one's body is disintegrating one can still be experiencing wholeness. Oftentimes many sick persons suffer so much more from mental anguish and guilt than from physical pain. And when such patients are able to unburden their sick minds, they experience peace, reconciliation and forgiveness. For such a healing to occur, forgiveness and reconciliation are crucial – both reconciliation with others and reconciliation with one's own past.

It is not enough simply to tell people that they are forgiven by a good and loving God, what most Nigerian TV preachers and healers do. They need to acknowledge their guilt, to ask for forgiveness (sometimes directly on the person whom they have hurt), and to forgive themselves.[18] Since as we

---

[17] Service Book of the Holy Orthodox-Catholic Apostolic Church, ed. and trans. Isabel Florence Hapgood, Englewood, N. J.: Antiochian Orthodox Christian Archdiocese, 1974, 355. It is noteworthy that apart from the "Our Father," the prayer of the publican and the words of the thief on the cross are the most repeated biblical prayers in Orthodox liturgy.

[18] S. M. Burns, "The Spirituality of Dying," in Health Progress, (September 1991): 50, quoted by V. Guroian, Life's Living toward Dying, 1996, 87.

have already noted there is a mysterious connection between individual sins (and bad habits) and sickness; then it may be necessary for pastors to remind their parishioners of the link between their behaviour and their sickness. This is not to say that we should casually equate sickness with punishment for sins. As we saw earlier, Jesus repudiates this inference (cf. Lk 13:3-4). Nevertheless, a deep interior connection of sin to sickness and death remains. On the contrary, Jesus himself underlines this synthesis of forgiving sins and healing. He surprises everyone when he tells the paralytic man who is brought to him for healing: "My son, your sins are forgiven" (Mk 2:5). Jesus explains the mysterious connection: "Is it easier to say to this paralyzed man, 'Your sins are forgiven,' or to say, 'Stand up, take your bed and walk'? But to prove to you that the Son of Man has the right on earth to forgive sins" – he turned to the paralyzed man – "I say to you, 'stand up, take your bed, and go home'" (Mk 2:9-11). Another case of forgiveness of sins mentioned in connection with healing is that of the man at the pool of Bethzatha (cf. Jn 5:14).

However, there is another dimension to personal sin and reconciliation, namely, the social. Personal sin begets corporate sin, and corporate sin begets personal sin. We pay the price in a broad spectrum of physical and psychological illnesses as well as mortality. Thus, many people become sick and are a source of frustration for others because they nourish grudges and bitterness in their hearts. Experience shows that people who are unable to cultivate healthy and healing relations with others are more than any other group vulnerable to illness of a psychosomatic nature such as stress and heart attacks.[19] On the other hand, full reconciliation with God, which depends, however, on reconciliation with one's neighbour and even oneself increases the chances to overcome not only psychosomatic but even somatic illness. No wonder Jesus links the forgiveness of our enemies with the Father forgiving us our own trespasses as well as his answering our prayers (cf. Mk 11:24-25). This explains also why the prescription in James (5:15b-16) is concluded with an admonition: "Therefore confess your sins to one another and pray for one another, that you may be healed."

---

[19] See B. Häring, Healing and Revelation, 1984, 22.

There is another implication to the social dimension of sin. Oftentimes, many people may look down on a sick or suffering person and consider him or her a greater sinner than themselves. A prayer from the Byzantine Rite of Holy Unction draws attention not only to the sins of the sick person but also the sins of the family and friends who gather at the bedside or in the Church. This attention to corporate sin is important for a Christian ministry for the sick and dying, because it helps to reduce the weight and guilt of failure on the sick and preclude their alienation from the healthy. Even more important is the prayer's view of the Church as a community of penitent sinners aware of their common frailty and mortality who are in the same bandwagon looking together to God for wholeness of souls and bodies.[20] The healthy are reminded in the said prayer that they are not so very different from the afflicted in their midst, and the afflicted are drawn back into the body that loves and forgives all of its members.

One final point that needs to be noted is that a serious illness may be a conversion experience that finds full expression in the sacrament of reconciliation celebrated as an authentic personal encounter with the risen Christ, the primordial sacrament. In cases of emergency or other serious pastoral situations, as indicated in the Celebration of Viaticum and Continuous Rite of Penance, Anointing, and Viaticum, the confession may have to be more generic. But often many of us overlook the model penitential services provided in the Rite of Penance in Appendix II. One of them is designed for the sick and is titled: The Time of Sickness is a Time of Grace. The examination of conscience clearly depicts the trials of the sick person living out the Christian commitment undertaken at baptism:

Do I trust God's goodness and providence, even in times of stress and illness?

Do I give in to sickness, to despair, to other unworthy thoughts and feelings?

Do I feel my empty moments with reflections on life and with prayer to God?

Do I accept my illness and pain as an opportunity for suffering with Christ, who redeemed us by his passion?

---

[20] Cf. Service Book of the Holy Orthodox-Catholic Apostolic Church, 347.

> *Do I live by faith, confident that patience in suffering is of great benefit to the Church?*
> *Am I thoughtful of others and attentive to my fellow patients and their needs?*
> *Am I grateful to those who look after me and visit me?*
> *Do I give a good Christian example to others?*
> *Am I sorry for my past sins, and do I try to make amends for them by my patient acceptance of weakness and illness?* [21]

So far, we have focused on the Christian practice rooted in the central theological principle, that sin, illness, suffering and death are all mystically related. That practice is penance as it has always been known and called. It is the healing sacrament directed explicitly towards the forgiveness of post-baptismal sins. Another central theological principle holds that healing and salvation are intimately connected. The practice corresponding to this second theological principle is premised in the salvific effects of the Incarnation. We shall explore this principle and its practice under the next subheading.

6.3 Suffering and Dying under the Sign of the Cross

Theodicy is an attempt to resolve the apparent contradiction between God's justice and goodness and the fact of suffering and evil in the world. There are differing opinions with regard to God and suffering in the world. According to Richard McBrien:

> *God deliberately, almost callously, inflicts suffering and pain upon us in order to teach us a lesson or gain some unknown greater good. For many of course, the very existence of evil (natural disasters, the terminal illness of a young child, the sudden death of a father or a mother, a brutal murder, an act of terrorism, Auschwitz) is the single most persuasive argument against the existence of God, or at least against the existence of the God of Christianity.*[22]

---

[21] Rite of Penance, Appendix II, 68.
[22] R. McBrien, Catholicism, San Francisco: Harper & Ray, 1981, 238; see also John Douglas Hall, God and Suffering, Minneapolis: Augsburg Publishers, 1986.

Two classical approaches to the problem of theodicy have been suggested: an Augustinian theodicy of free will that has been handed down in the Western Church and has found a contemporary exponent in Karl Rahner; and an Irenaean theodicy of development transmitted in the Eastern Church, and finds expression in the thought of Teilhard de Chardin.[23]

The Augustinian theodicy of free will looks upon evil as a privation of good. Originally, creation was very good (cf. Gen 1:28). It was human choice that brought suffering and radical evil into the picture. According to this view, evil can be distinguished between natural or moral evil. Suffering can also be distinguished according to intentional such as suffering which human beings inflict deliberately on others – massacre of innocent people by terrorists or wars or unintentional, for example, natural catastrophes – Hurricane, earthquake, fire, flood, and numerous incurable diseases like HIV/AIDS and cancer, etc. While there is a deep mystery in the unrelievable suffering and tragedy that comes from such catastrophes, the ones deliberately and systematically inflicted by some people on others are attributable to sin. The theodicy of free will has been criticized for being too static and for lack of sufficient understanding of history and eschatology. On the other hand, the approach recognizes the mysterious relationship between sin and sickness. Moreover, it rightly sees suffering and sickness as a result of the sinful disharmony in creation introduced by human free will.

The Irenaean theodicy is rooted in the hopeful theology of Irenaeus of Lyons (d.c. 202). It locates the perfect harmony and order of creation not at the beginning but at the end of history. It sees evil and suffering as an opportunity for growth and transcendence. Positively, this approach agrees with the thrust of salvation history, as well as a theology of hope and contemporary eschatology.[24] The approach has been criticized for its excessive optimism about suffering.

New insights on theodicy have been gained from process theology through its more dynamic view of God. God participates in the joy, pain and suffering of human beings. Thus, the history of the suffering in the world is in-

---

[23] M. Galligan, God and Evil, New York: Paulist, 1976, develops these two approaches.

[24] See J. Moltmann, Theology of Hope, New York: Harper & Row, 1967; E. Schillebeeckx, God the Future of Man, New York: Sheed & Ward, 1968.

cluded in the story of God because of the story of Christ's suffering. In the words of Whitehead, the foremost exponent of process theology: "God is the great companion - the fellow sufferer who understands."[25] But it is interesting to note that the Christian scriptures approach the reality of evil from an entirely different perspective, though it agrees to a large extent with the views of process theology. The New Testament's preoccupation is not to explain evil. There is nowhere it tries to offer a justification of God in the face of an evil world. Even when the early Christians encountered persecution or illness, they never asked, "How could God have let this happen?" As Walter Wink puts it:

> *The burning question for them was not why but how: How has God used this evil for good? How has God turned sin into salvation? How has God triumphed over the powers through the cross? Likewise, persecution did not evoke surprised reactions of "why me?" The early Christians expected to be persecuted; they were surprised when they were not! For them the question was not why but how long?*[26]

For the early Church, therefore, the problem of justifying the existence of evil in a world created by God did not exist. The early Christians never blamed God for their evil unmerited suffering. Their concern was how to overcome evil, not explain it. The Christian Scriptures make it clear that God knows about the suffering in the world. But human ways are not his ways and his thoughts are completely different from human thoughts. The tragedies and disasters of this world are often permitted to prevent human beings from forgetting that they are passers-by to a home in heaven. Whole nations and civilizations have been allowed to perish to teach humanity that a Supreme Being is in control. The situation, however, does not mean that God is aloof from the suffering of innumerable unnamed people who disappear into the mass cemeteries of the world.[27] On the contrary, God through Jesus Christ confronts the evil in the world head on. God "suffers"

---

[25] Whitehead, Process and Reality, 351 as quoted by J. Moltman, "The Crucified God": God and the Trinity Today," in the God Question, Concilium 6 (1972): 26-37.
[26] W. Wink, Engaging the Powers, Minneapolis: Fortress Press, 1992, 314.
[27] See A. Echema, "The Omnipotent God Vis-à-vis Human Suffering: The Church's Response," a paper delivered at the 16th CIWA Theology Week, Port Harcourt,

in the suffering of his Son.[28] In the suffering which Jesus endured in keeping with the will of God, the Father also suffered. If the Father suffered along with the suffering Son, then he also suffers when his other children suffer. In humanity's suffering the Father is deeply and painfully involved.[29]

The foregoing shows that human beings are responsible for their own problems, because human suffering has consequences. Surely, there are certain natural catastrophes which are difficult to explain. But if people stop killing one another and inflicting suffering on each other and begin to live together in peace with justice, it will be easier to find ways to respond to the world's unintentional catastrophic suffering. When people end the wars, the arms race, human conflict and the institutionalized violence of poverty and starvation, it may be possible to apply the resources, talents and money to find cures for such diseases as cancer, HIV/AIDS and to alleviate disaster in the face of natural events.[30] In other words, God never approves people killing one another or people suffering and dying in poverty and disease. Consequently, people should be mindful not to blame God directly for sickness or other forms of suffering, as if God were responsible. God reacts to and respects humanity's use and lamentable misuse of its freedom. On the contrary, God suffers and dies with all those who suffer and die in poverty and disease. And he dies in Christ Jesus.

The cross is God's justification of himself before human history so full of suffering. The cross demonstrates that God is not the Absolute that remains outside of the world, indifferent to human suffering. He is Emmanuel God-with-us, a God who shares the lot of humanity and participates in its destiny. The cross stands as the ultimate witness of God's reaction to human suffering. God takes on the suffering of the world upon himself. He is always on the side of the suffering and sick. His omnipotence is manifested precisely in the fact that he freely accepted suffering. The scandal of the

---

2005, 3.
[28] J. Moltmann, The Crucified God: The Cross of Christ as the Foundation and Criticism of Christian Theology, New York: Harper & Row, 1974, 243.
[29] Cf. J. Dear, The God Of Peace: Toward a Theology of Nonviolence, Maryknoll, New York: Orbis Books, 1994, 70.
[30] Ibid.

cross remains the key to the interpretation of the great mystery of suffering, which is so much a part of the history of mankind.[31]

The crucified Christ is proof of God's solidarity with humanity in its suffering. He is God's answer to the call of suffering humanity. God places himself on the side of humanity. He does so in a radical way: "He emptied himself, taking the form of a slave, coming in human likeness; and found human in appearance, he humbled himself, becoming obedient to death even death on a cross" (Phil 2:7-8). Christ could have chosen to demonstrate his omnipotence even at the moment of crucifixion. In fact, it was proposed to him: "Let the Messiah, the King of Israel, come down now from the cross that we may see and believe" (Mk 15:32). But he did not accept the challenge. The fact that he stayed on the cross until the end, the fact that on the cross he could say, as do all who suffer: "My God, My God, why have you forsaken me?" (Mk 15:34), has remained in human history the proof of God's solidarity with the suffering humanity. If the agony on the cross had not happened, the truth that God is love would have been unfounded.[32] Indeed, God is love and precisely for this he gave his Son, to reveal himself completely as love. "To the end" means to the last breath. "To the end" means accepting all the consequences of humanity's sin, taking it upon himself. This happened exactly as the prophet Isaiah affirmed: "It was our infirmities that he bore ... We had all gone astray like sheep, each following his own way. But the Lord laid upon him the guilt of us all" (53:4-6).

The suffering of God is the bedrock of the Christian faith and there is no way suffering can be fully understood except from the perspective of the cross. Pius Kii puts it thus:

> *The glory of the cross provides ... the only light by which we can appreciate the enigma of suffering, for the language of the cross (1 Cor 1:8) is the supreme wisdom in all that touches the destiny of man in his relationship to God.*[33]

---

[31] John Paul II, Crossing the Threshold of Hope, New York: Alfred A. Knopf, 1994, 62.
[32] Ibid; 66.
[33] P. Kii, The Healing Ministry, 2004, 163.

In the mystery of the cross, therefore, there is a meeting point between the suffering God and the suffering humanity. God not only shares our suffering and sickness in Christ, he empathizes with the suffering of every human being. In the words of Alban Goddier:

The cross forever proclaims the firm hope that suffering, even from an evil source, can be met by the love of God, transformed and used to defeat the evil from which it originated. The cross is a mystery, which holds together a multitude of paradoxes: defeat and victory, sickness and healing, disintegration and wholeness, fear and hope, death and life.[34]

However, God does more than simply suffering-with. His solidarity is not merely affective, it is equally effective. He strives with men and women against sickness and suffering.[35] In Christ even death no longer has the last word (Phil 2:6-11). This victory is promised to everyone who relies on him. Jesus fought against sickness and suffering as he cured the sick and against death as he even raised the dead. In the same way, every effort should be made to bring cure and healing to our suffering people. But both the healers and people need also to know that there is suffering that is redemptive. Cardinal Terence Cooke speaks convincingly about the meaning of human existence and warns against a "quality of life" ethic that devalues suffering: "Life is no less beautiful when it is accompanied by illness or weakness, hunger or poverty, physical or mental diseases, loneliness or old age."[36] Since the suffering and death of the humiliated God-man of Golgotha, suffering has assumed a different nuance in Christianity. That is why when we view our sickness and suffering from the perspective of carrying our cross and in participation with Christ, it becomes salvific. It is difficult to cope with suffering in its naked reality. Suffering is not sent by God and can never be a source of joy and strength. A Christian never looks for pain or sickness. As a matter of fact, everything possible is to be done to overcome such negative experiences, following the example of Christ himself, who

---

[34] A. Goddier, The Passion and Death of Our Lord Jesus Christ, New York: P. J. Kennedy and Sons, 1944, 325ff.

[35] J. C. Ike, "Faith in God Amidst Suffering in the World," in R. Madu and A. Echema (eds.), Essays in Honour of Very Rev. Msgr. Alphonsus Aghaizu, 2004, 145.

[36] Quoted by P. M. J. Stravinskas, Understanding the Sacraments, San Francisco: Igna-

could pray, "Father, if it is your will, take this cup from me" (Lk 22:42). But suffering discovered as the redemptive expression of love and transfigured by the love of Christ, can become the strongest expression of human solidarity, within the mysterious solidarity of God – through Christ – with us.[37] The Apostle of the Gentiles made this discovery and exulted: "Now I rejoice in my sufferings for your sake, and in my flesh I complete what is lacking in Christ's afflictions for the sake of his body, that is, the Church" (Col 1:24).

Our people need to be helped to see illness and healing from within the passion and resurrection of Christ. While seeking victory over illness through all means at our disposal, the Christian needs also to look at the cross of Jesus Christ. We need to have faith in the biblical God, who is faithful to his promises, to his covenant of love, powerful and wise, not in our own powers or even in our own faith. Nothing is impossible for God, even to raise the dead. In prayer, we should "let go and let God," turn to God with complete trust, pray for the sickness to leave us, and allow God to do the rest. "But may your will be done" (Matt 26:42). This should be the attitude of every sufferer who looks upon God for help.

It is the task of the Church and especially of all those who minister to the sick and the dying to help them see in their sufferings a loving Father and to awaken in them a hopeful conversation between them (sufferers) and a compassionate listener. The opening prayer of the Holy Mass for the Sick as found in the Sacramentary demonstrates the Church's faith and trust in God's healing care:

> *Father, your Son, accepted our sufferings to teach us the virtue of patience in human illness. Hear the prayers we offer for our sick brothers and sisters. May all who suffer pain, illness, and disease realize that they are chosen to be saints, and know that they are joined to Christ in his suffering for the salvation of the world.*

This prayer shows that healing and suffering are not mutually exclusive. The healing power of prayer and the sacraments are recognized, but not at the expense of the redemptive nature of suffering. As McManus puts it:

---

tius Press, 1997, 94.
[37] B. Häring, *Healing and Revealing*, 1984, 35; see also CCC, 1521.

A gospel of healing which excludes the spiritual value of suffering is not the gospel of Christ. Similarly, a gospel of redemptive suffering which excludes divine healing is not the gospel of Christ.[38]

6.4 Jesus' Ministry to the Sick

"Nothing is more certain about Jesus than that he was viewed by his contemporaries as an exorcist and a healer."[39] The ministry of Jesus is one of healing in the widest sense. All the sick that came to him or were brought to him in faith by their friends and relations were healed. He himself declares: "Those who are well have no need of a physician, but those who are sick; I came not to call the righteous, but sinners" (Mk 2:17). Thus, Jesus heals the lepers by touching them, thereby giving them the healing experience of human love and divine presence. He rescues men and women who were social outcasts in the society. He welcomes sinful women and treats them as persons, giving them back a sense of dignity. Similarly, he socializes and even eats with Levi-Matthew, the tax collector and his friends who are despised as sinners. Jesus went as far as even inviting himself to the house of Zacchaeus, one of those who were considered as exploiters and traitors. The magnitude of these healings shows that they were more than simple healing of illness. According to K. O'Rourke,

When the sick flocked to Jesus during his earthly life, they recognized in him a friend whose deeply compassionate and loving heart responded to their needs. These cures involved more than just healing sickness. They were also prophetic signs of his own identity and the coming of the kingdom of God, and they very often caused a new spiritual awakening in one who had been healed.[40]

The healings of Jesus are unmistakeable proof of his divine mission and power, but above all, they are signs of his divine-human love, a revelation of his compassion. By this unlimited compassion and total solidarity with

---

[38] J. McManus, The Healing of the Sacraments, Bandra: St. Paul's, 1993, 29.
[39] J. Meier, "Jesus," in The New Jerome Biblical Commentary, London, 1991, 1321.
[40] K. D. O'Rourke and P. Boyle, Medical Ethics: Sources of Catholic Teachings, CHA, St. Louis, 1989, 134.

the unclean, the poor, the sinner, he reveals the true image of God, the Father of all.

One of the most characteristic dimensions of Christ's healing ministry is that it differs greatly from the legends of pagan religions about their miracle workers or even that of Asklepius, the god of healing in the Ancient Near East.[41] These latter stories are exotic, playing to the gallery, while Jesus sternly rejects the devil's attempt to seduce him to perform miracles of a purely sensational kind. He equally rebukes the Pharisees and others who came "to test him, asking him to show them a sign from heaven" (Matt 16:1). David Stanley is also of the opinion that the evangelists do not see the healings of Jesus as a "means of publicizing or accrediting the message of Jesus, but as an integral part of that message itself." In other words, "these acts of healing possess a profound Christological significance for outweighing their 'marvellous' character."[42]

Even the evangelists' choice of vocabulary is significant. They deliberately avoid expressions which emphasize the spectacular, such as taumasia (stupendous events) or teras (extraordinary miracle) and prefer expressions like ergon (a work of deep meaning), dynamics (a mighty deed, energy), and semeion (a sign). These expressions show that they are manifestations of divine power and are simply good news in action.[43]

Despite all the efforts not to popularize Jesus' acts of healing, they remain central to the New Tesatament.[44] Mark's gospel alone records over twenty individual acts of healing, so that almost one-half of his gospel is given over to healing narratives. Likewise in the Acts of the Apostles the witness of Jesus' healing forms the integral part of Peter's Kerygma on Pentecost Sunday (cf. Acts 2:23) and elsewhere. It is, therefore, not in doubt that Jesus healed or how the healings happened. The question is what they mean. The encounter between John the Baptist and Jesus towards the end of John's ministry helps to throw light on the meaning of Jesus' healing activity. John the Baptist sends his disciples to ask Jesus: "Are you the one who

---

[41] F. Dölger, "Der Heiland," in Antike und Christentum VI, 4, Münster, 1950, 241-72.
[42] D. Stanley, "Salvation and Healing," The Way 10 (1970): 301.
[43] D. Stanley, "Salvation and Healing," 303; see also L. Monden, Signs and Wonders: A Study of the Miraculous Element in Religion, New York: Desclee, 1966.
[44] Cf. J. Kallas, The Significance of the Synoptic Miracles, London: SPCK, 1961; A.

is to come, or are we to wait for another?" (Lk 7:19; Matt 11:2-5). Jesus' reply, involving the categories of Isaiah 35, contains an imagery that goes beyond physical healing: the "blind" are able to see the glory of God, "lepers" are cleansed from their sins, "deaf" people hear the good news, the "dead" are raised to new life in Christ, and the "poor" become rich through the preaching of the gospel (cf. Lk 7:20-23). Equally significant are the seven signs of the fourth gospel, three of which are healing miracles. For instance, the man born blind (Jn 9:1-34) portrays Jesus as the light of the world; the raising of Lazarus (Jn: 1-44) points to Jesus as the resurrection and the life.

The healings of Jesus are, therefore, not just social helps to the individual sick persons. They are signs of the coming of God's kingdom proclaimed in the gospel as a new reign of peace and justice in which God will put an end to the ancient enemies of the human race, namely, sin and evil, sickness and death; indeed "the last enemy to be destroyed is death" (1 Cor 15:26).[45] The healing acts of Jesus are eschatological signs of his future Lordship of the universe. This reign is already with us but not yet in its fullest sense. The enemies are still active; many people are sick, some have died, evil still exists. These will not be wholly destroyed until the parousia when "death shall be no more" (Rev 21:4). Each healing is a partial victory over death. Thus, the blind man and Lazarus will eventually die, but the healing works on their behalf show, no matter how briefly, something of the healing transformation that will take place on the last day. In this sense then, "each healing of illness is a sign of that 'redemption of the body' (Rom 8:23) for which we must still wait in hope."[46]

Jesus' ministry to the sick is also closely related to the Paschal Mystery. Human wholeness is always a relative concept in this life. The ultimate healing transformation comes from suffering and death borne out of love. This is what the Paschal Mystery is all about. In this way, Jesus becomes the Risen Christ and we too can personally share in the Easter victory of

---

Richardson, The Miracle Stories of the Gospels, London: SCM Press, 1941.

[45] C. W. Gusmer, And You Visited Me, 1990, 150; also F. A. Sulivan, Charisms and Charismatic Renewal: A Biblical and Theological Study, Ann Arbor, Michigan: Servant Books, 1982, 164.

[46] J. I. Okoye, "Healing in the Bible," in BTS 21 (2001): 55.

the Lord. The Risen Lord confronts and consoles his disheartened disciples at Emmaus: "Was it not necessary that the Christ should suffer these things and enter into his glory?" (Lk 24:26). To the doubting Thomas he says: "Put your finger here, and see my hands; and put out your hand, and place it in my side" (Jn 20:27). Even in his glorified humanity the Risen Christ still bears the marks of his crucifixion. His very wounds are healing and life-giving (1 Pet 2:24): "Worthy is the Lamb who was slain, to receive power and wealth and wisdom and might and honour and glory and blessing" (Rev 5:12). We cannot understand fully the compassion with which Jesus healed the sick and ministered to the poor and the suffering unless we realize that his compassion is part of his readiness to accept the bitter suffering of the final passion. As Bernard Häring points out:

> *When healing the sick and proclaiming the Good News, Jesus, in a deep mystical sense, is constantly on the road to Jerusalem, on the way to the cross, knowing that the scandalous history of the murder of the prophets in Jerusalem will be re-enacted in him (cf. Mt 23:33-39). His passion, death and resurrection become the inexhaustible fountain of redemption and healing love for all generations.*[47]

For Paul suffering accepted in union with Christ fosters both personal growth in holiness and a union with the Crucified and risen one. This union begins at baptism (Rom 6:3-11) and glories in the cross (Gal 6:14). When we conform our sufferings to those of Christ, we participate in the eternal sacrifice for the salvation of all men and women. Although, Paul graphically depicts the sufferings that come from his apostolate, the celebrated "thorn in the flesh" (2 Cor 12:7) seems to include the misery that comes from ill health. In as much as it is wrong to exaggerate the spiritual importance of suffering as many saints in the past did, the equally opposite extreme that fails to see that the Easter issues forth from the passion of Good Friday is also unacceptable. It is in this perspective that we can understand Paul in the celebrated passage of sharing in Jesus' life-giving death and resurrection when he prays "that I may know him in the power of his resur-

---

[47] B. Häring, Healing and Revealing, 1984, 29.

rection, and may share his sufferings, becoming like him in his death, that if possible I may attain the resurrection, from the dead" (Phil 3:10, 11).

Similarly the theology of the cross of John's gospel further shows that Jesus' "lifting up" on the cross – a phrase that refers to the cross as both an instrument of torture and a way to exaltation – is the way in which Jesus will draw all people to himself (Jn 12:32). It is important to note that the motivating force behind the ultimate healing through suffering and death is love. John's gospel is clear on this radical love of Christ. In his account of the Last Supper and Passion, he writes: "Now before the feast of the Passover, when Jesus knew that his hour had come to depart out of this world to the Father, having loved his own who were in this world, he loved them to the end" (Jn 13:1). Jesus chose to die on the cross in order to demonstrate in the most radical way possible, the completeness of his love for humanity. However, the fact that God has identified with our suffering and dying in Jesus Christ does not mean that we no longer have to face sin, suffering or death. Suffering and death have eschatological dimensions that go beyond our temporal lives.[48] Christ's freely accepted death on the cross is a victory over mortality that makes nonsense of the claims and aims of all demonic forces which exert power over humanity. But Christ's supreme sacrifice does not dispense us from dying physically. Rather, because of Christ even physical death is placed within the context of a history of salvation. We are to see illness and healing from within the passion and resurrection of Christ. In this way, we shall heal what can be healed and be enabled to give meaning to what cannot be healed.[49]

The introductory paragraphs to the revised Pastoral Care of the Sick (nos. 1-4) on human sickness and its meaning in the mystery of salvation captures this paradoxical predicament of Christian existence confronted by illness. On the one hand, the Christian is challenged to make every honest effort to fight against sickness and restore wholeness in the name of Jesus. On the other hand, we are to realize that ultimate healing can never be found on earth but comes rather from loving communion in the Lord's

---

[48] See V. Guroian, Life's Living toward Dying, 1996, 95-96.
[49] Cf. B. Häring, Healing and Revealing, 1984, 14.

death and resurrection. This is the attitude that should guide all who seek healing as well as the healers themselves:

> *Part of the plan laid out by God's providence is that we should fight strenuously against all sickness and carefully seek the blessings of good health, so that we may fulfil our role in human society and in the Church. Yet we should always be prepared to fill up what is lacking in Christ's sufferings for the salvation of the world as we look forward to the creation's being set free in the glory of the children of God (cf. Col 1:24; Rom 8:19-21).*
>
> *Moreover, the role of the sick in the Church is to be a reminder to others of the essential or higher things. By their witness the sick show that our mortal life must be redeemed through the mystery of Christ's death and resurrection (no. 3).*

Suffering, therefore, has a redemptive value not only for the sufferer but also for the Church and the world.[50] The sick and the dying manifest in a profound way the presence of the Suffering Servant of God. For this reason, they are not to be considered a mere object of medicine, but have a dignity that is equal if not superior to those caring for them. No wonder Lumen Gentium urges that the Church "exhorts (the sick) to contribute to the good of the people of God by freely uniting themselves to the passion and death of Christ."[51] In the same way, John Paul II appeals to all those suffering: "We ask you who are weak to become a source of strength for the Church."[52]

6.5 Jesus' Ministry Continues in the Church

Jesus' ministry to the sick is continued in his Body, the Church, which received the charge "heal the sick" (Matt 10:8) from the Lord and strives to carry it out by taking care of the sick as well as by accompanying them with her prayer of intercession.[53] The Church has the mission to be and to

---

[50] Cf. CCC, 1505.
[51] Vatican II, Lumen Gentium, 11.
[52] John Paul II, Salvifici Doloris, 31.
[53] CCC, 1509.

become ever more visibly and effectively a sign of the kingdom, "a visible, efficacious sign" of salvation in all its dimensions. The Church fulfils this injunction from Christ at the interrelated levels: charitable or pastoral, charismatic and sacramental. The charitable (pastoral) ministry to the sick finds its model in the Good Samaritan (Lk 10:25-37) as the compassion a Christian should have towards a suffering sister or brother. Christ identifies himself with the sick: "I was sick and you visited me" (Matt 25:36).

The patristic Church seems to have understood the message of this gospel and put it into practice. Polycarp the bishop of Smyrna, writing to the Church at Philippi in the second century admonishes the clergy to "keep an eye on all who are infirm."[54] Similarly, the Apostolic Tradition of Hippolytus of Rome speaks of gifts for the sick as well as the consolation derived by a visit made by the local bishop, "for a sick man is much comforted that the high priest remembered him."[55] This ministry gave rise to the founding of Christian hospitals as early as 369 in Asia Minor by St. Basil, 375 in Edessa by St. Ephraim, and in Rome in the year 400, as well as the establishment of numerous religious communities dedicated to the care of the sick. This fact probably led Anthony A. Ojo to "consider the female religious as the charitable arm of the Church …"[56] The very French word for hospital, Hotel-Diew (God's hotel), reflects this concern of the Church. E. Baldwin testifies to the fact that the Church pioneered the very beginning of health care institutions and programmes:

Long before health care became a specific government concern it already had been given a high place in the Church's list of priorities. Many of the hospitals the world over were Church-sponsored.[57]

The Church sees its venture in health care facilities as an apostolate to the helpless, the sick, the infirm, the aged, and the dispossessed. Most of the

---

[54] The Epistle of Polycarp to the Philippians, Early Christian Writings, vol. 6, trans. M. Staniforth, New York: Penguin Books, 1968, 146.
[55] G. Dix (ed.), The Apostolic Tradition, XXX, 57.
[56] A. A. Ojo, "The Healing Imperative of the Gospel of Luke and its Relevance to the Nigerian Church," in A. D. Danjuma (ed.), The Catholic Biblical Apostolate, Lagos: Sovereign Ventures Press, 2003, 64.
[57] E. Baldwin, "Health Care and the Church," in New Catholic Encyclopedia, vol. 17, reprint 1981, 247-248.

early hospitals were associated with cathedrals and monasteries in order to serve both the spiritual and physical needs of the sick. Apart from the hospital apostolate, the Church extends its salvific mission to social and environmental issues which are easily overlooked, such as providing low cost houses for the poor, a more equitable distribution of food among the hungry, the prevention of drug and alcohol abuse, coping with AIDS and refugee problems, a responsible accountability of natural resources, etc. This explains why the Church's department of Justice, Development and Peace Commission (JDPC) wades into political and economic spheres of life. It is an integral part of the Church's salvific mission that it should care for the health of the society and culture within which the People of God live. In this pastoral ministry, all Christians are involved. According to the revised rites all Christians by virtue of their baptism participate "by doing all that they can to help the sick return to health, by showing love for the sick, and by celebrating the sacraments with them" (no. 34). They are to visit the sick regularly and share scripture and prayer with them. In a more intimate way, the Church's pastoral ministry is practiced by the family and friends as well as all who care for the sick and dying at home, in hospitals, hospices, and nursing homes.

In sum then, the purpose of the Church in establishing hospitals and other social institutions is to penetrate the secular society. These according to Vatican II are to serve as a leaven and as a kind of soul for human society as it is renewed in Christ and transformed into God's family.[58] The Catholic hospitals seek to be a place where the excellence of medical care, provided according to Christian principles will help the gospel spirit permeate and improve the temporal order. The aim of the Church is thus to heal and restore health and more importantly to prevent disease. As O'Rourke puts it:

> *The purpose of Catholic hospitals remains in accord with the Church's mission to bring the person of the healing Christ to people, to penetrate society with Christian values, and to work for bet-*

---

[58] Vatican II, Gaudium et Spes, 40.

ter society by striving for social justice in the field of health and care.[59]

We have already discussed in detail the charismatic ministry of the Church to the sick. This ministry has always been in the Church and still remains with it. In our day it is manifested in the lives of the saints, for example, miracle cures, pilgrimage shrines of saints and in the healing activities of Pentecostal and Charismatic groups. What remains to be emphasized once again is that charismatic gifts especially that of healing are given to the entire Church; they are at the disposal of the Church, and should never be used without reference and permission from the Church. The sacramental ministry is the liturgical expression of an overall concern of the Church for the sick. This ministry is celebrated in the sacraments of penance (reconciliation), anointing of the sick with its closely associated symbol of the laying on of hands and the eucharist. The first two we have examined at length. What perhaps remains to be repeated is the need to distinguish between care and cure. The anointing of the sick is not in competition with medical diagnosis and treatment, still less is it a magic to attempt a cure when all else fails. The "saving and raising up" spoken of in James refer to an integration of the situation of sickness within one's Christian life and commitment and actively bringing the meaning of Christ's death and resurrection to bear on one's own life-situation. In this regard the care of the Christian community, paralleling the physical care given by medical personnel, is crucial: the anointing is a sign (as every sacrament is a sign), given by the faith community and its leaders, of the strengthening and comfort of Jesus Christ.

As we have already noted sickness brings a crisis situation and a profound sense of isolation. In such a devastating condition, room must be given for the sick person to acknowledge anger, depression and pain. This is the role of the sacrament of reconciliation. The pastoral minister's choice of prayers from among the options offered in the ritual, and the sacramental act itself, should move the sick person towards a recovery of his or her own identity, a restored sense of communion with God and with others, a new integration

---

[59] K. O'Rourke, "Catholic Hospitals," in *New Catholic Encyclopedia*, vol. 17, reprint 1981, 275-276.

of one's unique situation, and ultimately a new sense of vocation, a new future. Since at times an overemphasized penitential character has been assigned to anointing, it needs to be pointed out that penance is the healing sacrament directed towards the forgiveness of sins. And as we have seen there is a mysterious relationship between sin and sickness, both of which are manifestations of evil in the world.

Closely related to the sacramental ministry to the sick is the gesture of the laying on of hands. Norman Cousins narrates the experience of a doctor who regularly lays hands on the sick as part of their medical treatment.[60] From medical reports it has been known that the last senses to die in us are the senses of hearing and touch. The imposition of hands is a basic sacramental gesture that features prominently in all the sacraments: the catechumenal liturgies, exorcisms, celebration of the sacraments of initiation; the epiclesis and final blessing of the Eucharist; the action that accompanies the prayer of absolution now restored in penance; the central sacramental sign of holy orders; and the blessing at marriages.[61]

The imposition of hands is the healing action par excellence in the New Testament. Godfrey Diekmann lists eighteen such instances of healing or raising from the dead in Mark's gospel (in twelve instances "touch," six instances of "laying on of hands"); in Matthew, twelve incidents (nine "touch," three "laying on of hands"); in Luke, ten instances (eight "touch," two "laying on of hands").[62] Jesus effected his healing miracles mostly with a touch or by laying of hands on the sick. Sometimes too many people were cured by merely touching him or his garment with faith:

> And wherever he came, in villages, cities, or country, they laid the sick in the market places, and besought him that they might touch even the fringe of his garment; and as many as touched it were made well (Mk 6:56).

In the tradition of the Church, the laying on of hands has often been associated with the application of the blessed oil. This was pre-eminently high-

---

[60] Cf. N. Cousins, Anatomy of an Illness, New York: W.W. Norton, 1979, 135.
[61] See G. Diekmann, "The Laying On of Hands: the Basic Sacramental Rite," in The Catholic Theological Society of America Proceedings 29 (1974): 350-51.
[62] G. Diekmann, "The Laying On of Hands in Healing," in Liturgy 25 (1980): 7-10, 36-38.

lighted by James and was testified to by Origen in the early third century as well as in the Ambrosian liturgy of Milan dating from the ninth centuries. In our own century, the laying on of hands was first restored to the anointing of the sick even as it was yet called extreme unction, in the 1952 edition of the Roman Ritual, where it accompanied the prayer of exorcism. It is given more prominence in the revised rites of 1972, where the introductory notes describe the sacrament of anointing as consisting "especially in the laying on of hands by the priests of the Church, the offering of the prayer of faith, and the anointing of the sick with oil made holy by God's blessing" (no. 5). While in confirmation, the gesture of the laying on of hands has been subsumed into that of anointing with chrism, the rite of anointing provides for a more explicit action of imposition by the presbyters in silence. The gesture follows after the litany of intercession before the blessing or thanksgiving over the oil. The rite of visitation of the sick also suggests that the priest conclude the visit by laying hands on the sick person's head. Other ministers to the sick are invited to trace the sign of the cross on the forehead of the sick person.

The Eucharist is the representation of the healing power of the Paschal Mystery. All other sacraments are ordered to it as Aquinas rightly noted.[63] It is a healing sacrament and the pledge of the ultimate resurrection of the whole person: "Anyone who does eat my flesh and drink my blood has eternal life, and I will raise him up on the last day" (Jn 6:54). We have already seen the tradition of communion of the sick and viaticum in earlier chapters. What is important for now is to underline the frequent mention of healing in the Eucharistic celebration and communion rite which many Christians unfortunately neglect. The Eucharist is a healing celebration.[64] Jesus describes the reason for his coming into this world thus: "That they may have life and have it abundantly" (Jn 10:10). He continues this mission of healing, consoling and liberating those bound by sin and sickness even today in a powerful manner, namely, through the sacramental encounter.

---

[63] T. Aquinas, Summa Theologica III, q. 65, a. 3.
[64] J. Brookman-Amissah, "The Eucharist as Healing Celebration," in J. S. Ukpong (ed.) et al, Jesus Christ: The Food of Life, 11th CIWA Theology Week Proceedings, Port Harcourt: CIWA Press, 2000, 222-231.

Apart from the sacraments being a means of salvation, they possess a healing power as the Cathechism of the Catholic Church says:

> *Sacramental grace is the grace of the Holy Spirit given by Christ and proper to each sacrament. The Spirit heals and transforms those who receive him by conforming them to the Son of God.*[65]

Of all the other sacraments, the Eucharist is the most central and fruitful sacrament of the saving-healing grace of God. Although, Jesus is present everywhere, he is really present in the Eucharist in a pre-eminent and unique way. The Eucharist is the unique sacrament in which not only grace is given but the author of grace himself.[66] The presence of Christ in the Eucharistic celebration is first and foremost for therapeutic purposes of forgiveness of sins and healing. Every Eucharistic celebration has a healing effect. This fact is often forgotten by those who are in the healing ministry, when they talk about what is wrongly referred to as "healing Mass."[67] But they will be surprised to see that throughout the celebration of the Eucharist, the Church is praying for healing and wholesomeness of body, soul and mind.

Already at the beginning of the Mass, the Penitential Rite, the presider may use the alternative rite of penance to ask the Lord for healing:

> *You were sent to heal the contrite.*
> *Lord, have mercy.*

Conscious of the fact that sin causes wounds and divisions in the Body of Christ, he continues to pray with the congregation:

> *Lord Jesus,*
> *You heal the wounds of sin and division.*
> *Christ, have mercy.*

The priest and the congregation may further pray as follows:

> *Lord Jesus Christ,*
> *You give us yourself to heal*
> *and bring us strength.*
> *Lord, have mercy.*

---

[65] CCC, 1129.
[66] Cf. Vatican II, Sacrosanctum Concilium, 7.
[67] A. Echema, "The Omnipotent God Vis-à-Vis Human Suffering: The Church's Response," 6.

Just before the reception of Holy Communion, the Church prays for the healing of the whole person. In one of the two alternative quiet prayers of preparation for communion the presider prays specifically for healing:

> *Lord Jesus Christ,*
> *with faith in your love and mercy,*
> *I eat your body and drink your blood.*
> *Let it not bring me condemnation*
> *but health in mind and body.*

The showing of the consecrated elements is accompanied by the rephrasing of the centurion's words: "Lord, I am not worthy ... but only say the word and I shall be healed." In the Lord's Prayer which precedes the above prayers, the congregation had prayed to be delivered from all evil. Praying for deliverance from all evil is integral to the Christian's work with Christ in the spiritual warfare. We live in a depraved world in which the Christian is surrounded and assailed with all kinds of evil, including attacks from evil spirits. The Church recognizes the need to pray against natural and man-made disasters, accidents, debilitating diseases such as HIV/AIDS, cancer and importunate death.[68] Not only does the Eucharistic celebration promise physical healing, it also assures healing for inner hurts, heartaches, frustrations, and disappointments in life for all those who pray fervently with expectant faith. Being the celebration of the sacrament of healing, the Eucharist is capable of healing our diseases, emotions, and restoring of broken relationships. The healing aspect of the Eucharistic celebration comes out more vividly in the liturgical prayers in Lent. McManus points out some of them especially in the Post-Communion Prayers:

1. *Lord, may our sharing in the mystery*
   free us from our sins
   and make us worthy of your healing
   (Friday after Ash Wednesday).

2. *Lord, through this sacrament,*
   may we rejoice in your healing power

---
[68] See J. Brookman-Amissah, "The Eucharist as Healing Celebration," 228.

and experience your love in mind and body
(Monday of First Week of Lent).

3. *Lord, our God,*
   renew us by these mysteries.
   May they heal us now
   and bring us to eternal salvation
   (Thursday of First Week of Lent).

Commenting on this last prayer Brookman-Amissah rightly points out that the word "now" in the prayer means "that the Church wants the Lord to do the healing 'now' and not some other occasion or time. There is opportunity for healing at every celebration of the Eucharist."[69] The Church also requests the Lord to continue his healing work within the community:

Almighty and eternal God,
you have restored us to life by the triumphant death and resurrection of Christ. Continue this healing work within us.
May we who participate in this mystery never cease to serve you
(Final Prayer of Good Friday Liturgy).

All these prayers for healing within the Mass show how firmly the Church trusts in God's healing power and love, and how it expects that healing power to be experienced in the Mass.

The ministry of the Church to the sick also finds liturgical expression in the revised Sacramentary, where special Mass prayers are provided for the sick, as well as in readings from the Lectionary.[70] The Entrance antiphon of the Mass for the Sick is taken from the Psalmist's cry for mercy and healing:

Have mercy on me God, for I am fading away.
Heal me, Lord, my bones are shaken ... (Ps 6:3).

The alternate antiphon is a recall of Psalm 53:4.

The Lord has truly borne our sufferings,
he has carried all our sorrows.

---

[69] Ibid; 229.
[70] Sacramentary, 32; Lectionary, 871-75.

As we have already seen the opening prayer of the Mass for the Sick is a testimony of the Church's faith and trust in the healing power and care of God. Furthermore, the most recent English revision, Pastoral Care of the Sick, has added special intercessions for the sick to be inserted into Eucharistic Prayers I, II, III. It also includes a special preface for the Mass in which the anointing takes place, the main body of which reads:

In the splendour of his rising
Your Son conquered suffering and death
and bequeathed to us his promise
of a new and glorious world,
where no bodily pain will afflict us,
and no anguish of spirit.
Through your gift of the Spirit,
you bless us even now,
with comfort and healing
strength and hope,
forgiveness and peace.

In this supreme sacrament of your love
you give us the risen body of your Son:
a pattern of what we shall become
when he returns again at the end of time (no. 145).

All the sacraments for the sick are not only actions of Christ but also acts of the Church; for the Church is the fundamental or primordial sacrament of the saving grace of Christ. This Church is more perfectly a Church when it actively engages itself in the salvation of its members, especially those who are sick and afflicted.

Summary

In this chapter we occupied ourselves with the theological meaning of sickness and healing. The Church as the living extension of Christ's saving mission on earth has the task of taking care of the People of God in all their conditions especially the poor, the afflicted and the sick. The Church carries out this purpose through its charitable (pastoral), charismatic and sacramental dimensions. But what does it actually mean to be sick? Illness ushers in a moment of crisis in a person, affecting his or her whole existence. For this reason, any attempt by the Church to bring cure or healing must consider the human person as a psychosomatic unity rather than following the old dualism between the body and soul. Against such dualistic tendencies are the insights gained from biblical anthropology, contemporary theological-anthropology (Rahner), and from depth psychology (Jung). All these insights caution against a one-sided approach to illness. Therefore, we need today a theology of healing that includes anointing and considers the sacrament as affecting the whole person.

As a result of the mysterious relationship between sin and illness, there is need for the sick person to repent, confess his or her sins and seek reconciliation with self, with fellow human beings and eventually with God. There is a close relationship between penance (reconciliation) and healing. All the rites for the sick and dying provide for the sacrament of reconciliation. Although there may be abuses whereby some people overemphasize sin and assume divine prerogative of judgment, the placing of repentance and forgiveness at the centre of the Church's ministry to the sick and dying still remains relevant and necessary. It has been known that many patients suffer more from mental anguish and guilt than physical pain. The approach is biblical. Jesus himself demonstrates the synthesis of forgiving sins and healing in the example of the man he cured at the pool of Bethzatha (cf. Jn 5:14). Moreover, sin has not only personal but social dimensions. It is, therefore, not enough to tell people that their sins have been forgiven. Sometimes, it may be necessary for them to confess such sins, ask for forgiveness and to forgive themselves.

A fuller theological meaning of illness is found in the cross of Jesus. The problem of theodicy notwithstanding, God remains a God who is in solidarity with humanity. While the Stoic's God was considered "perfect" because he was unmoved by human misery, the God of Christianity meets his own not as a stranger to their misery, illnesses and sufferings. On the contrary, he comes to us as the "One-of-us," as the Son of Man foretold by the prophet Isaiah: "He proved himself their Saviour in all their troubles. It was neither messenger nor angel but his presence that saved them" (63:8-9). God is deeply moved by human suffering and pain. He suffers with all those who suffer and die in sickness and he dies in Jesus Christ.

The cross is, thus, the meeting point between the "suffering God" and the suffering humanity. God shares our suffering and sickness in Christ. Since Christ conquered sin and death through his own suffering and death on the cross, suffering has become something salvific. For, the victory of Christ is promised all those who wait on him in hope. While Christians should struggle against illness and do everything possible to restore wholeness, they need to see whatever cannot be healed in the light of their participation in the redemptive suffering of Jesus Christ.

Christ himself did not do away with all suffering. He did not dispense humanity from dying physically, but he deeply changed the meaning and experience of sickness, suffering and death. By following the example of the Redeemer, mankind will be spared from all kinds of illness, suffering and from a meaningless death. The healers in Nigeria and their clients ought to know that healing and suffering are not mutually exclusive. The healing power of prayer and the sacraments are important, but not at the expense of devaluing redemptive suffering. But that Jesus was a healer par excellence is not in doubt. Even his contemporary critics are in agreement. He continued his healing works even as he hung dying upon the cross by forgiving those who crucified him, promising paradise to the repentant thief, and comforting his grieving mother by bequeathing John to take care of her. The healings, however, were more than mere healings of illnesses. They are also eschatological signs in the sense of the "already" and the "not yet." This singular fact distinguishes Jesus' healing works from those of pagan religions or even from the present day healers who play to the gallery and seek publicity. Even the evangelists' choice of words in describing these healing miracles is an indication that they are manifestations of divine power rather than mere spectacular and stupendous events.

Jesus' healing ministry is closely linked with the Paschal Mystery in which Jesus shows the depth of his love for the suffering and sinful humanity. Doing the will of his Father is an integral part of his readiness to accept the bitter suffering of the final passion and death. When we conform our sufferings to those of Christ, we participate in the eternal sacrifice for the salvation of all humanity. As it is usually said, there is no crown without the cross, just as there will be no Easter without the passion of Good Friday. Every Christian should see illness and healing from the point of view of the mystery of the passion, death and resurrection of Jesus Christ; which we partake in through our baptism.

Finally, Jesus' healing ministry is carried on by the Church, his body. On the pastoral (charitable) level, the Church reaches out to its sick members following the example of the Good Samaritan by providing hospitals, looking after the displaced and giving food to the hungry. The Church also extends its saving mission to the social and environmental issues such as politics, social infrastructure and opting for the voiceless. Summarily, the Church aims to penetrate the secular society through its hospitals and other social institutions. The other arm of the Church is its charismatic ministry to the sick. Here care must be taken since charisms such as healing and prophecy while they may be found in those who are ordained cannot be restricted to them. However, the exercise of all charisms is for the upbuilding of the Church. Therefore, they must be used in reference to and permission from the Church authorities. Today unfortunately, this wonderful gift with which the Church has also judged and selected its saints is being blown out of proportion by Pentecostal and Charismatic Renewal Movements and the healers.

The sacramental ministry is expressed and celebrated in the sacraments of reconciliation (penance), anointing of the sick with its closely associated symbol of the laying on of hands, and the Eucharist. Although, penance and anointing have been often confused throughout the history of the Church's sacramental system, both have their proper and crucial role to play especially with regard to the sick. It was this confusion that led to the association of the anointing ritual with deathbed reconciliation of penitents especially in the Middle Ages. This development also made anointing become "extreme unction" – a name that has plagued the sacrament till this day. However, the Church has undertaken to reform its rites and it does that in a most marvellous way in its elaborate reforms of the sacraments for the sick and dying. The new rites have been theologically and pastorally enriched even with ecumenical undertones. The aim of the Church's reforms is to make this sacrament more available to the sick and the dying. It is no longer the task of the priest alone but the entire Christians to take care of the sick. Closely related to anointing is the gesture of the laying on of hands. Although the symbolic gesture is still restricted only to the ordained, it is very biblical and therapeutic.

There is a close link between the Eucharist and healing. Not only that the Eucharist celebrates and gives grace, it makes the author of this grace present. The frequent mention of healing in the prayers of the Mass bears sufficient evidence even to those in the healing ministry that the Eucharistic celebration is for therapeutic purposes of forgiveness of sins and healing. The rites, thus, lay emphasis on bringing communion to the sick and aged who cannot be present at Mass. In addition, the Sacramentary contains a special Mass for the sick with prayers and readings. In the most recent English revision, Pastoral Care for the Sick, there are additional special intercessions for the sick to be inserted into Eucharistic prayers. All these reforms show the Church's concern for the sick and the afflicted. They also have pastoral implications. These will be considered in the next chapter.

Chapter Seven
Pastoral Implications (Practical Inculturation)

In chapter six of this book the theological meaning of sickness and healing was considered. This present chapter focuses attention on the pastoral implications. It is one thing to have the right formulation of the concepts and their implications for the sacrament of the anointing of the sick. It is another thing to put these into concrete pastoral practices. For instance, after over thirty years of the official reform of this sacrament, most Catholics not only in Nigeria, but elsewhere in the world are still ignorant of the content and structure of the new rite. My experience in the chaplaincy of the Heart of Jesus Hospital Dernbach, Germany is that most Roman Catholics still cling to the pre-Vatican II (Medieval-tridentine) titles for this sacrament, "Extreme Unction" or "Last Rites," which terminologies in fact appear nowhere in the new rite. Despite the efforts of the Church to reform the sacrament of the anointing of the sick, its actual application and practice has remained problematic. Both the clergy and laity have continued to misunderstand anointing within the entire rite of the Pastoral Care of the Sick. Instead, healing ministry has become the order of the day. But as we have seen both anointing of the sick and charismatic healing are not in opposition to each other. On the contrary, they are aspects of the holistic ministry of healing of the Church.

In addition to the proliferation of the charismatic healing ministry is the communal anointing whereby some priests indiscriminately anoint everybody both old and young, sick and healthy that attends the Mass for the Sick. All these are indications of the confusion that still compounds the fifth sacrament of the Church. We shall start, therefore with the clearing of this confusion by examining the misunderstandings of the sacraments in general and that of the sacrament of the anointing of the sick in particular. This confusion leads to certain abuses in the celebration of the anointing since people are still operating in the frame of the old terms used to describe the sacrament before the reforms. This will bring us to practical inculturation where we shall make concrete suggestions for the further enrichment of the sacrament of the anointing of the sick according to African culture and values. Furthermore, we shall undertake a healthy self-critique of the Church's healing ministry, for we think that the hospital ventures should be balanced with the pastoral care of the sick and the aged. Finally, the present day healers – both Catholics and non-Catholics - will be placed side by side with Jesus Christ, the real Healer to see how they are following the master in spite of their claims.

7.1 Misunderstandings of the Sacraments

Right from its inception anointing of the sick has posed a problem both in its conception and implementation. For instance, what is a priest to do when stopping at the scene of an accident? Is he to indiscriminately anoint the injured victim in every instance, just to make sure? When is the best time to administer the sacrament in a hospital? Is the emergency room always the best place, provided there is time to see the patient afterwards? Should the sick be anointed upon every admission to the hospital? These are some of the questions bothering the ministers of anointing. They have their roots in the magical conception of the sacrament. But what is the actual place of sacraments in the life of the Church? What is the "thing-ness" (kpim) of the sacraments and their working?

One major characteristic feature of the Catholic Church is its strong sacramental system which is integral to the very nature of the Church. However, this sacramental ministry remains in solidarity with the rest of the Church's mission, for the Church does not exist only to dispense sacraments. When sacraments are viewed in isolation from the rest of the Church's mission, they become wrongly conceived "as the sole vehicle of the salvific plan of God, quite unrelated to a sense of being Church."[1] To correct such an erroneous view, one must keep in mind that the primordial sacrament is Jesus Christ himself in his incarnate risen humanity. There is no sacrament without Jesus. The Church is only the visible continuation of the risen Christ. In the words of Michael Lawler,

---

[1] C. W. Gusmer, And You Visited Me, 1990, 176.

The man Jesus is the sacrament of God. The Church is the sacrament of the risen Jesus, and, therefore, also of God. The solemn ritual actions of the Church are the sacraments of the presence and the action of Christ and of God.[2]

In this framework of the sacraments, there are other requirements for them to work. Faith is indispensable without which nothing happens. This faith comes from hearing the word of God proclaimed in the gospel. That is why the new rite emphasizes the unity between word and sacrament which underlies the set pattern for every sacramental celebration. The Church's sacramental system and the celebrating assembly are complementary. In other words, the primary locus of the Church is the worshipping assembly.[3] The institutional dimension must not displace or overshadow the community of faith in whose service institutional forms exist. The sacraments in this perspective are the symbolic expression of what it means to be Church. They are the Church's most intense self-expression and realization, but they do not exhaust the total activity of the Church. Other dimensions of the Church include proclamation based on the scriptures, ethics which refers to the Church's commitment to justice, advancing the reign of God on earth, witness of life and mission. Any overemphasis on one of these dimensions is at the expense of the others. One must avoid the overvaluation of one category to the detriment of the other. As Louis-Marie Chauvet puts it:

Because the sacraments are seen as "means of salvation" and because they act "ex opere operato," one has such a trust in them that they tend to occupy the whole sphere of Christian life. In this perspective, which verges on magic, the model Christian is the "practicing" Christian.[4]

With regard to the sacrament of the anointing of the sick, this will mean that it is to be seen complementarily with the Church's wider pastoral ministry to the sick and the aged. Indeed, the "ex opere operato" efficacy of the sacraments has often been overstated and misinterpreted in a mechanistic,

---

[2] M. G. Lawler, Symbol and Sacrament, 1987, 46.
[3] Cf. A. Echema, "The Liturgical Assembly in the Third Millennium: The Nigerian Perspective" in R. Madu and A. Echema (eds), Essays in Honour of Msgr. Alphonsus Aghaizu, 2004, 77-94.
[4] L. M. Chauvet, The Sacraments: The Word of God at the Mercy of the Body, Col-

automatic fashion by post-Tridentine manual theology. The Council of Trent employed this phrase in reaction to the extremes of the Reformers' sola fides position, which held that sacraments were effective only because of the faith response of the recipient. On the contrary, the Council Fathers maintained that priority of grace, the initiative of God in the sacraments, before anything else the sacraments are actions of Christ. The opus operatum (the object) and the opus operantis (the subject) are not in opposition; rather the two elements should be seen as complementing each other in any sacramental encounter and not conflicting with one another. The former refers to the divine and objective efficacy of the sacraments as effective signs of grace. They are basically efficacious signs of the divine transforming Presence which reaches their goal unless we frustrate God's designs by putting obstacles in the way. The latter (opus operantis) concerns the graced human response and involvement. The recipient of any sacrament is not just passive; sacraments are also signs of faith. They require a mutual and covenantal presence which implies conversion and commitment on the part of the recipient. The overlooking or outright neglect of the opus operantis - the recipient subject has often led to the mechanical, magical handling of the sacraments. Let the priest for example, happen to chance upon the dying victim of an accident and give this person extreme unction in extremis, and the person is believed to be automatically saved or at least surer of being saved. The same thing applies to the unbaptized child in danger of death.

It is obvious how such conceptions favour certain questionable representations of the efficacy ex opere operato of the sacraments. Evidently the insistence on the objective efficacy of the sacraments is done at the expense of the concrete existential subjects, who are not taken into account. It is true that the old cathechism requires that the recipient have the "piety" and the "right intention" in order to receive the sacraments fruitfully. But this has nothing to do with the "nature" or the "being" of the sacraments but only with their "well-being." In the 1947 cathechism's sixteen lessons on the sacraments, the word "faith" never appears; the same is true of "Church" (except once to designate it as an institution into which baptism

---

legeville, Minnesota: The Liturgical Press, 2001, 40.

incorporates its members). The only instance where the concrete subjects are taken into account is the conditio sine qua non, that they will not place any obstacle (mortal sin or canonical sanction forbidding access to the sacraments) to the reception of grace that comes down through the sacraments).[5]

One of the merits of Vatican II is its insistence on liturgical celebrations being seen as a dialogical graced human encounter with the mystery of God.[6] Following this understanding, the revised rites recommend the earliest possible moment for anointing in the case of serious illness and for viaticum when the dying Christian is still conscious and able to enter into the sacramental experience.

Another misunderstanding of the sacraments is their reduction to a one-to-one transaction between the minister and the subject or recipient. This individualistic approach does violence to the assembled worshipping community that celebrates the sacraments. But to correct this private tendency which was inherited from the Middle Ages as a result of the excessive emphasis placed on the role of the priest, Vatican II reaffirms the communal nature of Christian worship. The Constitution on the Sacred Liturgy states:

Whenever rites, according to their specific nature, make provision for communal celebration involving the presence and active participation of the faithful, it is to be stressed that this way of celebrating them is to be preferred, as far as possible to a celebration that is individual and, so to speak private.[7]

In the same way, the introductions to the revised rites always contain an extended treatment of Offices and Ministries which includes the baptized members of the faithful. For the Council Fathers as well as for the new rites, baptism rather than ordination is the common denominator for all Christian ministries. They recognize the diversity of gifts within the liturgical assembly which symbolize and represent the diversity of talents and gifts within the one body of Christ. The liturgical assembly becomes the principal agent in the liturgical event and the principal minister to which all other liturgical ministries are ordered. The priest is more properly called

---

[5] L. M. Chauvet, The Sacraments, 2001, XV-XVI.
[6] See P. Fransen, "Sacraments, Signs of Faith," in Worship 37 (1962): 31-50.
[7] SC, 27.

the presiding celebrant, for all the participants are celebrants according to a diversity of roles and ministries.[8] Unless the communal aspect of the anointing of the sick is rediscovered, the sacrament will "remain mired in the misconception of being last rites, a hasty timed curative to the departing soul, a gesture moving entirely in one direction from the priest to the passive recipient."[9] But as we have seen the reformed rites see in the sick person a living sign, a sacrament, an event disclosing the truth that Christianity trusts God to reveal himself in suffering.

7.2 Abuses in the Celebration of the "Last Rites"

It is not an exaggeration to say that of all the sacraments, the anointing of the sick is probably the least understood, the most uncommunally and most unliturgically celebrated. The sacrament of anointing continues to be misunderstood by all those (and these are in the majority and include both the clergy and laity) who still cling to the pre-Vatican II terms "extreme unction" or "last rites." In addition, there are people who still consider the sacrament as a kind of religious pronouncement of death, so that sending for the priest automatically means arranging for the funeral[10] as it was wrongly understood in the past.

Anointing has remained the most uncommunal of sacraments. Many Catholics in particular and people generally view sickness as private and somehow shameful.[11] Such feelings can easily go against a person's desire to be part of a communal celebration of the sacrament. However, this situation is now changing. Today one observes communal celebrations of anointing in

---

[8] Cf. K. F. Pecklers, "The Liturgical Assembly at the Threshold of the Millennium. North American Perspective," in M. R. Francis and R. E. Pecklers (eds.), Liturgy for the New Millennium: A Commentary on the Revised Sacramentary, Collegeville, Minnesota: The Liturgical Press, 2000, 54.

[9] B. T. Morill, "Christ the Healer: A Critical Investigation of Liturgical, Pastoral, and Biblical Sources," in Worship 79 (2005): 413.

[10] Jean-Marie Lustiger, Stärkung fürs Leben: Über das Kranksein und das Sakrament der Krankensalbung, München: Verlag Neue Stadt, 1991, 6; see also G. Ikeobi, "Healing and Exorcism: The Pastoral Experience," 1992, 58.

[11] Cf. D. B. Moris, Illness and Culture in the Postmodern Age, Berkeley: University of California, 1998, 64-65, 245.

some hospitals, parishes, dioceses and at pilgrimage centres like Lourdes, Fatima, etc. The only danger in such group anointing is the tendency to trivialize sickness and even the sacrament itself, whereby everybody is anointed irrespective of age and seriousness of the illness.

Anointing has been the most unliturgical of the seven sacraments. This problem is compounded by priests darting into sickrooms for a quick dabbing with oil. All these call for certain concrete and practical suggestions which are believed will obviate these abuses and improve the celebration of the sacrament of anointing.

7.3 Inculturating Anointing of the Sick

Although, many official Church documents since the Second Vatican Council[12] have always emphasized the need of inculturation, it has remained one of the greatest challenges for the Church on the continent in this third Millennium. The 1994 Synod for Africa on several occasions stressed the particular importance of inculturation and called on the bishops and episcopal conferences to take the task very seriously.[13] Already the challenge to the African local Churches is clearly expressed in the Instrumentum Laboris of that Synod:

Those responsible in pastoral matters should analyze the nature of inculturation of Christianity in Africa and its capacity to constitute vibrant ecclesial communities, the role of the laity, the response to the thirst for spiritual experience and the Word of God as well as the reply to be given to the vital questions posed by suffering, sickness and death.[14]

In a continent where the lives of its citizens are closely connected with sickness, suffering and death, it is not surprising that the questions about healing abound. But since the Synod for Africa, almost twelve years ago, the aspirations and wishes of the people in Africa seem not to have

---

[12] SC, 37-40.
[13] Ecclesia in Africa, 59-62.
[14] 1994 Special Assembly for Africa of the Synod of Bishops, Instrumentum Laboris,89.

changed. While some local Churches like the former Zaire now the Republic of Congo have responded positively to this call to inculturation, others are yet to show any signs that they have heard the call at all. In Nigeria, for example, there are some local efforts at inculturation, though these are done mostly by individuals who are gifted. There is hardly any coordination as a Church. In fact, there is very little encouragement or support of radical inculturation by the clergy, individual bishops, or conference of bishops.[15] This situation explains why local efforts by pioneers have only a very limited scope. As long as they are not officially taken over by the Church's hierarchy, they remain private matters. Following the example of SC 37-40, the Sacred Congregation for Divine Worship has continued to show attitude of openness to matters of inculturation. In its *De Benedictionibus*, promulgated on May 1984, we read:

> *It is for episcopal conferences to examine with care and prudence that which it could be good to accept from the traditions and genius of each people, and thus to suggest other adaptations that might be thought useful or necessary.*[16]

Such a statement is good news. The authorities responsible for Catholic worship in Rome now recognize how difficult it is to impose a universal ritual. They are inviting the Churches to adapt and inculturate the Roman rites for their people. It is a challenge to the local Churches in Africa to construct African rituals, which are then to be submitted for the approval of Rome. For this to be realized, ad hoc commissions, according to national or regional groups should be created, promoted with determination and above all supported in both the pastoral and financial spheres. Commissions have been set up in the past which in the end have achieved nothing apart from elementary working methods. Others simply died naturally because of lack of financial support. By and large, the task of inculturation remains an urgent one and which a people must do for themselves. It is never done in proxy. What is needed now are actions, not words. We, therefore, propose a

---

[15] See E. E. Uzukwu, Worship as Body Language: Introduction to Christian Worship: An African Orientation, Collegeville, Minnesota: The Liturgical Press, 1997, 272-274.

[16] Rituel Romain, Chalet-Tardy, 1988, 13.

few concrete actions in the practical inculturation of the sacrament of the anointing of the sick.

7.3.1 Use of Locally Produced Oil

Aware of the pastoral needs and the difficulty involved in obtaining the olive oil, (the prescribed matter for valid administration of the sacrament of anointing) in some part of the world, Pope Paul VI, in his Apostolic Constitution allows the use of "another kind of oil provided it is obtainable from plants, and similar to olive oil."[17]

Among the Igbo of Nigeria, the oil extracted from palm kernel is an easily available commodity. This oil is generally acknowledged as being curative and is often used as an antidote for convulsion. It would certainly satisfy the requirement of Paul VI's Constitution.

7.3.2 Sacramental Use of Oil Blessed by the Bishop

In the first 800 years the practice of self-application of oil existed provided that it was blessed by the bishop. People brought their own oil on Holy Thursday to be blessed after which they went home with it like holy water for their private use or other's needs. It would seem that today, the rediscovery of this old practice has become necessary. Already many people bring their own oils from Lourdes, Jerusalem, Fatima, Rome, and so on for blessing. There is resurgent use of oils in the form of aromatherapy, vegetarianism, and massage in the latter half of the last century. Significantly, much of the prescriptive and marketing language used to describe these oils is drawn from sacramental language. Oils, the advertisements say "revitalize," "refresh," "renew," and "restore," they contribute to a sense of "well being." Generally speaking, most of the health uses of oils are beneficial and seem to answer people's needs. Since of all the sacraments, oil is the one that takes most account of our outward bodies, it will be appropriate that a renewed revival of the sacramental practice using oil in the Church

---

[17] Paul VI, Apostolic Constitution: The Sacrament of the Anointing of the Sick, Nov. 30, 1972.

should build on people's already positive experience of oils. Sacramental practice relating to oil should aim to be broadly based and empowering, keeping the benefits of oil in people's own hands. As the sacrament that most relates to the sense of touch and healing, people should be allowed to use it themselves.[18]

7.3.3 Lay Anointing

It is not widely known that the lay people can bless sick people and others. According to canon 1168 certain sacramentals can be administered by lay people who posses the appropriate qualities, provided these are in accordance with the liturgical books and subject to the judgement of the local ordinary. These may include the distribution of ashes on Ash Wednesday, parents blessing their children, an extraordinary minister of the Eucharist blessing a communicant. The code leaves no doubt that lay people can also bless. Certainly, the request for a blessing from God does not accomplish "more" if it is given by a priest. It will be a magical notion to suppose that a papal blessing has more power than, for example, parents' blessing of their children.[19]

There is in the Roman Ritual a blessing for olive oil (or other vegetable oil) called the oil of Gladness which is a special sacramental that lay people can use for healing and other suitable purposes. This is not the official sacrament of the anointing of the sick but it affords the lay people an opportunity to exercise the ministry of healing by virtue of their baptism and confirmation. They are empowered by the Holy Spirit. But they need also the permission of their local ordinaries or conference of bishops to exercise such powers. There are various times when lay people can pray over each other and use the blessed oil: home visitations, visits to sick people and prayer meetings. This blessed oil can be used in ministering to emotional, spiritual and relational wounds and these cases are so important in the Afri-

---

[18] See R. Abrams and H. Slim, "The Revival of Oils in Contemporary Culture: Implications for the Sacrament of Anointing," in M. Dudley and G. Rowell (eds.), The Oil of Gladness: Anointing in the Christian Tradition, London: SPCK, 1993, 169-175.

[19] H. Vorgrimler, Sacramental Theology, Collegeville, Minnesota: The Liturgical

can communitarian society and Nigeria in particular. In ministering to someone who is broken-hearted, one can anoint the person over the heart while prayers are said to heal the brokenness. In praying for the healing of memories, the lay minister can anoint the supplicant's forehead.[20]

Thus, without prejudice to the rulings of canon 1003, which stipulates that the ordained priest is the ordinary minister of the sacrament of anointing, the "lay anointing" which pope Innocent I so highly commended could be rediscovered in Nigeria. John Anyanwu argues that in traditional society and in modern medical care the practitioners of traditional medicine and medical doctors first administer their drugs personally to their patients and entrust the rest to be administered later to the relations of the sick with definite and clear instructions. Similarly, pastoral workers and the lay faithful who visit the sick and the infirm and pray with and over them could anoint such patients with the blessed oil.[21]

7.3.4 Anointing of the Sick and Liturgical Celebration

Apart from the provision of communal celebrations by the new rite, the anointing of the sick is properly a liturgical and communal celebration. But oftentimes this sacrament has remained very skeletal and a quick action due mainly to the postponement of anointing to the very last breath. The celebration may take the following format: The setting is the sickroom or house of the sick. Family members, friends and other Christ's faithful are in attendance. The celebration begins as usual with the sprinkling of holy water. After the greeting and penitential rite, follows the reading either from the gospel or any other passage from the bible. This is supposed to be carefully chosen beforehand to suit the condition and circumstance of the sick. A short but well prepared homily follows. Then, come a period of silence. A song or chorus may follow; after which comes prayer of intercession. Those present are to take up prayer points directed mainly on the sick.

Press, 1992, 317.
[20] J. Healey and D. Sybertz, Towards an African Narrative Theology, 1996, 312-313.
[21] J. E. Anyanwu, "Pastoral Liturgical Care of the Sick: Problems and Prospects," a paper delivered at the 9th CIWA Theology Week, 9.

Following the examples of our traditional pattern of prayer and those of the Pentecostal and Charismatic groups, the ills that we suffer and the forces that act upon us could be mentioned by name. It is not enough to simply recite the ritual prayer over the sick; for at times such ritual prayers are of a universal nature and application and need to be contextualized. In addition, it may be necessary to name explicitly in a loud and intelligible voice those formidable forces, for example, malevolent spirits, witchcraft, demons, etc. which the African believes cause illness to ward them off. One of the major criticisms of the Roman rituals and pattern of worship is their precision, skeletal and general nature. These do not seem to satisfy the religious emotions of the African who is said to be temperamental, celebrative and verbose (but not in a pejorative sense). There is, therefore, an urgent need to inculturate these rituals in order to enhance a more meaningful communal participation of all at their celebration.[22]

The rite continues as usual until the final blessing. All those present could be allowed to lay hands on the sick person. This is a demonstration of community witness and solidarity with the sick and a powerful communication of God's loving mercy and concern. This gesture provides a remarkable opportunity for reconciliation should there be anyone with grudges against the sick person. In view of the aggressive incursions of the various African Independent and Pentecostal Churches with their healing ministry featuring constant laying on of hands, our lay faithful should be empowered to exercise this ministry for which they have a right to by virtue of their baptism.

7.4 Ongoing Catechesis on the Revised Rites

There is a general ignorance of the content and structure of the reform of the sacrament of anointing among the Nigerian Catholic clergy and laity. Traditional Catholics still associate this sacrament with ministering to someone who is very ill and close to death. The syndrome of the "last rites"

---

[22] Cf. N. I. Ndiokwere, The African Church Today and Tomorrow, vol. 2, Enugu; Snaap Press, 1994, 98.

is still sitting fixed in the psyche of the people. In order to overcome this syndrome, there is need for an ongoing catechesis for updating the theology and praxis of the sacrament. This can take the form of preaching, teaching and periodic seminars and workshops both at the diocesan and provincial levels.

On the parish basis, the Sunday Eucharist is a good opportunity to preach on such themes like the Church's ministry to the sick, the mystery of death and other healing ministries. The Sunday Lectionary readings afford the priest enough materials from which to choose and build his homily or sermon. The general intercessions should regularly include petitions on behalf of the sick of the parish, who, could be mentioned by name. It is the duty of the pastor to enlighten the laity on the importance of the care of the sick and above all on the general pastoral ministry to the sick and the infirm.

In addition, there is need for constant seminars and workshops both at parish and diocesan/provincial levels. Competent experts should be invited to discuss themes such as clinical pastoral and health issues, health environment, positive value in sickness and human suffering, a team concept of ministering to the sick, the emergence of Eucharistic ministries and ministers to the sick, the care of the dying, the hospice movement, and so on. These themes should be discussed in the context of the culture of the people. As we saw earlier, the traditional medicine men and women command a lot of respect and influence among the people. African traditional medicine and treatment involve interesting characteristic features which could be and should be taken up by the Christian liturgy for the sick in black Africa. But these need to be studied and integrated into the Christian rites. These educational programmes should include not only instruction, but also actual practice or field experience lest they degenerate into a merely academic exercise.

However, the last point is necessary for this generation of seminarians who are in the theological formation. Attention needs to be paid to the Lord's mandate for the Church to heal the sick as an essential part of its mission. Even the manuals of moral theology and specific treatise on medical ethics whose prevailing approach has been one of casuistry need to be updated and revised in the ongoing orientation of the seminary curriculum. The seminary formators should discuss the phenomenon of healing with the seminarians in an unbiased way. The formation of such groups like the "Leadership Charismatism" of Bigard Memorial Seminary Enugu should be extended to other major seminaries if they do not already have one with competent direction of chaplains. This will help the future priests to cope with these movements when they eventually enter the pastoral field and will equip them with leadership qualities, so that "we do not become madder than those we want to cure of insanity."[23]

7.5 Healthy Self-Critique of the Church's Healing Ministry

It has often been said that the mainline Churches care only for the healthy, the rich and the active but neglect the sick, the poor and the infirm or the handicapped. The type of care we are talking about here is quite different from the provision of hospitals, health care, old people's homes and hospice facilities. I am sure most people will agree that the Catholic Church has excelled more than any other Church, governmental or non-governmental organizations in this area. What the Church has done in the service of the sick deserves unreserved admiration.

However, most of these hospitals and institutes for Medicare today no longer serve the original purpose for which they were set up by the early missionaries. The same could be said of mission schools and other institutions. As Häring rightly observes, "the chief weakness was probably that mission hospitals and clinics generally followed the modern technical medical model."[24] Most of these establishments today have become as expensive as any government or private sponsored ones. They are now mere ventures rather than ministries. This is understandable due to the explosive increases in the cost of maintaining this type of institution which include the infrastructure, personnel, houses, salaries of workers, transport, office equipment, insurance, etc. In a situation where the Church is poor because its faithful are mostly poor folk, being citizens of poor nations and conti-

---

[23] T. Onoyima, "Priestly Formation, Charismatism, Pentecostalism and the Healing Ministry: New Trends in African Christianity," 2001, 269.
[24] B. Häring, Healing and Revealing, 1984, 6.

nent, it is not surprising that the Church cannot dispense health care free of charge. To worsen the case the governments who should help are so corrupt and unaccountable. Instead of maximizing the scarce resources, they use them to enrich themselves and their families. Consequently, even the poor had to pay in order to keep these institutions functioning. "Thus hospitals originally erected for the poor had to serve the privileged class more than the very poor."[25]

But the type of care we mean here goes beyond hospital cure or modern medicine, which deals with sick organs rather than with the sick person as a whole human being. The type of pastoral care we mean takes the psycho-somatic-spiritual health of the person into consideration. The Church can do more in this area whereby the priests take the pastoral care of their parishioners very seriously. They should show willingness and interest in their sick parishioners by paying them regular visits with Holy Communion in the hospitals and homes. This is an important apostolate which many priests have neglected for too long, which if taken seriously will reduce significantly the myriads of the faithful who throng the so called centres of healing or prayer ministry in search of help and miracle (- or magic?). It will help to check the increase in the number of those being fed with religious soporifics by opportunistic religious ministers (including Catholics), who are exploiting the people's gullibility and craving for the miraculous and magical.[26]

However, this task is no longer exclusively for priests alone. The revised rites enlarged the concept of Offices and Ministries for the sick to include all baptized faithful. All Christians by virtue of their baptism participate by doing all they can to help the sick return to health. They are to show them love and be willing to celebrate the sacraments with them. According to the rites, "one of the animating principles that have guided the preparation of the new rites is to encourage the people of God to understand and participate more fully in these sacred celebrations."[27] Apart from the indispensable role which the family and friends play in the care of the sick, the Christian community and the lay apostolate organizations are all involved in this

---

[25] Ibid.
[26] C. J. Uzor, Living Between Two Worlds, 2003, 433.
[27] The Rites, vol. I, VII.

apostolic outreach. These lay apostolic organizations include the Legion of Mary, Society of St. Vincent de Paul, Catholic Charismatic Renewal and Hospice Movements, etc. Indeed these groups have really made a lot of achievements in the pastoral care of the sick, the aged and the handicapped, although the over enthusiasm of some of the groups have often brought them into conflicts with the parish priests. Be that as it may, this does not detract from the good work they can and are doing in the Church. What is needed is the coordinating role of the priest. The priest must be there with his presence in order to give the close supervision that some of the groups require not with the aim of clamping down but to humanely direct and advice them. He should coordinate the activities of the different sodalities so that there is no unhealthy rivalry among them. Above all, there is need for "collaborative ministry" between the clergy and the laity in this apostolate.[28] The Church places a high premium on collaboration and co-responsibility. Hence it calls on the lay faithful to collaborate according to their talents and the spiritual gifts committed to them by God. The decree Ad Gentes underlines the importance and indeed the irreplaceability of the laity in the missionary activity of the Church when it says:

The Church is not truly established and does not fully live, nor is a perfect sign of Christ unless there is a genuine laity existing and working alongside the hierarchy.[29]

To my mind, it is this pastoral diakonia to the sick, which is more personal, more humane but communal and therefore African in approach that is lacking in the Church's charitable and hospital apostolate. For a long time the integration of the meaning and role of healing within the indivisible mandate given to the Church to proclaim the message of salvation and to heal has been neglected. Today, however, much has been done, and more can still be done to overcome this dichotomy. The new approach is the de-emphasis on the Cartesian dualism which speaks of "pastors of souls," thereby thinking only of souls and salvation in heaven. The other extreme

---

[28] See A. Echema, "Collaborative Ministry in the Church Family," in F. A. Adedara (ed.), Church Leadership and the Christian Message, Ibadan: Stirling-Horden Publishers, 2004, 88-102; also his "Collaborative Ministry and Extraordinary Ministers of Communion," a paper delivered at the 20th Annual Cathan Conference, Tansi Seminary, Onitsha.

will be to consider only the horizontal dimension of human well-being and justice. The good news is that these divisions and compartments are giving way to a holistic understanding of human beings in their totality of body and soul.

7.6 Present Day Healers and the Example of Jesus

One fact that needs to be noted is that healers have always been in existence even in the time of Jesus. As we saw earlier in the Patristic era, Church leaders both in the East and West kept admonishing their people not to put their trust in the incantations of sorcerers and magicians. The reference of Jesus to the casting out of demons in Luke (11:19-20) or the caution to his followers to "beware of false prophets who come to you in sheep's clothing but inwardly are ravenous wolves" (Matt 7:15) shows that there were some who practiced the trade in his own time. In other words, right from the beginning of time, there have been "healers" - genuine and fake ones. What is happening in the present day is not new and there is no proof that it is worse than it was in the past.

However, our people need to know that there is a very tiny demarcation between religion and magic since both have to do with the invisible. This calls for caution not to fall prey to human designs and fake healers and prophets. Jesus remains the measure and example on which healers need to look upon and imitate. How did he heal? What was his motive and method of healing? I think this is where our so called present day healers must learn a lot if they are genuine and want people to take them seriously. Jesus shows us right from the beginning of his mission how to remove the main obstacles from participation in his healing-saving mission by saying "NO" to the temptation to seek and offer material security, "NO" to vanity and purely exhibitional religion, and "NO" to any kind of power or authority linked with the "prince of this dark world" of power and violence (cf. Lk 4:1-13; Matt 4:1-11). He teaches his disciples the kind of authority they are to exercise among them, namely, the authority of the "Suffering Servant of

---

[29] Vatican II, Ad Gentes, 21.

God," servant of the poor, of the outcast, the sick and the downtrodden. He tells them that it should not be so with them as it is among the nations where the domineering styles of authority: arrogance, exploitation, oppression, manipulation and deception are the order of the day. Should such authority be exercised in the name of religion, the situation will even be more severe. That is why he emphatically teaches them that their mission of sharing in the proclamation of the Good News and the healing of the sick presupposes commitment to simplicity and humble service (cf. Lk 9:3; 10:3ff). Their whole conduct should be in imitation of the Son of Man.

It is not surprising then, that when the seventy-two returned from their first preaching and healing journey and exultantly reported that even devils submitted to them, Jesus counselled them to rejoice, rather, "that your names are enrolled in heaven" (Lk 10:17-20). This same attitude is even more evident when he praises the Father for having revealed his mysteries only to the humble ones, who are conformed with him to whom the Father reveals himself completely (cf. Lk 10:21-24). This calls for a totally new way of life for all those involved in the mission of proclaiming the Good News and diakonia of healing.

In spite of the warnings of the master, most healers today carry on their trade regardless of these counsels from our Lord. Yet they claim to be following and working in his name. One of the major criticisms of the healers (both Catholics and non-Catholics) is the air of exhibitionism and at times playing to the gallery. Their actions most times lack the humility urged by Jesus Christ. They advertise themselves and their miraculous powers and induce their clients to do the same through testimonies. Oftentimes most of these self-acclaimed miracles are fake and stage-managed; they are unsubstantiated by any medical certification, which makes them spurious and dubious. It is such suspicious claims that must have led Anatole France to say that if one could not show him that an amputated leg has been restored, he would not believe in miracles.[30] This is, however, an extreme case of unbelief and a proud challenge to God. Miracles do occur even on daily basis; not only on healing centres but everywhere and usually without pub-

---

[30] A. France, Le Jardin d' Epicure, quoted by Ivo da C. Souza, The Healing Ministry, 1999, 52.

licity. And as we said before, many and most of the events of healing can be explained by psycho-somatic medicine and by the findings of logotherapy. But that neither diminishes their value as faith healings;[31] nor does it warrant the type of excitement that they generate.

Again, Jesus the healer par excellence is totally different. He abhors publicity and would often command those healed not to tell anyone about their cures. He even hid himself from the people who wanted to make him a king on account of his wonderful works. (cf. Jn 6:14-15). But it is not so with our present day priest-healers. They ignore these living examples of Jesus in blind imitation of their fundamentalist Pentecostals. Even the fatherly advice of the Nigerian bishops that "great discipline is to be observed to discourage testimonies which aim at exciting admiration and the adulation of the minister"[32] seems to fall on deaf ears. Being enriched through exploitation of desperate and distressed people, some priest-healers parade themselves as deities and defy the authority of their local ordinaries. Many of them are too conscious of their "power" forgetting that what ever they claim to have is a gift (charism) from God. This is not surprising when as Uzukwu says an individual combines in himself "the power of seers, healers and priests representing God."[33] But there is no way a gift can become greater than the Giver. No matter how powerful healers may claim to be, they "are at best nurses who are assisting the great physician. It is Christ the doctor, who does the healing."[34] Or as the French Surgeon, Andre Palev puts it: "I dressed the wounds, God healed them." Similarly, a Latin adage expresses the same truth thus: "Nature heals, the physician cures/takes care" (Natura sanat, medicus curat). In other words, it is God who heals and to him belong all glory and honour.

Of all the accusations levelled on the present day healers, the association of the healing ministry with lots of money and material possession seems to be the worst evil. Even Catholic priests who are in the ministry are not different from their Pentecostal counterparts. They seem to show little re-

---

[31] B. Häring, The Sacraments in a Secular Age, Slough: St. Paul Publications, 1976, 243.
[32] Guidelines for the Healing Ministry in the Catholic Church in Nigeria, 4. 3d.
[33] E. E. Uzukwu, A Listening Church: Autonomy and Communion in African Churches, Maryknoll: Orbis Books, 1996, 124.

straint in receiving "thank-offerings of grateful votaries" which in most cases they themselves induce. Some go to the extent of charging stipulated amount of money for "special Masses" (healing Mass), consultation, thanksgiving, appreciation, "one out of ten" (Otu uzo n'uzo iri) and the innovation these days of paying tithe in the Catholic Church.[35] In spite of their philosophical and theological studies these priests forget the sin of simony which the Church frowns at and the Lord's admonition that freely you have received, and freely you should give (cf. Matt 10:8) which was repeated so often by the Fathers in the Patristic period. Even the example of Elisha who refused to accept silver and gold from Naaman (2 Kgs 5:15-19) does not appeal to them. The words of the Psalmist are proved right: "In his wealth man lacks wisdom. And he is like beasts that are destroyed" (49: 20).

Since the love of having increases by having (Amor habendi habendo crescit), many of these healers are ready to do anything, even to deceive in order to maintain their status quo. For instance, they promise the impossible to their clients who in their desperation believe them. They claim to heal AIDS, tumour, provide security, success in business, in examinations, promotion in work places, prosperity, provide jobs, children to barren women, husbands to young ladies, etc. This wide range of promises (which in most cases are empty promises) explains why persons of varying social and economic positions flock to these ministries. Indeed, oftentimes, these promises fail and the healers turn round to blame their clients of lack of faith thereby harming people's faith and spiritual life instead of helping it. Persons who are not healed go away with the impression that they lack the faith they should have, or that God does not love them as he obviously loves those who have been healed.

In addition, many of these healers have sent people to their untimely grave by advising them to disregard any symptoms they may have, and to show their faith by not taking their medicine or seeing their doctors.[36] Many sick

---

[34] P. Amakiri, Divine Healing, Benin City: Totan Publishers, 1987, 30.
[35] Cf. K. Chigbo, Catholic Healing Ministry on Fire, Enugu, 1997, 40, quoted by M. C. Obiagwu, "Healing Ministry in the Church in Igbo Society of Nigeria," in BTS 21 (2001): 103.
[36] See T. Onoyima, "Priestly Formation, Charismatism, Pentecostalism and the Heal-

people have been known to get worse or even died of diabetes because the healers encouraged them to stop anti-diabetic drugs/insulin as a sign of faith. They have forced such patients to make a false decision between faith and science or set up prayer (supernatural) in opposition to medicine (natural). This is a false theology of healing, unless a person is genuinely inspired by God to rely solely on prayer and not to see a physician. There is no opposition between medicine and faith or prayer. The bible itself holds the medical profession in high esteem even at a time when medicine was in its infancy and was little more than the art of the apothecary. Thus, the Book of Sirach (Ecclesiasticus) in the second century BC admonishes:

Hold the physician in honour, for he is essential to you, and God it was who established his profession. From God the doctor has his wisdom, and the king provides for his sustenance. His knowledge makes the doctor distinguished, and gives him access to those in authority. God makes the earth yield healing herbs which the prudent man should not neglect. Was not the water sweetened by a twig that man might learn his power? He endows men with the knowledge to glory in his mighty works, through which the doctor eases pain and the druggist prepares his medicines; Thus God's creative work continues without cease in its efficacy on the surface of the earth. My son, when you are ill, delay not but pray to God, who will heal you: Flee wickedness; let your hand be just, cleanse your heart of every sin; Offer your sweet-smelling oblation and petition, a rich offering according to your means. Then give your doctor his place lest he leave; for you need him too. There are times that give him an advantage, and he too beseeches God. That his diagnosis may be correct and his treatment brings about a cure. He who is a sinner toward his Maker will be defiant toward the doctor (38:1-15).

The hagiographer believes that prayer is therapeutic. He admits that the Creator heals through the skills of the physician and through meditation. Medicine and prayer are not opposed. On the contrary, the doctor, the nurse and the healer form God's healing team.[37] Paul recommends wine for the

---

ing Ministry," 2001, 273-274.
[37] See F. MacNutt, Healing, 1987, 265.

stomach trouble of Timothy (cf. 1 Tim 5:23). Fortunately, doctors themselves recognize the limits of medical art and pray or invite the relatives and friends of the patients to pray. This is where the services of the Charismatics, the Legionaries, etc. are needed: to visit the sick at home, in hospitals and hospices in order to pray for them. Any opposition between prayer for healing and medicine is against common sense and against the scriptures. Sometimes God cures directly through prayer; at other times, through nature, assisted by physicians. A healer should not tell the patients to stop taking their drugs, except through a special inspiration from God. But inspirations are not daily occurrences. God does not work like that in all cases. Those healers who give the patients such advices are only sowing seeds of confusion, self-condemnation in the patients not cured, which eventually results in greater anxiety and sleepless nights. This in turn leads to lower resistance of the sickness and eventually to untimely death.

Apart from these few abuses mentioned above, there are myriads of other aberrations of healers and their healing ministries. We have discussed some in the course of this book and there are others not touched. The abuses are legion. We mentioned these ones only to highlight how they are completely against the witness of the gospel and all that Jesus taught and did. However, beside the abuses are also positive contributions which the Catholic healing ministry and the popular Charismatic movement have brought to the Church. Prominent among these is the area of inculturation. The liturgy of the Mass is celebrated today all over Nigeria with joy and life. The beating of drums and the accompanying dance with the clapping of hands have really made the celebration of the Mass lively and festive. Anyone who has had the experience of the celebration of the Mass in Europe will automatically see the stark difference. The Mass for the sick has been inculturated to suit the aspirations of the people, unlike the usual cold and monotonous way. Although, there have been syncretistic tendencies in some areas, the deviations do not justify the baby being thrown away with the bath water.

Another good thing that has happened among Catholics since the advent of Charismatics and healing ministries is the ability to pray better. It was this singular purpose that led people like Godwin Ikeobi to start what he called "Tuesday Prayer Group." It is doubtful to say whether the same purpose motivates the rest of them today to start ministries. However, one observes that Catholics who in the past were cajoled as lukewarm and unfamiliar with the bible have now become experts in quoting the bible and leading in public prayers. In the prayer of the faithful today, it is wonderful to see how our Catholics participate actively, spontaneously and inspiringly. They are no longer shy or ashamed to render prayers for themselves and for others. Again much catechesis needs to be done in this area. For example, the new fashion of beginning prayer with "In the Name of Jesus" (Obu n'aha Jesus); "In the precious Name of Jesus" (Obu n'ike di n'obara Jesus) instead of the traditional and correct way of "In the Name of the Father ...," the indiscriminate and frequent calling of God's name, commanding him and apparent physical manipulation of the Holy Spirit with numerous invocations and incantations; and of course the phenomenon of speaking in tongues need to be moderated. These are the results of the epic mimicking of the Pentecostal TV fundamentalist preachers.[38]

Finally, it must be observed to the credit of the healing ministry and Charismatic groups that the Church has now been made relevant to our people. They now see God as one who is very near to them, ready to solve their problems and heal their sickness and not a God who is very distant, beyond the reach of human beings. All these are a big challenge to the Roman Catholic Church as well as other mainline Churches to re-examine their pastoral and liturgical approach so far. They should find out what the legitimate needs of the people are that they are lacking. Above all, it calls for a patient dialogue between the Church and the priest-healers. This has already started with the number of conferences being organized among Nigerian theologians and theological institutes and the epoch making National Theological and Pastoral Seminar on Healing Ministry organized by the Catholic Bishops' Conference of Nigeria (CBCN) in 1992. This conference eventually gave rise to the Guidelines for the Healing Ministry in the Catholic Church in Nigeria issued in 1997. There should be more and more of such dialogues, for as Hilary Achunike says "mere control will not solve the problem."[39] Perhaps what the Italian novelist Alberto Moravia said in

---

[38] A. Echema, "Pastoral Administration of Sacraments and Sacramentals: Abuses," 2004, 51-52.
[39] H. C. Achinike, The Influence of Pentecostalism on Catholic Priests and Seminari-

1972 should guide our bishops in the handling of the religious issues like the healing ministry. According to him, "it is dangerous to destroy a religion at a single blow, rather than allow it to die from old age and unreality ..."[40]

I personally believe that when our people in Nigeria particularly and Africa generally come of age, through good government, education, gainful employment, living humanly and not barely surviving, are provided with functioning infrastructure like schools, hospitals, good roads, electricity, water, healthy environment, manageable family, etc. all these scrambling for healing and demonic pursuits will become a thing of the past. At least they will be reduced to their barest minimum.

Summary

This chapter treated the practical inculturation of the sacrament of the anointing of the sick. Since the sacrament is still surrounded with a general misunderstanding concerning its meaning and practice, we started by clearing some of the confusions. It became clear that the misunderstandings could be seen within a larger context of the crisis of sacraments in general. For instance, there is a growing dissatisfaction today with the entire sacramental system throughout the Catholic world. People are now reconsidering the place of the sacraments in the life of the Church, the "thing-ness" (kpim) of the sacraments and the meaning of sacramental grace, ex opera operato efficacy and the overly individualistic conception of the sacraments. In the case of the anointing of the sick, such misunderstandings have led to its reduction to a merely skeletal and magical nature. Priests can just dash in and dash out of the sickroom of patients believing that once the right prayers are said in the right order, anointing the stipulated parts of the body, the magic is wrought.

Today, things have changed. With the new insights gained from the natural and human sciences concerning the social dimension of disease (the so-

---

ans in Nigeria, 2004, 83.

[40] Cited in David Lamb, The Africans; Encounters from the Sudan to the Cape, Lon-

matic symptoms or processes making a person sick) and illness (the sickness as it functions in the total life of the person – physically, psychologically, interpersonally, economically), anointing of the sick is no longer as simple as it used to be. Therefore, the Church needs to seek new ways of implementing the new rites, and their proper liturgical celebrations. This need is even more urgent for the Church in Africa, where the sacrament of anointing of the sick is facing a lot of challenges from the new phenomenon of healing ministry, Charismatic and Pentecostal groups. This calls for the inculturation of not only the oil (the approved matter of the sacrament) but also the entire liturgical celebration in a way that anointing becomes truly Christian and authentically African.

In this regard, we proposed the use of locally produced oil, allowing Christians the personal use of blessed oil as it was done in the first 800 years of the Church, the empowerment of the pastoral workers to anoint and lay hands on the sick, and making the celebration of the anointing of the sick more communal rather than individualistic and magical. This proposal for communal celebration should not be confused with the indiscriminate anointing of large numbers but rather refers to the active participation of the faithful during the celebration.

In order to constantly update and renew the implementation of the rites, ongoing catechesis through preaching, teaching, seminars, workshops, and retreats are indispensable. These must be laced with practical and field experiences, so that they do not appear too academic. The seminary curriculum needs to be reoriented from time to time to introduce future priests into pastoral challenges especially those posed by the new phenomenon of healing ministry.

The Church's healing ministry so far was x-rayed and a proposal of balancing the hospital apostolate which the Church has so marvellously done with a pastoral care of the sick was made. The two are not the same: the former focuses more on the sick organ of the body; the latter is more holistic and takes care of the whole person as a human being. Moreover the obligation to carry out the pastoral care of the sick lies no longer on the priest alone but the entire members of the Christ's faithful. However, the priest remains

---

don: Mandarin Paperback, 1990, 141.

the coordinator of the ministries but with an open mind for collaboration with other extraordinary ministers.

The chapter ends with a critical evaluation of the present day healers. Jesus Christ, the Healer par excellence is presented as the standard on which all healers are measured. It is observed that overemphasis on and fascination with the gift or charism of healing has led to a neglect of the Giver. This has brought other numerous abuses. But as the Latin adage goes "abuse does not destroy use" (Abusus non tollit usum), especially when besides the abuses, there are equally other gains accruing from the ministry. More importantly too, we observed that religious ideas die hard, and therefore, are better allowed to die naturally from old age and unreality, rather than through the force of law or decree. Consequently, a patient dialogue remains the best pastoral option and approach to solve the problems of priest-healers and their ministries.

General Conclusion

We have come to the end of our investigation. I am sure that I have written things which some will agree with; I suspect I have also written certain things others may deplore; and undoubtedly I have left out some things untouched. But this has been more than a thrashing out of some disturbing practices or a presentation of my own personal wish. That is why we started with the contextual pastoral situation of the Church in Nigeria, which mirrors also the same scenario in the whole of Africa. In that context, we saw why the new phenomenon of healing flourishes with its attendant abuses.

The various attitudes towards sickness and healing were also surveyed, noting particularly how these concepts have developed over the years. Certain human conditions can influence for better or for worse certain illnesses as well as their cure or healing. This explains why people whose community and family ties are strong experience pain less frequently and less intensely than people whose community and family ties are breaking down. The same could be said also of people with strong faith, determination to survive and, of course living in healthy environment. These categories of people have a better chance of avoiding illnesses, resisting diseases, and eventually recovering quicker than their counterparts.

The biblical data show that God is the healer par excellence (OT); while doctors, physicians and prophets who perform works of healing are doing so as God's vice-regents. Jesus continues the healing work of his Father (NT) in which all diseases, demons, and all kinds of ailments are conquered. Similarly, healing activities are witnessed in the apostolic age through the hands of the apostles who wrought "many signs and wonders among the people, so much so that the sick were even taken out into the streets and laid on beds and sleeping mats in the hope that at least the shadow of Peter might fall across some of them as he went past" (Acts 5: 5-14).

However, in the early Christian community, there is a little shift in emphasis. The power to heal which it had received from Jesus still persists but is now proclaimed and realized in an anointing with oil. And from now onwards, the Church tries to find in the classical texts of Mark 6:7 and James

5:14-15 the origin and institution of the sacrament of the sick. It is usually said that Mark insinuated this institution, while James commended and promulgated it to the faithful.[1]

The history of the fifth sacrament of the Church is characterized by change and the meaning and function of the sacrament varied according to these changing ideas. At one stage, precisely in the Scholastic period, the sacrament became confused with deathbed penance and was regarded as a sacrament of the dying. Thus, the sacrament earned its famous, though erroneous name of "extreme unction," a name that has coloured it to this day.

The Church undertook a reform course to save the sacrament and restore it to its original aim. The reforms enriched the sacrament theologically, pastorally and ecumenically. Despite these efforts, anointing has remained problematic and seems to be in conflict with the healing ministry in our day. Many priests and laity today seem to believe more in the physical healing through faith and prayer with total disregard of the Church's sacrament which also speaks of healing but in a more holistic manner. This has created a lot of confusion and brought abuses in the Church in Nigeria and Africa in general.

These abuses notwithstanding, we insist that anointing of the sick remains important and is desired by many Christians who are sick and dying. The healing ministry is equally relevant and needs to be handled with care. The abuses and misunderstandings surrounding the fifth sacrament can be corrected through ongoing catechesis, preaching and teaching. It is not enough simply to change the name from extreme unction or last rites to anointing of the sick. Being perhaps the most liturgically deprived of all the sacramental celebrations of the Church, anointing of the sick needs to be stripped of its quasi-magical and mechanistic nature. In addition it needs to be inculturated in order to make it relevant to the Christians in Nigeria. We, therefore, made certain suggestions which include the use of locally produced oil, allowing for lay anointing, imposition of hands on the sick by ministers, and communal celebration of this sacrament rather than the private business of the priest and the sick alone.

---

[1] DS, 1695; cf. also DS 1716.

The hospital apostolate of the Church no matter how marvellous it may be is not enough and does not exclude the pastoral dimension which involves all Christians. The role of the sodalities in the Church especially those whose charisms are directed on the sick and dying should be enhanced to reach such people. Already some of the groups like the Charismatics and the healing ministry have distinguished themselves in this regard. We are all reaping the wonderful fruits, such as the love of the Word of God, love of prayer, serenity, courage to face problems of daily existence, etc. On the contrary, the over-zealots among them have brought in abuses. But we cannot quench the movement of life, of grace, of healing and stop all healing ministries. Healers and people should be initiated with sound theology and practice (orthodoxy and orthopraxis). Otherwise, people will be leaving the Church and joining the sects.

The Second Vatican Council speaks of these gifts and urges the bishops to use their discernment and discover the popular religiosity:

In any case, judgement as to their genuineness and proper use belongs to those who preside over the Church, and to whose special competence it belongs, not indeed to quench/extinguish the Spirit, but to test all things and hold fast to that which is good" (cf. 1 Thess 5:12, 19-21).[2]

We are witnessing a "new Pentecost," we are living in the era of the Spirit moving in today's sickly world.

When people outside the Church think about Catholics, invariably their thoughts turn to our constant involvement with the sacraments; and rightly so. Yet the question still imposes itself: Why this preoccupation with sacraments? Some centuries ago, St. Ambrose put it succinctly and powerfully: "You have shown yourself to me face to face, O Christ; it is in your sacraments that I meet you."[3] I wish our sick sisters and brothers a similar experience in the sacrament of the anointing of the sick, rather than giving in to the wonder stories of the modern faith-healing by revivalist preachers and self-proclaimed healers.

---

[2] Lumen Gentium, 12.
[3] Quoted by M. J. Stravinskas, Understanding the Sacraments, 1997, 118.

Bibliography

1. Sources

Apostolic Tradition of Hippolytus. English translation with notes in Geoffrey J. Cuming, Hippolytus: A Text for Students. Grove Liturgical Study No. 8, Bramcote, Notts. : Grove Books, 1976.

Augustine. City of God, XXII, 8. Trans. by Walsh and Honan, D. New York: Fathers of the Church, 1954.

Caesarius of Arles. Sermons. Critical Latin Text in Morin, G. (ed.) Sancti Caesarii Arelatensis Sermones. 2Vols. Editio altera, Corpus Christianorum 103-104, Turnholt: Brepols, 1953.

Catechism of the Catholic Church, Chicago, Illinois: Loyola University Press, 1994.

Denziger, H. and Schönmetzer, A. (eds.). Enchiridion Symbolorum. Definitionum et Declarationum, 35th ed. Freiburg: Herder, 1967.

Die Sorge der Kirche um die Kranken (Hrsg.) Die deutschen Bischöfe, April 20, 1998.

Dix, Gregory (ed.). The Apostolic Tradition. London: SPCK, 1968.

Early Christian Writings. The Apostolic Fathers. Trans. by Maxwell Staniforth. New York: Penguin Books, 1968.

Flannery, Austin (ed.). Vatican Council II. The Conciliar and Post-Conciliar Documents. Northport, New York: Costello, 1975.

Guidelines for the Healing Ministry in the Catholic Church in Nigeria, issued by the Catholic Bishops' Conference of Nigeria (CBCN), September 14, 1996.

Innocent 1. Letter to Decentius of Gubbio. Latin Text in PL 20: cols. 556-557.

John Paul II. Apostolic Letter Salvifici Doloris, February 11, 1984.

_____ . Encyclical Letter Ecclesia in Africa, September 14, 1995.

Ministry to the Sick (Episcopal). New York: Church Hymnal Corporation, 1977.

Neuner, J. and Dupuis, J. (eds.). The Christian Faith in the Doctrinal Documents of the Catholic Church. Westminster, Md.: Christian Classics, rev. ed., 1982.

Occasional Services. A Companion to the Lutheran Books of Worship. Minneapolis, Minnesota: Augsburg, 1982.

Ordo Unctionis Infirmorum Eorumque Pastoralis Curae. Vatican City: Typis Polyglottis Vaticanis, 1972.

Palmer, Paul F. Sacraments and Forgiveness. Sources of Christian Theology, Vol. 2. Westminster, Md.: Newman Press, 1959.

Pastoral Care of the Sick: Rites of Anointing and Viaticum. Washington D.C.: ICEL, 1982.

Paul VI. Apostolic Constitution Sacram Unctionem Infirmorum, November 30, 1972.

Rituale Romanum Pauli V Pontificis Maximi Iussu Editum, Rome, 1614.

Rituale Romanum. Editio prima juxta typicam Vaticanam. New York: Benziger Brothers, 1953.

The Rites of the Catholic Church as revised by the Second Vatican Council, Vol. 1. Collegeville, Minnesota: The Liturgical Press, 1990.

2. Literature

Achunike, Hilary C. The Influence of Pentecostalism on Catholic Priests and Seminarians in Nigeria. Lagos: Rex Charles & Patrick, 2004.

Anyanwu, Cyprian. The Rites of Initiation in Christian Liturgy and in Igbo Traditional Society. Frankfurt: Peter Lang, 2004.

Brookman-Amissah, Joseph. "The Eucharist as Healing Celebration," in Ukpong, Justin S. (ed.) et al. Jesus Christ: The Bread of Life, 11th CIWA Theology Week Proceedings. Port Harcourt: CIWA Press, 2000, 222-231.

Chauvet, Louis-Marie. (ed.) et al. Concilium: Krankheit und Heilung 34 (November 1998).

_____. The Sacraments: The Word of God at the Mercy of the Body. Collegeville, Minnesota: The Liturgical Press, 2001.

Chibuko, Patrick C. "HIV/AIDS and the Healing Mission of the Church Today: Reversing the Stigma of the Scourge," in BTS 25 (2005): 42-67.

Chukwuezi, Anelechi B. Odenigbo 2004, Ahuike: Ike Ogwu na Ike Ekpere, Owerri: Assumpta Press, 2004.

Collins, Mary. "The Roman Ritual: Pastoral Care and Anointing of the Sick," in The Pastoral Care of the Sick: Concilium 2 (1991): 3-18.

Diekmann, Geofrey. "The Laying on of Hands in Healing," in Liturgy 25 (1980): 7-10, 36-38.

Dudley, Martin and Rowell, Geoffrey (eds.). The Oil of Gladness: Anointing in the Christian Tradition. London: SPCK, 1993.

Echema, Austin. "Collaborative Ministry in the Church Family," in Adedara, Francis A. (ed.). Church Leadership and the Christian Message. Ibadan: Stirling-Horden Publishers, 2004, 205-215.

_____. "Pastoral Administration of Sacraments and Sacramentals: Abuses," in Jiwike, Maurice (ed.). The Challenges of the Pastoral Ministry in a Pluralistic Society. Owerri: Assumpta Press, 2004, 34-56.

_____. "The Omnipotent God vis-à-vis Human Suffering: The Church's Response," being a paper delivered at the 16th CIWA Theology Week (2005).

_____. Corporate Personality in Traditional Igbo Society and the Sacrament of Reconciliation. Frankfurt: Peter Lang, 1995.

Fink, Peter E. (ed.). Anointing of the Sick: Alternative Futures for Worship, Vol. 7. Collegeville, Minnesota: The Liturgical Press, 1987.

Geißler, Heiner. Was würde Jesus heute sagen? Die politische Botschaft des Evangeliums. Berlin: Berlin Verlag, 2004.

Goddier, Alban. The Passion and Death of Our Lord Jesus Christ. New York: P. J. Kennedy and Sons, 1944.

Greshake, Gisbert. "Extreme Unction or Anointing of the Sick? A Plea for Discrimination," in Review for Religious 45 (1986): 435-451.

Groen, Basilius. "The Anointing of the Sick in the Greek Orthodox Church," in The Pastoral Care of the Sick: Concilium 2 (1991): 50-59.

Guroian, Vigen. Life's Living toward Dying. Grand Rapids: William B. Eerdmans Publishing Company, 1996.

Gusmer, Charles W. "I was Sick and You Visited Me: The Revised Rites for the Sick," in Worship 48 (1974): 516-525.

_____. "Liturgical Traditions of Christian Illness: Rites of the Sick," in Worship 46 (1972): 528-543.

_____. And You Visited Me: Sacramental Ministry to the Sick and the Dying. Collegeville, Minnesota: The Liturgical Press, 1990.

Häring, Bernard. Healing and Revealing. Slough: St. Paul Publications, 1984.

_____. The Sacraments in a Secular Age. Slough: St. Paul Publications, 1976.

Hastings, Adrian. African Catholicism: Essays in Discovery. London: SCM Press, 1989.

Healey, J. & Sybertz, D. Towards an African Narrative Theology. Nairobi: Paulines Publications Africa, 1995.

Ike, Jude C. "Faith in God amidst Suffering in the World," in Madu, Raphael and Echema, Austin (eds.). Essays in Honour of Very Rev. Msgr. Alphonsus Aghaizu. Owerri: Assumpta Press, 2004, 137-146.

John Paul II. Crossing the Threshold of Hope. New York: Alfred A. Knopf, 1994.

Kii, Pius. The Healing Ministry. Lagos: Planet Press, 2004.

Kübler-Ross, Elisabeth. On Death and Dying. New York: Macmillan Publishing Co., 1969.

Lawler, Michael G. Symbol and Sacrament: A Contemporary Sacramental Theology. New York/Mahwah: Paulist Press, 1987.

Leijssen, Lambert. "Die Krankensalbung: Eine Neue-Interpretation aus dem heutigen Kontext heraus," in Liturgisches Jahrbuch 45 (1995): 152-177.

Lustiger, Kardinal Jean-Marie. Stärkung fürs Leben: Über das Kranksein und das Sakrament der Krankensalbung. München: Verlag Neue Stadt, 1991.

MacNutt, Francis. Healing. Notre Dame/Indiana: Ave Maria Press, 1974.

_____. The Power to Heal. Notre Dame/Indiana: Ave Maria Press, 1977.

Manus, Chris U. (ed.) et al. Healing and Exorcism: The Nigerian Experience. Enugu: Snaap Press, 1992.

McManus, Jim. The Healing of the Sacraments. Bandra: St. Paul's, 1993.

Milingo, Emmanuel. The World in Between: Christian Healing and the Struggle for Spiritual Survival. New York: Orbis Books, 1984.

Mitchell, Nathan. Cult and Controversy: The Worship of the Eucharist Outside Mass. Collegeville, Minnesota: The Liturgical Press, 1990.

Moltmann, Jürgen. The Crucified God: The Cross of Christ as the Foundation and Criticism of Christian Theology. New York: Harper & Roy, 1974.

Ndiokwere, Nathaniel I. Search for Security. Benin City: Ambik Press, 1990.

Nwabekee, Aloysius. "Liturgical Formation in the Seminary," in Okeke, Valerian (ed.). Bigard Diamond Jubilee Essays. Nsukka: Fulladu Publishing Company, 2001, 237-266.

Nwaigbo, Ferdinand. "Today's Quest for a Synthesis of Wholeness and Healing in African Church and Culture," in BTS 21 (2001): 10-43.

Nwosu, Vincent A. (ed.). Prayer House and Faith Healing. Onitsha: Tabansi Press, 1971.

Obiagwu, Marius C. "Healing Ministry in the Church in Igbo Society of Nigeria: It's Pastoral Contributions and Possible Pastoral Challenges," in BTS 21 (2001): 59-132.

Okoye, John I. "Healing in the Bible," in BTS 21 (2001): 44-58.

Onoyima, Taddeo. "Priestly Formation, Charismatism, Pentecostalism and the Healing Ministry: New Trends in African Christianity," in Okeke, Valerian (ed.). Bigard Diamond Jubilee Essays. Nsukka: Fulladu Publishing Company, 2001, 267-280.

Onyenemegam, Justin O. Pastoral Care of the Sick in Igbo Community-Nigeria. Rome: Typo-Lithografia, 1985.

Palmer, Paul F. "The Purpose of Anointing the Sick: A Reappraisal," in Theological Studies 19 (1958): 309-344.

_____. "Who can Anoint the Sick?" in Worship 48 (1974): 81-92.

Poschmann, Bernard. Penance and the Anointing of the Sick. New York: Herder, 1964.

Power, David N. "The Sacrament of Anointing: Open Questions," in The Pastoral Care of the Sick: Concilium 2 (1991): 95-107.

Probst, Manfred and Richter Klemens (Hrsg.). Heilssorge für die Kranken. Freiburg: Herder, 1975.

Scanlan, Michael. Inner Healing: Ministering to the Human Spirit through the Power of Prayer. New York: Paulist Press, 1974.

Schockenhoff, Eberhard. Krankheit – Gesundheit – Heilung: Wege zum Heil aus biblischer Sicht. Regensburg: Verlag Friedrich Pustet, 2001.

Shorter, Aylward. Jesus and Witchdoctor: An Approach to Healing and Wholeness. New York: The Liturgical Press, 1985.

Souza, Ivo da Conceicao. The Healing Ministry. Santa Cruz, Goa: New Age Printers, 1999.

Stravinskas, Peter M. J. Understanding the Sacraments: A Guide for Prayer & Study. San Francisco: Ignatius Press, 1997.

Umoren, Anthony I. Jesus and Miracle Healing Today. Ibadan: Intec Printers, 2000.

Uzukwu, Elochukwu E. A Listening Church: Autonomy and Communion in African Churches. Maryknoll, New York: Orbis Books, 1996.

Uzukwu, Elochukwu E. Worship as Body Language, Introduction to Christian Worship: An African Orientation, Collegeville, Minnesota: The Liturgical Press, 1997.

Ziegler, John. Let them Anoint the Sick. Collegeville: The Liturgical Press, 1987.

IKO – Verlag für Interkulturelle Kommunikation

Obiora F. Ike (ed.)
Globalization and African Self-Determination
What is our future?
Ezi Muoma – Afrika verstehen, Vol. 3
321 S., € 24,90, ISBN 3-88939-753-0

Okpe Nicholas Ojoajogwu
Social and cultural Identity of an African Society
The Igala People of Nigeria
316 S., € 22,90, ISBN 3-88939-803-0

Patrick Chukwudezie Chibuko
Keeping the Liturgy alive
An Anglophone West African Experience
192 S., € 21,90, ISBN 3-88939-704-2

Joseph Okechukwu Offor
Community Radio and its Influence in the Society:
The Case of Enugu State - Nigeria
Ethik – Gesellschaft - Wirtschaft, Vol. 14
336 S., € 26,80, ISBN 3-88939-661-5

Patrick Chukwudezie Chibuko
Liturgy For Life
Introduction to Practical Dimensions of the Liturgy
178 S., € 14,90, ISBN 3-88939-777-8

George Nnaemeka Oranekwu
The Significant Role of Initiation in the Traditional Igbo Culture and Religion
An Inculturation Basis for Pastoral Catechesis of Christian Initiation
Ezi Muoma – Afrika verstehen, Vol. 2
268 S., € 24,90, ISBN 3-88939-710-7

Simeon Onyewueke Eboh
An African Concept of Law and Order
A Case Study of Igbo Traditional Society
244 S., € 19,90, ISBN 3-88939-695-X

Simeon Onyewueke Eboh
African Communalism
The Way to Social Harmony and Peaceful Co-Existence
Onuganotu Lectures, Vol. 3
264 S., € 21,95, ISBN 3-88939-715-8

Simeon Onyewueke Eboh
Inalienability of Land and Citizenship in the African Context
Unity and Diversity in the Age of Globalisation
Onuganotu Lectures, Vol. 4
2005, 246 S., € 19,90, ISBN 3-88939-780-8

www.iko-verlag.de
Find all current titles – visit us!